PN 81 .B29 1995

Bakhtin in contexts

B⟨

IN

D1056755

Rethinking Theory

GENERAL EDITOR

Gary Saul Morson

CONSULTING EDITORS

Robert Alter
Frederick Crews
John M. Ellis
Caryl Emerson

Bakhtin
in Contexts

Across the Disciplines

Edited by

Amy Mandelker

With an Introduction by

Caryl Emerson

Northwestern University Press
Evanston, Illinois

Northwestern University Press
Evanston, Illinois 60208–4210

Library of Congress Cataloging-in-Publication Data

Bakhtin in contexts : across the disciplines / edited by Amy Mandelker
; with an introduction by Caryl Emerson.
    p.   cm.— (Rethinking theory)
    ISBN 0-8101-1268-X.—ISBN 0-8101-1269-8 (pbk.)
    1. Criticism.   2. Bakhtin, M. M. (Mikhail Mikhaïlovich),
1895–1975.   I. Mandelker, Amy.   II. Series.
PN81.B29   1995
801'.95—dc20   95–23880
                                                                    CIP

The paper used in this publication meets the minimum requirements of the American National
Standard for Information Sciences—Permanence of Paper for Printed Library Materials, ANSI
Z39.48–1984.

Contents

Acknowledgments

Gary Saul Morson's article, "Prosaic Bakhtin: *Landmarks*, Anti-Intelligentsial-ism, and the Russian Countertradition" first appeared in *Common Knowledge* 2 (Spring 1993): 35–74. It is reprinted here with the permission of the author.

Dale E. Peterson's "Response and Call: The African American Dialogue with Bakhtin and What It Signifies" first appeared in *American Literature* volume 65, no. 4 (Dec. 1993): 761–74. It appears here with the permission of Duke University Press.

Vincent Crapanzano's article, "The Postmodern Crisis: Discourse, Parody, Memory," first appeared in *American Anthropology* 6 (1991): 431–46. It appears here with the permission of the American Anthropological Association.

John Dore's article, "The Emergence of Language from Dialogue" was orig-inally published under the title "Monologue as Reinvoicement of Dialogue," in *Narratives from the Crib*, edited by Katherine Nelson (Cambridge: Harvard University Press, 1989), 231–60. It is reprinted here with the permission of the author.

Amy Mandelker's article, "Logosphere and Semiosphere: Bakhtin, Russian Organicism and the Semiotics of Culture," was first published in a shorter form under the title, "Semiotizing the Sphere: Organicist Theory in Lotman, Bakhtin, and Vernadsky," in *PMLA* 109, no. 3 (May 1994):385–96. It appears here with the permission of the Modern Languages Association.

Introduction: *Dialogue on Every Corner, Bakhtin in Every Class*

Caryl Emerson

It should come as no surprise that the Bakhtin boom in post-Communist Russia has had a different trajectory from our own domestic American one. At one point, however, the two paths intersect: here as well as there, Bakhtin is no longer perceived primarily as a *literary* critic. On American campuses this can be explained in part by the fact that literature itself is ceasing to be the central concern of many prestigious and trendsetting literature departments—whose members seek, through ambitious multicultural curricula, a more direct impact on real-life worlds. To those inclined to such politicization, Bakhtin seems to offer inspired support. Read in the spirit of liberationist ideology, his irreverent ideas on the novel and on the potential of carnival appear to invite a release from institutional constraints, from closed-down words, from the isolation and irrelevance of much academic thinking, and from all those conventions that continue to keep the marginal and unofficial at bay.

In Russia, Bakhtin is being read in quite a different key. To ex-Soviet philosophers and literary specialists, the phenomenon of a "radically politicized literature" is so repellently familiar from their own Stalinist past that they now take special pains to locate, among their rehabilitated and canonized scholars, methods or worldviews that offer an alternative to power-centered reading. It is precisely Bakhtin's advocacy, in his early writings on ethics, of "self-reliant," personally negotiated, and apolitical values (in lived lives as well as in literary texts) that has captured the imagination of Russians—and that now seems so desirable and so genuinely revolutionary. Consider, for example, the following portrait of Bakhtin taken from the opening pages of a 1991 monograph entitled *Culture, History, Personality: An Introduction to the Philosophy of the Act*, by the aesthetician and moral philosopher Aleksei Shevchenko. He notes that Bakhtin's early philosophical writing "seems remarkably contemporary, a sort of optimistic antithesis to the spiritual paralysis of the 1970s. Full of an irradicable faith in the limitless potentiality of any human being who acknowledges his absolutely unique irreplaceability . . . [it expresses long-awaited truths that could not be elaborated] in the social space of hurrah-collectivism, and for that reason had seemed somehow sinful and impermissible."[1] Shevchenko would doubtless find Bakhtin studies in the West a peculiar, even an incomprehensible, body of work. For many of our most prominent scholars who are working with Bakhtin's ideas tend toward a brand of "hurrah-collectivism" that incorporates Bakhtin's ideas into one or another suprapersonal theory. Russian Bakhtinists, in contrast, have long been easing out of their master's legacy a sort of neohumanism, usually liberal in spirit and often religiously informed.

The contributors to *Bakhtin in Contexts: Across the Disciplines* partake of both these critical sensibilities, American and Russian. All are skeptical of the harsher, less flexible forms of social and literary theorizing. But their work has been affected to differing degrees by the insight—or corrective—offered their discipline by Bakhtin's profoundly antitheoretic mode of thought. One way of understanding this difference was provided by Stephen Toulmin, in a 1993 essay entitled "The Marginal Relevance of Theory to the Humanities."[2] In this essay, Toulmin argues against the commonly held view that our experiences (and perhaps even our perceptions) occur to us already "theory-laden," that is, "shaped by intellectual standpoints that are essentially arbitrary." Theory, according to Toulmin, is at its best when it serves formal and paradigmatic knowledge, like the stuff of mathematics or geometry. But individual life-events and learning are rarely "knowledgeable" in that way; they serve *phronesis*, practical character-building, the cultivation of memory and moral judgment. Toulmin insists that the proper realm of the humanities is always ongoing experience—and *experiences* are almost never the same as *experiments*.

Since this volume investigates Bakhtin's influence across several fields in the humanities and social sciences, a brief review of Bakhtin's ideas on the subject might be useful. In a late (1974) essay that is remarkably consonant with Toulmin's argument, Bakhtin asked how the humanities, the *"human* sciences," differed from the exact or natural sciences.[3] And he offered this convenient distinction: in the natural sciences, at least at their purest extreme, there is only one consciousness at work—an astronomer at work on a star, a geologist at work on a rock, a chemist at work on a molecule. In the humanities, by contrast, there are always at least two consciousnesses: that is to say, all texts talk back. Each text has its own voice or personality behind it, and that voice is constantly saying: I am more than your analysis says I am; my words or images mean something other than what you just said they mean. Therefore, merely to extract my "intent"—merely to recuperate what my author put into me—is not enough; in fact, that is a very impoverished view of intentionality, for in the humanities it is assumed that authors *intend* their texts to mean something more, and different, to each person who reads, views, or experiences them. All this is to suggest that there is an essential difference between the way two consciousnesses interact with one another and, say, the way one consciousness interacts with a rock, or the way two rocks interact with each other. Of course, Bakhtin adds, we can always *choose* to treat conscious living matter as an inert thing. But that is probably not what the humanities are designed to do best.

Although they vary in their suspicion of impersonal paradigmatic thinking, the contributors to the present volume would agree with Bakhtin on this question of "texts talking back." Some of them, and especially the authors grouped in Part 1, "Bakhtin and Literary Studies," carry a skepticism against fixity and systematization into the very fabric of their argument. The opening essay by Gary Saul Morson, for example, locates Bakhtin's thought precisely in such an unpredetermined, open-ended matrix of values and multiple perspectives—what he calls the "prosaic" countertradition of prerevolutionary Russian literary and intellectual history. The next two entries discuss Bakhtin's contributions to literary genres outside Russia. The first, by the classicist R. Bracht Branham, returns (with more precision than Bakhtin had mustered) to the question of the European novel's untidy genesis out of ancient epiclike forms, attending especially to the shift from oral to written discourse. The second, by the Slavist/Americanist Dale E. Peterson, can be seen to "mirror" (or rather to reverse the flow of) Branham's task, although at many centuries' remove and on another continent. To understand the genre of contemporary American Black discourse, Peterson argues, we must first of all grasp its absolute orality—which means adjusting our critical grip (so comfortable and secure when visited upon the fixed written text) so as to accommodate the improvisation, rapid pace, and performative mastery indispensable to even the simplest genres of aestheticized oral communication. The final entry in Part 1, by Lisa Eckstrom, deals directly and in detail with one author and his literary oeuvre: Henry James, whose *Portrait of a Lady* and *Golden Bowl* represent painfully nuanced variations on the "chronotope of the threshold." Drawing on Bakhtin, Eckstrom offers a corrective to Martha Nussbaum's pathbreaking work on the Jamesian novel as "moral philosophy by other means."

Part 2, "Bakhtin and Social Theory," turns to disciplines located at the edge of the humanities. For the fields of sociology, anthropology, linguistics, and semiotics—while not wholly "exact sciences" in either Toulmin's or Bakhtin's sense of the word—do reward a higher degree of generalizing or structuralizing on the part of the scholar than is expected from our novel-reading authors in Part 1. Such scholars are thus more likely to treat their data as "experiments." Many researchers in these disciplines have found Bakhtin a welcome interloper—or, perhaps better, Bakhtin's thought has provided them with a new sort of self-consciousness. His skepticism of single-authored systems softens their methodologies, introduces humility, encourages their statistics and quantified conclusions to "talk back."

Stanley Aronowitz is an excellent case in point. A sociologist working from a neo-Marxist position, he provides an enthusiastic appreciation of Bakhtin's humanizing effects on a discipline much given to positivism, formalism, and faceless modernisms of various sorts. Aronowitz notes with approval that the Bakhtinian subject is socialized without being relativized; this concept of self, embedded in a concrete "biological-social chronotope," makes possible the breaking down of boundaries between the natural and human sciences and between nature and history. Thus does Aronowitz snatch Bakhtin back from the brink (or taint) of the modern. In a more cautious essay, Vincent Crapanzano shows how Bakhtin's ideas of dialogue and "the Third" can enrich the otherwise bleak, impersonal mechanics of postmodernist discourse.

In his contribution, the linguist John Dore gives us a microhistory of an infant's evolving crib talk. The genre is familiar, but Dore's use of Bakhtin is wonderfully syncretic. From his initial Vygotskian hypothesis that what we hear as a young child's monologue is not (as Piaget presumed) egocentric speech but in fact "reenvoiced dialogue," Dore proceeds to analyze recorded speech events in light of Bakhtin's theory of speech genres. In his scheme, a child's verbal maturation is less a matter of mastering words than it is learning how to construct one's own "compositional unities" within others' communication patterns, that is, learning how to become an *agent* in situations that might otherwise disorient or overwhelm. The concluding essay, by Amy Mandelker, moves us beyond the crib to questions of almost cosmic scope, the semiotics of culture as understood by Bakhtin and Iurii Lotman. And yet the intimate perspective is not lost: her argument is grounded in fine-grained physiological structures, some as individualized as the human brain. Again the natural and the human sciences interact—more strangely and speculatively, perhaps, than we are accustomed to seeing in our Western laboratories, but very much in the Russian tradition. Drawing on comments made by Bakhtin late in life, Mandelker constructs something like an ecology of consciousness, compatible (although not coincident) with Lotman's own theories of the semiosphere, logosphere, and their related realms of biosphere and noösphere. This intersection of concerns occurs late in the respective careers of both scholars, at a time when Bakhtin was writing as a culturologist and Lotman was gradually "organicizing" his originally structuralist thought.

The literary scholars and social theorists represented in this collection are united in one important way. All of them aim to "de-automatize" our responses to familiar Bakhtinian vocabulary by constructing a set of terms or methodologies that are more interesting, complex, and potentially useful to cultural criticism than those flattened-out catchwords we now meet at every step in the humanities, words that now anesthetize us rather than communicate a concrete point of view: *dialogue, polyphony, chronotope, the carnivalesque.* The authors also explore, through their mainstream subject matter as well as their own fraught maneuverings close to the border of various disciplines, the danger of "absolutizing the derivative"—that is, the danger of confusing the critical term with the whole and actually existing entity—in any field where theory has taken hold.[4] For what can ultimately be said of a theoretical approach to the world? We cannot help being drawn to it, we feel clean and on top of things with a general impersonal concept in hand, but all the same most of our texts will continue to slip out from under us because "not all experiences are experiments."

Each of these essays will now be discussed in more detail. Where appropriate, the larger implications or problems raised by these entries will be juxtaposed to a debate or a representative essay among Russian scholars also at work on Bakhtin's legacy. For to our very good fortune, a full picture of "Bakhtin in contexts" is gradually and belatedly coming to include an intellectual exchange with a scholarly community in Bakhtin's own homeland that, in the past half decade, has become unprecedentedly diverse. Both sides are the poorer for failing to engage it.

Bakhtin and Literary Studies

Gary Saul Morson opens his essay on just this note, the need to understand Bakhtin's "radical difference from us." By "us" Morson means theoretically minded academics in humanities departments across the country, whom he profoundly distrusts to the extent that they substitute collective identity for individual responsibility and tend to confuse (or conflate) the ethical with the political. The paradoxical trajectory noted at the beginning of this introduction (Americans celebrating radical groupthink, Russians rediscovering the value of more modest, gradualist, individuated human goals) becomes for Morson the scaffolding for a series of telling, precise observations on Bakhtin's powerfully "prosaic" place in the Russian world—a world all too often abandoned, in Russian minds and our own, to revolutionary ecstasy, apocalypse, maximalism, and titanic heroism.

We first learn what Bakhtin was not. Not a Marxist, not a Formalist, not a structuralist or a modernist, Bakhtin in Morson's portrait of him is compared in spirit and conviction with a group of eminent Russian thinkers of neoidealist, generally liberal views, who in 1909 published a scandalous volume of essays entitled *Vekhi* (Landmarks). These seven essays were united in their dissatisfaction with the Russian radical intelligentsia, whose personal habits, lazy mental reflexes, extremist worldviews, policy of total noncooperation with the tsarist regime, and arrogant pretensions to global salvation through personal sacrifice were all roundly and ungenerously condemned. The lineaments of this Russian *intelligent* is also Morson's major target. He argues persuasively that the young Bakhtin's case against "theoretism" and his insistence upon an individual's "nonalibi in existence" were most likely assembled in the polemical afterglow of the exposé so deftly enacted in *Landmarks*—whose worst predictions, to the horror of its contributors, were realized in October 1917, when Bakhtin was still an undergraduate classics major at Petrograd University.

Out of this *Landmarks* material Morson then unfolds an idea that has been the implicit one dominant in much of his own work over the past two decades: that of a "counter-" or "nonintelligentsial" tradition in Russian literature, of which Bakhtin is an important antitheoretic patron saint. Citing copiously from Herzen, Turgenev, Chekhov, the polyphonic pages of Dostoevsky, and Tolstoy, Morson designs an ethics made up of small tasks, immediate kindnesses, constant opportunity for choice, humility before the complexity of everyday living, and faith that the potentials of the present will lead to an open future—qualities that, taken together, constitute what Morson calls prosaics. These pragmatic and benevolent features are also definitive for what Bakhtin considers the fully "novelized" novel, and they are a factor in all occurrences of authentic love. For in such an understanding of ethics, that is, within such prose narratives and under such conditions of love, *time matters* to an excruciating degree. People, culture, material resources, are loved for what they are right now, loved as they are found, worked with and "lingered over" rather than sized up and sacrificed in the urgent, instantaneous categories so favored by the Tristan and Isolde plot as well as by the political fantasies of the radical intelligentsia—for whom human and nonhuman products were valued "by their potential for apocalyptic destruction or utopian transformation." Here we see evidence of Morson's recent fascination with the interrelations between literary genres and the ethical implications of time.[5]

It could be argued that Morson, and the *Landmarks* authors as well, are too harsh on the intelligentsia. For its ranks, of course, included many thinker-activists of great personal discipline, of learning and high moral fiber, who simply saw no "prosaically ethical" way out of what they perceived as the everyday horrors of Russian imperial politics. These men and women were in principle unwilling—or in practice unable—to endorse as morally sufficient Tolstoy's aristocratic anarchism, Chekhov's exquisite aestheticization of the tiny, private, often hopeless domestic scene, or the liberals' sorely tried patience with piecemeal legal reform. It should be noted, for American readers who seek some familiar analogue in our own culture, that however vehement their case against the nonprosaic vices of the radical intelligentsia, the famous Russian philosophers who wrote for *Landmarks* had little in common with pragmatic empiricists such as Charles Sanders Peirce or William James. In a prosaic no-nonsense way, our pragmatists taught (and to a large extent Bakhtin did too) that ethical life had to be justified minute by minute, "from the bottom up"; for the Jamesian pragmatist, truth was created in the process of verifying hypotheses, and thus truth was what "worked" in a given situation. By and large, the *Landmarks* authors were more idealist in their orientation. They saw a return to *objective* values—distant, disinterested, noneudaemonic, and true regardless of their utility—as key to the moral life and as answer to the "subjective materialism" of their time.[6] With these reservations, however, it must be said that the wholesale indictment of "radical intelligentsialism" that Morson delivers so eloquently in this essay appeals to many disillusioned Russian intellectuals today. The reasons are many, and they transcend any simple contempt for the crude and violent lessons of the failed Russian revolutionary experiment. As has been argued by the best American minds working in Russian philosophy today—George Kline, James Scanlan, and Andrzej Walicki—the problem consists not so much in Russia's supposed paucity of liberal secular thinkers (for she is exceedingly rich in such thinkers) as in a century of political and societal dictates that have narrowed, distorted, and caricatured those thinkers' work. Russia has long known a "West within," and now that communism has passed, this native Russian option can and should be restored, free from any taint of "alien" or "bourgeois" borrowing. It could be argued that among the most pressing tasks of current Russian scholarship is to resurrect Peter Struve's project in *Landmarks*, which was to "challenge the professed genealogy" of the Soviet-Russian revolutionary pantheon that had so greedily "bolshevikized" nineteenth- and twentieth-century thinkers and sucked so much complex talent into its simplifying maw.

To restore a heritage to its full complexity is only part of the task, however. Morson correctly notes that the neoidealists of *Landmarks* were eloquent in their irony and critique and often deficient in "fleshed-out, viable alternatives" to what they deplored. This complaint has been voiced in the ex-Soviet context as well, where, not surprisingly, formal freedom for the word has proved much easier to install than the habits or institutions necessary to employ free words responsibly. In a trenchant article entitled "The Russian Idea: The Temptations of Spirituality," which appeared in 1992 after the first wave of *Landmarks* reprints had subsided, the Petersburg historian Alexander Shchelkin addressed just this concern. He remarked ruefully that the most prominent *Landmarks* thinkers, themselves disillusioned former members of the intelligentsia now moved by more contemplative and de-bureaucratized models of the virtuous life, "not only renounced the politics of revolutionary fanaticism but renounced politics in general"—and thus could prove dangerous inspiration for the present, post-Communist day.[7] Although Shchelkin arguably misrepresents the overall spirit of the *Landmarks* volume, his anxiety is real: disdain for the spirit of compromise and a belief that systems of governance can dispense with well-differentiated power relations was, to the extent the *Vekhi* authors endorsed those ideas, misleading advice.

Morson's application of "prosaics" to Russian cultural history is a good corrective, although Bakhtin must be invoked with care. Bakhtin's early ethical teachings, so refreshingly free of suprapersonal constructs or gestures toward utopia do indeed provide abundant guidelines for spiritual and behavioral "literacy" in everyday life. But the extant writings contain only the most rudimentary and abstract comments on organized political activity as such; although in the early 1920s Bakhtin had projected a large work on moral philosophy with one of its four parts devoted to "the ethics of politics," it is now assumed that he never completed the study.[8] As Morson and I have argued elsewhere, Bakhtin conceives of the human being as a creature of intimate gatherings, as a communicating (or communing) animal, and not primarily as a *political* animal. When admirers of his thought smuggle politics into his scenarios, more often than not the result is appallingly contrary to Bakhtin's overall ethical orientation. (We witness just such distortion, for example, when carnival is attached to the spirit of Marxian revolution or when Bakhtin's rogues, jesters, and fools are celebrated as "the organized voice of the oppressed.") Distrustful of all thinking via large groups or masses, suspicious even of representational procedures (which he considered insufficiently personalistic and wanting in humility), Bakhtin gives us little by way of concrete recommendations for achieving a workable institutional pluralism.[9] Morson acknowledges this fact. The great value of his contribution lies in its recuperation of a nonintelligentsial tradition for Russian culture and its placement of Bakhtin within that tradition—while recognizing the immense distance that still remains between those virtues and a prosaically viable daily politics.

If Gary Saul Morson interacts with the concerns of his text as a novelistic author (or novelistic hero) would do, in a zone of contact "maximally close to the present," then Bracht Branham adopts the philological distance of the author of an epic. His essay "Inventing the Novel" is the work of a classicist looking at Bakhtin *as* a classicist. He finds there much to recommend in big categories and blunt historical dynamics, but he is vexed, as many in his field have been, by Bakhtin's summary attitude toward smaller historical shifts or refinements. Seeing in Bakhtin a masterful corrective to both Marxist and early Formalist theories of literature (each of which ignored, in its own way, the mediating function of genre), Branham takes a closer look at some of the famous essays that launched Bakhtin as a theorist of the novel in the West: "Epic and Novel," "Toward a Prehistory of Novelistic Discourse," and the book-length essay on the chronotope. In those essays, it will be recalled, Bakhtin discusses the genesis of postclassical genres in very broad sweep, invoking a dramatic and anthropomorphized cast of actor-agents. "Novelization" invades the placid domain of the epic. The result, in Bakhtin's scenario, is an explosion of looser, more penetrable forms: the chance-ridden Greek romance, the Roman comic novel, autobiographical narrative, and biographical genres of varying degrees of self-consciousness. Branham considers this leap "from heroic verse to comic prose" too abrupt in Bakhtin's rendition. Bakhtin, Branham argues, is too casual in his distinction between Greek and Roman traditions of fiction; his readings are too closely tied to an a priori faith in the transformative power of polyglossia and laughter. Indeed, so passionate is Bakhtin about those two virtues that he considers them beyond dispute and in need of no defense in a history of the evolution of literary form.

Branham's revisionism centers on the genre of the Greek romance. He argues that this genre is best *not* understood as a single "post-epic" category, classified together with its purported Roman counterpart, the novel of Petronius. For in contrast to the somewhat stylized, "staged" romance, the racy everydayness of

The Satyricon is meant to be read privately to oneself; its stories are the province of a narrator who is as irreverent, as highly personalized and unpredictable, as each individual reader. In contrast, the Greek romance—for all its adventures, escapes, and scary episodes "in the nick of time"—remains solidly in the Panhellenic tradition. Markers of oral transmission are still in place; its beautiful, virtuous heroes and heroines are fully conventional and "ready-made"; its settings are "modernized versions of the 'absolute past' of epics," and its "cultural memory is personified by the Muses." Branham concludes, against Bakhtin's spirit, that the Greek romance is less the first step en route to the novel than it is "a kind of prose epic." It was the Romans who first submitted this genre, and its parent the epic, to that subversive parody so marvelously realized by Petronius. This development was due not only to the mythic, irresistible forces of laughter and multilanguagedness in the younger empire (as Bakhtin implies) but also to the growth of literacy and the institutionalization of rhetoric and philosophy in rapidly maturing Roman culture.

Branham's overall project is larger than his brief essay suggests. Its first achievement is to confront head-on what might be called the covert, Hegelian-style anthropomorphism of Bakhtin's literary history, his impatience to see all of literary history unfolding toward the Spirit or Hero of the Novel immanent in it. Bakhtin often practiced this sort of imperialism on behalf of his favorite genre in his middle, quite maximalist years.[10] Branham properly resists this implicit teleology—or at least brakes and tempers it. Unlike Bakhtin, he does not assume that all epic-style literature, as it survives into a postclassical world, eventually comes to sense its own smug self-enclosure as a disability and thus anticipates its "liberation" by the ascendant novelizing impulse. Instead, Branham allows the Greek romance to drag its feet, remain behind in familiar plots and characters, savor the virtues of the old epic world. As he intimates, literary evolution more resembles a mixing pot than a single undeviating drive toward individuation or freedom. Indeed, elsewhere (and specifically in the chronotope essay) Bakhtin himself endorses a more flexible position on the coexistence of archaic and modernizing genres. But in "Epic and Novel" and other teleological essays from the high Stalinist years upon which Branham draws, that more flexible, tentative voice is in abeyance.

A second and related issue raised in Branham's essay concerns Bakhtin's predilection, as literary historian, for the very large scope—which, for all Bakhtin's massive learning, makes imprecision and overstatement inevitable. Branham wonders how we, as literary scholars, might best benefit from such research practices. For judged by the whole of his corpus, Bakhtin is eclectically interdisciplinary: a psychologist, moral philosopher, and student of consciousness in his early period; he only later attached those interests to literary scholarship. On this matter Bakhtin himself was quite explicit: according to recently published interviews from the early 1970s, Bakhtin always considered himself "a philosopher and a thinker" who used literature as a rich pool of examples and as a safe haven from politics.[11] The word *myslitel'* (thinker) has special resonance in Russian academic culture. "Thinkers" can be eclectic and eccentric; they are more free than scholars to transcend established methodologies or disciplines. In Bakhtin's case, the term suggests a person who is less concerned to apply his thought to illuminate literature than he is to utilize literature, selectively and at a high level of inspiration, to illustrate his thought. It is of some interest that Bakhtin's lofty self-appellation and intellectual trajectory have now become his identifying marks rather than his flaws.

But it will surprise no professional classicist that Bakhtin's breadth and provocative imprecisions do not sit well with the majority of traditionally trained philologists in classics departments, here or abroad. Although Bakhtin on Menippean satire has always been popular in academe, classicists—who tend to be conservative by principle, temperament, and methodology—have only recently taken a serious look at Bakhtin's many other bold hypotheses about the ancient world. (In 1993, a special issue of the classics periodical *Arethusa* was devoted to "Bakhtin and Ancient Studies: Dialogues and Dialogics."[12]) In post-Communist Russia as well, according to one academic insider, references to Bakhtin in the research of senior classicists are few or absent altogether; what references there are often occur in the safe context of a critique or survey of Western Bakhtinian readings. This same scholar notes that her Russian colleagues who specialize in the ancient world tend to focus on individual works or authors, or on stylistic and prosodic detail; their work and Bakhtin's belong to "different optics, different scales." To most of them, Bakhtin's far-flung general theories "sound too loud and pretentious; and here it appears that the researchers are correct."[13] These Russian criticisms, not entirely unjust, are familiar to the American classicist community out of which Branham writes. His essay is an attempt—difficult and largely successful— from within the profession to affirm Bakhtin's broad scope while introducing a concrete corrective.

Unlike the classicist instance, Dale Peterson's Bakhtinian discussion of Black literary voices, "Response and Call: The African American Dialogue with Bakhtin and What It Signifies," has no conceivable professional Russian counterpart. Why this is so is itself an intriguing question. A huge multicultural empire comes apart, and its separate ethnic groups achieve freedom of the word almost overnight. Where are the theorists? There have been superb ethnologists among Soviet scholars: in the 1920s and 1930s they helped craft written languages for many non-European Soviet peoples, whose local literatures were then subsidized and loudly celebrated throughout the Stalinist period. To be sure, an edge of colonial patronizing could always be felt. As is the case with Western empires, in Great Russia too a deep provincialism and naive racism has coexisted easily with cosmopolitan pretensions—with the added complication in the Russian instance of a rhetoric of Communist internationalism, that omnipresent background din, which preached that ethnic difference would be dissolved eventually in classless social harmony. But as regards the complex problem of Blackness, our histories have been profoundly different. In the nineteenth century Alexander Pushkin, Russia's greatest poet, prided himself on being one-eighth Ethiopian, the great-grandson of an African prince; such genealogy was exotic and regal. In the twentieth century, however, xenophobic nationalism and resentment of Communist subsidies to the so-called third world have reinforced traditional Russian racisms. And Russia, of course, never had an indigenous Black population whose very language and interaction with fellow citizens had been shaped by the awful reality of race-based slavery.

For all these reasons, Peterson's essay cannot find its Bakhtinian equivalent on the multiracial soil of the former Soviet Union. Here an important methodological point must be made. The best argument against applying Bakhtinian ideas to "creole" or dialect studies was provided by Bakhtin himself. He specifically withdrew his insights about dialogic language from anything as crude and cosmetic as the surface features of a given dialect. In his Dostoevsky book, for example, Bakhtin noted that in terms of "speech dialect" Dostoevskian heroes do indeed all sound alike; in those novels, "there is significantly less language differentiation, that is, fewer language styles, territorial and social dialects, professional jargons and so forth, than in the work of many writer-monologists" (in that latter group of "monologists" Bakhtin includes Leo Tolstoy as well as the great Russian master of *skaz*, Nikolai Leskov).[14] One should not confuse mere reified and externalized "speech characterizations" with a genuine polyphony or individuality of worldview, Bakhtin cautions. For the authenticity and quality of these inner worldviews are measured not by specific words, sounds, syntax, or semantic content—formal matters, which linguists are qualified to assess—but by the *dialogic angle* at which one consciousness is juxtaposed to another.

It is precisely this focus on the "dialogic angle" of discourse between Blacks and Blacks, and between Blacks and Whites, that makes Dale Peterson's essay so accomplished an application and extension of Bakhtin's thought. For he does not discuss Black English as a *language* (although such technical linguistic studies have been undertaken, drawing usefully on Bakhtin and Voloshinov). What interests Peterson is what had always been of primary interest to Bakhtin: not the phonemic envelope, sound rhymes, or repeating features of an utterance but its dialogic orientation, especially when produced under conditions that require constant mental agility and alertness from both speaker and listener. Producers of such utterances communicate in a "tension-filled environment"—as Bakhtin was fond of putting it—and are thus maximally sensitized to the contours of their own and others' words.

Peterson suggests that the fifty-year time lag between Bakhtin's texts and their reception on Western soils has brought real benefits. As do Aronowitz and Crapanzano in their respective essays, Peterson claims that our present poststructuralist, postdeconstructionist climate makes Bakhtin the perfect mediator between old and new methodologies: he desires to loosen up the sign, yes, but not entirely and not indefinitely. Rather than the extreme, aggressive gestures of either fixing down or freeing up a text, Bakhtin is content to "ventilate" it. Utterances have more on their minds than mere power; as Abraham Lincoln once said, "Most people are about as happy as they make up their minds to be," and Peterson would say the same about an utterance even in the mouths of persons with slavery in their past. It is as free as it makes up its mind to be. "Tricky, artful, evasive, obviously hyphenated," African American writing fascinates because it requires so much subtle, unrelieved work to keep the interlocutor simultaneously engaged and at bay. But the main thrust of Peterson's essay is probably not there. His primary task is to interrogate those two gifted scholar-critics, Henry Louis Gates Jr. and Houston A. Baker Jr., who have been instrumental in helping non-Black communities appreciate the artful, tricky, performative "street-smart signifyin'" of Black texts.

What does Peterson find in the writings of these two prominent Black critics? The same awkward moment that comes upon us when we wish to seal in place a political gain made during the process of carnival. It will not stick; and if it did stick, it would cease to be true to its own inner dynamic. Yet to get any serious thing done, one must call "a willful halt to dialogic tensions." (As Peterson points out, such a halt to the sassy give-and-take conventions of oral dialogue seems all the more necessary in the larger context of American culture, where *entertainment* has long been the accepted mode of Black expression.) The critics are all caught in this paradox. But fortunately, primary fiction writers know what the critics must forget: that all "mouth-to-mouth appropriations" are highly unstable and anxious things. Double-voicedness liberates everything from everything else, constantly. Peterson puts this wisdom well when he quotes Janie Starks, heroine of Zora Neale Hurston's *Their Eyes Were Watching God*, walking by the village gossips after telling them her story: "Ah see Mouth-Almighty is still sittin' in de same place. And Ah reckon they got *me* up in they mouth now." To be sure, it is the business of any critical establishment—backed up by academic hierarchies, professional etiquette, and long-term tenures—to insulate itself somewhat from being up in the mouth of someone else. But dialogic literature itself cannot hide there. Peterson intimates that African American fiction, with its fiercely speakerly texts, can help us remember the feel of that primary vulnerability.

In her "Moral Perception and the Chronotope: The Case of Henry James," Lisa Eckstrom provides the sole essay in Part 1 devoted to a close reading of a single novelist. Her task is complex, what might be called "Bakhtin revisionism of the second degree." She presumes, and then partially undoes, an implicit parallel between the writings of the American philosopher Martha Nussbaum on Henry James and Bakhtin's ruminations on the spirit of the novel.[15] The convergences are indeed striking. Both critics can be read as moral philosophers who approach their favorite novels as "philosophy by other means," that is, as studies in perception designed to encourage in their readers qualities of moral attention through an "intense scrutiny of particulars."[16] The nineteenth-century novel is a rich site for exploring human indeterminacy and ethical fine-tuning. Both Nussbaum and Bakhtin intimate that we structure our art and our lives in overlapping zones, answerable to each other, and that this is a human good. For however extensive and nonschematic novelistic language might seem, it is in fact highly efficient moral philosophy—that is, it is perfectly suited to the particularized tasks of building a real-life self in open time—and this competence is due to the fact that discourse in the novel is so noncompressible and radically unparaphrasable. The close readings that both critics produce presuppose that literary theory can do without politics (can in fact do *better* without politics) but will fare poorly without an ethical philosophy.

Against this shared background, Eckstrom rethinks Bakhtin's idea of the nineteenth-century novelistic chronotope. She shows how the "threshold chronotope"—not the one Bakhtin applies to Dostoevsky's overheated scenarios, but a chronotope related to the more sober "architectonic" environment of Bakhtin's early writings on ethics—works more subtly in Henry James than Nussbaum has allowed. Bakhtin's "architectonics" (his attempt to ground Kant's categorical imperative in the concreteness of an individual life) finds a natural home in the nineteenth-century novel. But Eckstrom pushes further and adduces more difficult test cases than Bakhtin is inclined to do in his study of Dostoevsky. If moral knowledge does indeed lie in concrete perception and in complexly prosaic details of timing and intonation, then no one-way passage across a boundary will elucidate that knowledge. In fact, the whole idea of linear progress toward a resolved position cannot do justice to the pain, confusion, and cost exacted in genuine visitations of moral choice. In close readings of scenes from *The Portrait of a Lady* and *The Golden Bowl*, Eckstrom demonstrates how James increasingly traps his protagonists on lingering threshold chronotopes rich in transitional moods and moral dead ends. "Flashes" of insight are reduced to uncertain and inarticulate "flickers"; what ought to be instantaneous or epiphanic thresholds leading to comprehensive vision are in fact governed by uneasy "chronotopes of the vigil"; and the heroes and heroines who participate in these opaque scenarios cannot be said to "perceive" themselves more clearly as they grope their way toward the light. Nor are the victories they achieve necessarily an improvement or clarification. They are ethically correct holding patterns, whose price can often be a long-term anesthetization of feeling and a willful, partial suspension of consciousness. Echoing Nussbaum's collection of essays *The Fragility of Goodness*, Eckstrom concludes that Henry James, in his last novel, portrays "the fragility of moral cognition."

In her application of a revised "threshold chronotope" to analyze dialogic interaction in two novels by James, Eckstrom parallels the efforts of Russian scholars who are adjusting Bakhtin's time-space markers to accommodate classic modern novels in the West that Bakhtin himself did not address. (Perhaps the most interesting project in this regard is Sergei Khoruzhy's strikingly Formalist commentary to his acclaimed Russian edition of James Joyce's *Ulysses;* Khoruzhy reads Leopold Bloom's single day in Dublin as the product of a post-Einsteinian worldview, a dense, interwoven matrix of liberated and autonomous chronotopes, each of which is present in the novel not as a given characteristic of the genre but as the self-conscious application of a device.[17]) In a larger sense, however, Eckstrom is contributing to a Russian project now several years under way: the thickening and, as it were, "darkening" of Bakhtin's image and a soberer view of his more ecstatic categories.

How are Bakhtinian categories being darkened in the post-Communist period? As Russians discover that the free word does not guarantee any miracles—that in fact the Russian word is en route to becoming the same indifferent and devalued thing that we in the West have long known words to be—and as they learn that democracy is less a matter of utterances than of procedures, Bakhtin's heretofore benevolent, at times even utopian, optimism about dialogic language begins to lose some of its inspirational naïveté. Dialogue among speaking parties always keeps things going at some level, yes, but in this world we muddle down as often as we "make sense"—and in threshold situations it is very easy to evade and to lie. The recent publication of excerpts from Bakhtin's crumbling wartime notebooks (1943– 46) reinforces this more circumspect attitude toward the moral corruptibility of language.[18] "The lie is today's most ever-present form of evil," Bakhtin wrote, in a series of increasingly ominous ruminations on a theme he apparently was outlining for future research. "The phenomenology of the lie. Its extraordinary heterogeneity and the subtlety of its forms. Reasons for its extraordinary omnipresence. The philosophy of the lie. The rhetorical lie. The lie in artistic form." Keeping in mind Eckstrom's treatment of the compromised, fragile "threshold chronotope" in Henry James, we might consider Bakhtin's belated intimation that even the prodigious verbal resources of the novel cannot be relied upon to guide us, in all situations, toward a life that is "finely aware and richly responsible." As Bakhtin wrote during a sober moment in 1943: "The word does not know whom it serves. It emerges from the dark and does not know its own roots. Its serious link with terror and violence. The authentically kind, unselfish, and loving person has not yet spoken, he has realized himself in the spheres of everyday life, he has not attached himself to the official word, infected with violence and the lie; he is not becoming a writer."

Bakhtin and Social Theory

In the opening essay of Part 2, "Literature as Social Knowledge: Mikhail Bakhtin and the Reemergence of the Human Sciences," Stanley Aronowitz places Bakhtin in the context of anglophone cultural criticism. This move mirrors Gary Saul Morson's placement of Bakhtin in the Russian historical context in Part 1. The trajectories of our two countries are so very different, however, that the portraits of our subject that emerge from these two essays are not at all the same. Russians need little persuading on the issue of art's dominant role in life (the question there is, "Can there ever be a real life as attractive and compelling as art?"); and Aronowitz, a Western sociologist with Marxian leanings, activates potentials in Bakhtin quite different from those drawn upon by Morson, a literary scholar who explicitly leans toward liberal pluralism. Morson demonstrates how Bakhtin's concretely personalist ethics were shared by many Russian literary masters and eminent social critics, in conscious or unconscious resistance to that cluster of myths and convictions we recognize as the Russian utopian-collectivist tradition. For his part, Aronowitz is concerned to establish that artistic works are reliable sources of social knowledge (Russians would never feel the need to test that assumption) and that Bakhtin's idiosyncratic approach to language and literary art makes available to us "a critique of historicism from the perspective of a new conception of historicity."

Aronowitz's task is immense and here only sketched. He notes engagingly at one point that "Bakhtin gets us to think in his categories." Indeed, in this essay success on that score is profound. To appreciate its extent, we must remember the services that a thinker like Bakhtin can offer a leftist social scientist in the West during our current trivialized era of the "postmodern." Bakhtin's thought is not Stalinist or socialist-realist; in fact, it is on record as being against those things. But neither can it be assimilated smugly to the "robber-baron capitalist" ideology that now, after the debacle of communism, has commercialized and restratified Russia to a scandalous extent in the minds of many of her citizens. Bakhtin is nostalgic for an earlier time, when earnest conversation and continual eye contact could keep the rhetorical lie out of private lives. Although against theoretism, Bakhtin was still an ameliorist social visionary; himself no Marxist, the social and ethical contours of his thought were nevertheless shaped in the more diversified 1920s, when a concept like "Marxist-Leninist humanism" could still be taken seriously by Russian thinkers of good will. (On the question of Bakhtin's own politics there is little doubt, however. When queried on this point by a close friend near the end of his life, Bakhtin answered: "Marxism? Never. Like many others I was interested in Freudianism and even spiritualism, but I was never a Marxist, never in the slightest."[19]) Aronowitz is drawn to this potential in Bakhtin, even if Bakhtin himself did not acknowledge it, and he enlarges on the contribution that an ideal, and idealized, "Marxist-Leninist humanist" might have made to the sociology of knowledge.

Aronowitz begins by assessing the strengths and weaknesses of the best that mainstream Marxism could offer by way of twentieth-century literary critics: Georg Lukács. Lukács, however, was still caught in a "realist epistemology"—by which Aronowitz means that he developed a theory of narrative but not a theory of language. When theories of language did come on the scene, they tended to be structuralist, like that of Roland Barthes. According to Aronowitz, Bakhtin combines the best of old and new by offering "a theory of language that privileges agency over structure while working with, but not within, linguistic boundaries." But this is not all: through his concept of the chronotope (and especially the carnival chronotope, with its emphasis on cyclicity and regenerative folklife), Bakhtin makes available "an incipient theory of the relation of nature to human interaction."

The idea that Bakhtin's chronotope is somehow an "ecological" structure mediating between natural and human worlds is not immediately persuasive, given that Bakhtin is everywhere so taken up by the advent of consciousness. But it turns out that Aronowitz is making a looser claim: that the very structure of the chronotope is a standing challenge to the natural sciences, which too often are unwilling to acknowledge the uncontestable fact that within their domain as well, "evidence is heavily mediated by interpretation." Bakhtin puts to the test "the positivist doctrine of authentication through experiment" across a whole spectrum of academic disciplines (or in Toulmin's terms invoked at the beginning of this introduction, the chronotope, more efficiently than any other analytic category, persuades us that "not all experiences are experiments"). According to Aronowitz, the carnival chronotope in particular can teach the contemporary social historian very useful truths and methodologies.

The reasons for his preference are clear. First, Bakhtin's carnival invokes a social, not an individual, chronotope (with the emergence of the individual person as organizing principle, Bakhtinian "series" are replaced by "voices"). Second, carnival appears to contribute to the "neo-Marxist critique of modernity"—but at the same time it is reassuringly and productively historical, fused with real, everyday commoners' time—for carnival rhythms and folkloric time, although cyclical, are *not* static. Aronowitz's endorsement goes further. Drawing on the interlocking nature/nurture matrices in the Rabelais book and on Bakhtin's own early interest in the biological chronotope, he suggests that the hypothesis of "heterotrophic sources of life" worked out in the 1920s—a sort of synchronized or horizontalized Darwinism—set a precedent for rethinking the entire nature/history boundary, and thus also for rethinking the divide between the natural and human sciences. (Aronowitz would find more concrete support for this "ecological" hypothesis in Bakhtin's late writings from the 1970s; see Amy Mandelker's discussion of Vernadsky and Bakhtin in the final essay of this volume.)

In the welter of present trends in social criticism, what appeals most of all to Aronowitz is Bakhtin's relentless antiformalism—and Bakhtin's even more daring antimodernism. We detect here a certain nostalgia for more responsible, better-anchored times; this theme will resurface, in a very different context, in Vincent Crapanzano's essay on the postmodern crisis. And as the Communist East continues to implode, this point is worth emphasizing. For a certain class of social theorists in the West today, there remains something earnestly old-fashioned and nontrivial about the sympathies, subject matter, and beneficiaries of classical Marxism: its emphasis on "real material conditions," on collective affinities, and its constant reference to "the people" (as opposed to the artist or the self-destructing avant-garde). Bakhtin was "a religious individual," Aronowitz admits, and "profoundly at odds with postrevolutionary Russia"; yet he was smitten by the force of everyday things and "influenced by Marxism's *intention* to deliver literature from its formal bonds, especially in his attempt to develop a truly social theory of literature in which . . . whole discourses and even sentences embody the dialogic principle." This reading is open to debate. On the inspirational aspects of Marxism for Bakhtin, maybe yes, maybe no; Bakhtin himself denied any such influence. As regards literary production in his own century and its liberation through a materialist aesthetic, we know that Bakhtin had a thorough scholarly knowledge of Symbolist poetry and its successor movements in Russia, but as far as we can tell, he was profoundly unresponsive to the major works of twentieth-century modernism.[20]

How might a current Russian intellectual react to Aronowitz's appreciation of Bakhtin? Certain aspects would probably appear strange. Whereas Aronowitz praises Bakhtin's flexible and creative use of history, it was, as we noted above, precisely Bakhtin's loose, often impressionist historical terminology and methodology that was criticized in the Russian scholarly press in the mid-1960s, when the revised Rabelais and Dostoevsky studies were published. Most contested, probably, would be the rosy reading that Aronowitz gives to carnival. By now, American readers have had a taste in English of those contemporary Russian Bakhtinists, often very sympathetic to (and literate in) French cultural theory, for whom the Rabelais book delivers in spirit and in substance not a joyous or liberating thesis but a grimly serious Stalinist one—as in, for example, Mikhail Ryklin's essay "Bodies of Terror," on the carnivalized terror inscribed in Moscow Metro sculpture.[21] Since Ryklin's essay, the Russian critique of Bakhtinian-Rabelaisian carnival has broadened.

One example will suffice. In the second issue of *Bakhtinskii sbornik* (1991) the Petersburg intellectual historian Konstantin Isupov discusses what he calls "the Bakhtinian crisis of humanism."[22] His starting point is the exceedingly harsh judgment passed on Rabelais by one of Russia's great philosophers of culture, Aleksei Losev, in his book *The Aesthetics of the Renaissance*.[23] According to Losev, Rabelais gives us a picture of the inversion, destruction, and parody of Renaissance humanism, not its heroic realization. The Abbey of Thélème, where one neither prays nor works, is in Losev's view a dystopian parody of a functioning human community; and when examined closely, Losev sees in those much admired hero-giants Gargantua and Pantagruel nothing more than coarse, grasping, cowardly nihilists with no "truly durable perseverance to their natures." Furthermore, Losev contends, "corporeality" in Rabelais is at a far extreme from the grace, proportionality, and intelligence of the Renaissance body. Bodies in Rabelais are presented as "idea-less, empty, devoid of content, far from any artistry," and whatever ideas do connect with them are petty and dehumanized. Obliquely sparring with Bakhtin, whose examples he everywhere turns to negative effect, Losev concludes (and Isupov later approvingly cites): "If one takes Rabelais's realism in all the fullness of its content, what emerges is an extremely vile and repellent aesthetic, one which, of course, has its own logic, but this logic is repellent. . . . Rabelais's realism is the aesthetic apotheosis of all vileness and obscenity. Whoever is pleased to consider such realism progressive, go ahead and so consider it."

Losev's Communist-era critique of Rabelais—although not quite on the level of "this is a dirty book"—is not original; it was, after all, against such mainstream fastidiousness that Bakhtin's study made its own spectacular mark. Of interest to us here is Isupov's use of this negative assessment in the Russian post-Communist context. The Morson and Aronowitz essays make Bakhtin's humanism a central value, although those two American critics realize that value very differently. From within their zone, Isupov's despair strikes a sour and unsettling note. Isupov aims to describe Bakhtin's attitude toward humanism and finds it deeply ambivalent. What is his argument, and how might it speak to Western scholars rethinking the Bakhtinian carnivalesque?

In the still pre-Stalinist 1920s, Bakhtin and his colleagues were working out the proper relationship of "I" to "other." At the time, Isupov reminds us, a Christian "liturgical-sacrificial" model of service held sway; the I was seen as assembling itself out of others, who in turn retained a form-shaping power to finalize the I. The discovery of the dialogic nature of language modified this scenario in a positive, stabilizing direction. For in polyphonic construction—characteristic of both the novel and the human personality—what comes to anchor the I, even in its collective or choral mode, is *memory*. Over time, therefore, and regardless of the pain involved, we cannot help coming to know and answer for what is "our own." Isupov intimates that this knowledge is the minimal unit of humanism.[24]

In Bakhtin's book on Rabelais, however, there is an abrupt undoing of this ethos, "a loss of the very principle of 'one's own.'" The I simply "falls out of the problematic zone of Bakhtin's vision," Isupov notes. He then asks why Bakhtin might have departed so utterly from his early Christian anthropology. Because, Isupov surmises, the new choral I did not need it. Bakhtin effectively returns the conscious I, which is a fallen and articulate Adam, to a prelapsarian state where it blissfully knows nothing of good or evil; it reenters a "carnivalized Eden or Paradise." But Isupov hastens to add that this carnival Eden could just as easily be experienced as a carnivalized hell.[25] After all, the only resident within the Garden with any real knowledge is the Serpent. Its laughter is neither human nor humanistic but, ringing out boldly and facelessly on the Edenic equivalent of the public square, simply satanic. This "demonic humanism" is in fact Rabelais's chosen path, Isupov concludes. Its proper fruit is not the body warmth of Bakhtin's folk carnival but the exquisitely voided spaces of Baudelaire's *Les fleurs du mal.*

Such readings of Bakhtin are recent fare. When Russia was still part of the Soviet Union and the "simple folk" (the "masses") still a category that all writers had to emulate, Bakhtin *Festschriften* ran cheerful entries on Breughel's canvases as a hymn of praise to "Rabelaisian-type" peasants, whose ample backsides and bosoms Bakhtin, supposedly, would have eulogized. Celebrations of that sort are now in much shorter supply. And although, as we shall see in this volume's final essay, one can indeed construct a sort of human ecology out of Bakhtin's final philosophical writings, many Russian Bakhtinists would find strange the idea that carnival per se—with its absolute irresponsibility toward both human and nonhuman environments—could give rise to ecological visions reconnecting humans and nature (and especially visions of the ecstatic sort Aronowitz so praises in *Rabelais*). In fact, such readings might soon become the province solely of Bakhtin's carnival-folklore fantasy and of our own highly distanced, insulated extracts of his thought in the West.

It is equally instructive to read Vincent Crapanzano's essay, "The Postmodern Crisis: Discourse, Parody, Memory," against the background of Russia's present and continuing post-Communist crisis. For in recent years there has been an explosion of discussions of the "postmodern" in the Russian press, to which, at last, almost everything is permitted. At one pole is practice: the rush of new, earnest, often naive journals and anthologies devoted to integrating, as fast as possible so as not to fall further behind, the terminologies and gurus of continental (and especially French) cultural thought. The Russian critical lexicon employed here is shocking and hybrid; the titles and themes—dying, sex, desire, torture, slippage, authorlessness, disease—all terribly familiar. At the other pole is theory. The established professional journals, which, since the advent of freedom for the word, routinely do retrospectives on the fate of disciplines in the humanities, have assessed the phenomenon of postmodernism carefully, but often dismissively.

One such forum, "Postmodernism and Culture," appeared in the journal *Questions of Philosophy* in March 1993.[26] "The word 'postmodernism' lost its seductive nuance of originality extraordinarily quickly in our criticism," the opening panelist remarked. Its appeal in the West, where hi-tech gadgets are within everyone's reach, might be worthy of study—but only at a distance; the West's consumerized economies can afford to place aesthetic emphasis "not on depth or intensity but on slipping over the surface . . . [on] the rapid flipping of channels with the help of a remote-control unit, where the spectator's pleasure consists largely in the very process of pressing the buttons." But Russians—on this point the panelists tended to concur—always return, sooner or later, to a form of realism. They understand well the Fathers-and-Sons rivalry of the current *isms* because their experience has taught them to distrust all *isms*; they see the old-fashionedness of all binary oppositions. Postmodernism can teach the Russians (with their proclivity for depth and intensity) one important lesson, however: how to philosophize intelligently about art as *process*. One panelist remarked that the great "philosophers of becoming"—Bergson, Husserl, Merleau-Ponty, William James—had not been taken seriously enough on Russian soil; there needed to be more discussion of philosophy and artworks as *events* rather than as things. With his pragmatic ethics and his consciousness-centered, open-ended view of verbal art, Bakhtin is splendidly situated to contribute to this debate.

Crapanzano's essay is a welcome mediator between these two poles of the Russian response to postmodernism. On the one hand, there is mimicry and a rush to catch up; on the other, the traditional Russian route of exceptionalism (we translate you Westerners more than you translate us; you produce partial truths whereas we assimilate and integrate; our path is so different you cannot know it; consequently we are exempt from judgment). Crapanzano aims neither to endorse nor to reject the postmodernist perspective. His task is much more subtle and difficult: namely, to find in this perspective something complex, interesting, potentially creative. Here, despite his well-documented disinterest in both the ethics and the formalized aesthetics of the modern/postmodern, Bakhtin proves an unexpected ally.

Crapanzano begins by summing up what postmodernism has come to mean in a single metaphor: the supplanting of the ruin—which at least had real substance and historicity—by "the quotation, the trace, really a pseudo-trace." Our world has become one in which all accounts are artifice, where we sense "a far-reaching discontent with . . . the conventions of historical, indeed, at times it seems, of any kind of understanding." His godterm (and here we detect common ground with Isupov's reading of Bakhtin's humanistic dimension) is *memory*, surely one of the more beseiged concepts in the postmodern matrix. Memory, in Crapanzano's definition, is "a structural precipitate of any dialogic engagement in which a change of perspective or the illusion of a change of perspective occurs." We recall crucial intersections and interactions, whose sequencing then helps locate us in the world. But this engagement and its subsequent narration registers only if there is an "authoritative function," the Third, which "mediates any interlocution." Partly an enabling device and partly an appeal, the Third is "metapragmatic" to the extent that it determines how our communications with others are authorized and understood. How this Third works in practice is Crapanzano's narrower focus. Where does Bakhtin come in? The connection is not made explicit in this essay, but we might do so here.

Bakhtin's several references to a "third" are part of his lifelong devotion to "outsideness," that is, his belief that we must assume an external position vis-à-vis things we wish to understand. Although he nowhere develops its implications with Crapanzano's thoughtfulness or detail, Bakhtin uses the word *third* in two quite different senses. First there is his discussion, in his "Notes made in 1970–71," of the "noumenal" vantage point we occasionally posit to help orient ourselves when comparing and juxtaposing phenomena. "There exists an abstract *position of a third party* that is identified with the 'objective position' as such, with the position of some 'scientific cognition,'" Bakhtin writes. But he is quick to limit the applicability of this "third party" to those exchanges where mere recognition rather than genuine dialogic understanding is sufficient: "It is justified only in those situations . . . where the integral and unrepeatable individuality of the person is not required, that is, when a person is, so to speak, specialized, and reflects only one part of his individuality detached from the whole, . . . not as *I myself* but 'as an engineer,' 'as a physicist.'"[27] To appeal to the Third in this context is to be businesslike, opportunistic, automatized, and unchallenged in one's identity and modes of communication. In Crapanzano's terms, this would cover those ordinary, consensual exchanges where the Third "is usually taken for granted or easily negotiated."

But Bakhtin introduces the term in a second, more passionate sense, which is the one Crapanzano finds especially congenial. I have in mind Bakhtin's idea of the *nadadresat* or "superaddressee," whose identity and capacity to understand is specifically and, one might say, even rapturously individuated. If the "second" in any dialogue is the actual addressee "whose responsive understanding the author of the speech work seeks and surpasses," then the Third is the superaddressee, not necessarily present to us in an immediately available time and space but present as a consciousness "whose absolutely just responsive understanding is presumed, either in some metaphysical distance or in distant historical time (the loophole addressee)."[28] (In Bakhtin's scenarios, one must never forget, we always have a "loophole"—that is, the right to answer back ourselves and the right to dismiss the fear that we might speak into a void.)

At different times, Bakhtin writes, this "invisibly present third party who stands above all the participants in the dialogue" can be God, the Absolute, the dispassionate court of conscience. But for each speaker who shapes an utterance in its direction, this Third is always of maximum authority and authorizing power. In Crapanzano's scenario, it is precisely this figure that is lacking in postmodernist landscapes; in fact, participants on such ground have given up on the possibility of such a figure. In his usual benign fashion, Bakhtin does not investigate those potentially vexed situations where participants in an exchange each acknowledge radically different Thirds. (Bakhtin's grim wartime notes on the word as Lie, so uncharacteristic of his work as a whole, might have been a starting point for such investigations.) But Bakhtin does equate the generalized "absolute absence of a third party" with an "absolute lack of being heard," which for him is one definition of hell.

Crapanzano will not give up so easily. The absence of a mutually agreed-upon Third, something that stands a chance of integrating individuals, institutions, and nation-states, is indeed a challenge. Since we communicate creatively with others only when not everything is in question at once, such a lack is especially painful during any angry and unstable "postcolonial period," that is, during "cross-cultural exchanges before they are routinized." But Crapanzano argues that therein lies (if one wishes to bend over and pick it up) the potential of the "postmodernist moment." For what marks most "exchanges during periods of crisis" is just this absence of a stabilizing Third "to whom rhetorical appeal can be made": law, grammar, the words of the fathers, or our own words of yesterday. The same absence, although less well understood, can be said to mark moments of "creative fervor." Crapanzano affirms that most dialogue (inner and outer) does take place with each participant anticipating the other's response and being molded by it. But there are also dramatic moments "like conversion, a sudden insight, an epiphanous experience, a new way of seeing things," that are triggered by the other party but neither foreseen nor legitimated by that party. Crapanzano intimates that with the proper qualities of discipline and imagination, the Third can be *productively* eclipsed. Possible at last is something radically different, stunning, new.

Crapanzano is not naive about the dangers involved. When the Third is eroded or depleted, discourse can quickly lose its bearings: there is the illusion that anything goes, and equally disruptive, we begin to confuse prescriptive and descriptive statements. Crapanzano demonstrates how a stable, authoritative Third for all parties in an exchange makes flexibility and tolerance possible. Paradoxically, its absence or attenuation does not make us more free but, in many instances, makes us more prone to fundamentalist thinking. Fundamentalism is in fact postmodernism's shadow.

To tack things in place in a postcolonial, postmodern world, Crapanzano writes, we often adopt the "egalitarian pretense." Pretending that we all share the same views, rights, and universals can indeed work when no great passions are involved. But Crapanzano then treats us to an account of an academic conference with international delegates (Chinese, Indian, American) that blew up badly, even with all the conventional politeness and constraints that such gatherings observe. (The contrast here with Peterson's analysis of Black texts is sobering; and we are reminded of the blessing—no weaker word will do—conferred on all parties by the parodic two-way double voicedness of those dancing, speakerly narratives.) Crapanzano ends on a cautious note. In this Thirdless era, he remarks, it is no simple task to avoid "the enchantment of retrogressive movements": fundamentalism, racism, nationalism. To save ourselves from those movements we will retreat to such emptied-out terms as history, which "poses no threat" precisely because it was the demise of such explanatory megaschemes that marked the onset of postmodernism in the first place. He then concludes: "When universalist narratives, like the Marxist, lose their legitimacy as metanarratives, then history becomes an evacuated symbol of only rhetorical or pragmatic interest."

Need it be so? Here Crapanzano's thoughtful but perhaps overanxious con-clusion begs for an epilogue out of Bakhtin's own arsenal. Must history claim an encompassing authority or else be "evacuated" of meaning? In his final texts, Bakhtin suggests a way out—or rather, he suggests a way of looking at the broad sweep of history that is less teleological than his earlier schemes of the 1930s (that huge Hegelian-like Unfolding of the Novelist Spirit that Bracht Branham properly questions in his reconsideration of postclassical narrative) but that is nevertheless not anarchic. This is Bakhtin's concept of "great time." Bakhtin mentions the term briefly and with a sort of ecstatic vagueness in his final essay, "Toward a Methodology for the Human Sciences" (1974). "The mutual understanding of centuries and millennia, of peoples, nations, and cultures, provides a complex unity of all humanity, all human cultures . . . and a complex unity of human literature," he writes. "All this is revealed only on the level of great time. . . . Contexts of understanding. The problem of *remote contexts*. The eternal renewal of meanings in all new contexts. *Small time* (the present day, the recent past, and the foreseeable—desired—future) and great time: infinite and unfinalized dialogue in which no meaning dies."[29]

What exactly this distinction between "great" and "small" time might mean has engaged a number of contemporary Bakhtin scholars in Russia, ever eager for philosophical exits from the falsehood of Communist historical projection. For our purposes a general gloss will suffice. In what I take to be the spirit of Bakhtin's phrase, "great time" is some temporal level where all unexpressed or potential meanings are eventually actualized, where every idea finds a context that can justify and nourish it. Great time is neither abstract, nor ahistorical, nor systematic; it is simply an open—and very long—sequence of concrete historical moments. Each of these moments came to pass because of specific local conditions, some willed, others given; having come to pass, it always leaves some unique, potentially productive residue.

As an organizing idea for history, "great time" does indeed seem rather naive and accretive, unworthy of the synthesizing powers of philosophy. But as with so many of Bakhtin's prosaic insights, the commonsensical position had to be reconquered precisely from the heights of philosophy. We must remember that Bakhtin, in this instance resembling our American pragmatists, began his career in an era obsessed with mathematical essences, functions, and formal categories such as sets, fields, groups.[30] And not unlike the young Wittgenstein, Bakhtin's response was to embrace the *relationalism* dominant for his time while decisively rejecting the *system* that so often and automatically went with it. And why, indeed, must relationships, to be real, arrange themselves into systems? In great time, standards of measurement are always multiple. Events do not need to obey a single algebra nor respect closure; they recombine endlessly, generating "inconsistencies" and introducing the new. In this great time, our *present* time does not enjoy any absolute privilege. (Such "presentism" is what Bakhtin would have found unsatisfactory about current aggrieved readings of Mark Twain as a racist or Shakespeare as a sexist: the proper study of literature should make us *suspicious* of the impulse to measure the products of past culture by the socially or politically correct standards of the present. It certainly should not license us to do so.[31])

But one must ask: can Bakhtin's capacious, tolerant concept of great time— where "every idea finds its homecoming festival"—really satisfy our need to think through the events of the world historically? On what level do events in great time communicate with one another? Do they have a language in common, and can cultural memory be sustained on that thin minimum of mere open-minded sequence plus indispensable (yet so heterogeneous, so often unexpected) residue— and residue, what is more, that is ever at the mercy of my own uncertain, individual efforts to grasp and apply it? Perhaps, in short, some sort of "systems thinking" is essential to guarantee continuity and to generate what Crapanzano has called the Third? Questions such as these now occupy Russian culturologists investigating Bakhtin's legacy. In considering the potential—not only the superficial irritation— of the "postmodern moment," these Russian scholars would find in Crapanzano's work a new and most congenial angle of inquiry.

Crapanzano's essay adopts the widest possible global perspective for dialogic communication. John Dore's contribution, "The Emergence of Language from Dialogue," is located at the other end of the spectrum—"how language functions and how it is structured in a recurring scene from one family's daily life." He is concerned with narratives from the crib: how an infant, Emily, with continual support in the form of self-conscious dialogue from her parents, talked herself into going to sleep alone.

The methodology and psycholinguistic assumptions of the essay come from Gregory Bateson, Lev Vygotsky, and Bakhtin. The triad is a compatible one. For if Bateson's "ecology of mind" still appears loose, exotic, and clinically imprecise to some American linguists and behavioralists, to Russian theorists this approach is absolutely mainstream. Soviet and post-Soviet scholarship has been traditionally strong in child psychology, alert to the effects and prerogatives of the social collective, and is long accustomed to considering pedagogy a profession worthy of the highest academic respect (a status that greatly impressed John Dewey when he visited the Soviet Union during its first decade). Soviet scholars take as obvious and noncontroversial what Dore pleads for at the end of his essay: "a theory of the interaction between how the child acquires language cognitively and how a society acquires the child functionally."

Lev Vygotsky, a devoted, flexible Marxist and brilliant improvisator, worked out his hypotheses on child language acquisition in the 1920s and early 1930s. Among his primary targets were the language-learning maps of Sigmund Freud and Jean Piaget—and especially the latter's concept of "egocentric speech," that stage when young children "talk to themselves." According to Piaget, egocentric speech is intermediate between autistic play and reality-oriented "practical thought." In the spirit of Freud's pleasure and reality principles, Piaget assumed that a child's thinking is initially autistic (that is, "monologic" vis-à-vis the child's own needs and self-generated fantasies) and that this thinking becomes realistic only under imposed social pressure, as it were, unwillingly. With his Marxist convictions, Vygotsky was unsympathetic to the idea that an individual might be reluctant to adjust to its environment and that reality, work, and social intercourse were somehow not "pleasurable." He took it for granted that, as human animals, we *want* to adjust to our environment and to become effective agents in our world; to do so, he surmised, we utilize the most sophisticated tool at our disposal, which is language. Vygotsky thus reversed the directional flow of Piaget's dynamics. He demonstrated that when children talk to themselves they are not externalizing private impulses but internalizing dialogues that they have heard from those who surround them; at the proper time in the maturation of a child, these inner dialogues then become tools for self-persuasion and logic formation. Such a dynamic is Dore's starting point. To be sure, Vygotsky's findings have received previous confirmation on this score from American linguists. The special virtue and innovation of the present essay, however, is its coupling of the Vygotskian language-learning scenario with Bakhtin's ideas about genre.

For Bakhtin, learning a language is a fraught and long-term process. The least of its many tasks is mastering vocabulary lists or abstract rules of grammar. The key to language competence, rather, is to master the "speech genre" (the relatively stable, typical "forms for constructing the whole" that guide us in our acts of utterance) that is appropriate to a given communicative situation. Any language's repertoire of these genres is intimidating and vast—and literacy in them is not easy to achieve.[32] People with an excellent formal command of a language, Bakhtin notes, can often "feel quite helpless in certain spheres of communication" because they do not know how to grasp in time, and then to personalize with sufficient flexibility and grace, the social templates proper to a speech exchange. All infant children, of course, "feel quite helpless" in precisely this way vis-à-vis the dialogues that surround them. To enter the flow of "speech communion" (as Bakhtin would put it) is for them a lengthy, anxiety-producing, exhilarating process.

John Dore sets himself the task of transcribing Emily's breakthrough to a dialogic "speech genre" that gives her some control over a portion of her world. As in any Vygotskian scenario, biological maturation and social interaction must mesh in order that development can move forward with sufficient creative energy. Since such meshings take place not in one's reservoir of mastered skills but in one's "zone of proximal development," and since this zone is marked by the hazard and risk of trying things out beyond one's present means, firmness must be tempered with indulgence, reassurance, bribes. Dore catalogs the parents' input into these cribside dialogues as of three types: "negotiatory," "obligatory," and "promissory." As Emily matures, she tranforms, via her own "processes of imitation and creation," the "authoritative discourse" that she hears from her father into increasingly complex, derivative "monologues" (the term, of course, is a misnomer) that are for her "internally persuasive."

Dore documents only seven months—albeit seven crucial months—of Emily's development. But he assures us that the formation of confident speech genres takes many years. For us grown-ups as well, mastering the necessary speech genres is the task of a lifetime. For Dore reminds us that although "a perfectly grammatical sentence" can be produced by even a very young child, a "perfect genre performance" can almost never be achieved. But achieved perfection serves little purpose, for either child or adult. At stake in these exchanges are the more important skills of negotiation and identity-formation, and these qualities are always in transition.

How would the Russians read Dore's essay? Now that "monologic discourse" has fallen into such low repute in the former Soviet Union, Vygotsky's humanistic pedagogy (with its Marxism underplayed and its connection with Bakhtin empha-sized) is receiving a fresh look by Russian scholars. Indicative of recent work is an essay that appeared in *Questions of Philosophy* in the spring of 1993, "Experience and the Drama of the Development of the Personality (Vygotsky's Final Word)."[33] Its author, Mikhail Yaroshevsky, takes up Vygotsky's early, abiding fascination with drama—and here we can detect the aesthetic underpinnings that make the cribside research of John Dore so suggestive and creative.

Throughout this essay, Yaroshevsky labors to make Vygotsky more of a humanist than a Marxist. Those two categories were not unalterably opposed in the 1920s when Vygotsky was at work, but in the current Russian climate, of course, the distinction is a charged one. Yaroshevsky stresses the extent to which Vygotsky always resisted deterministic, stimulus-response models. In place of the Pavlovian reflex (essentially the mechanical reception of a signal), Vygotsky posited a more complex and holistic "experiencing of an object" that he called the "speech reflex" or speech reaction.

The inspiration for "experience" thus understood came from Vygotsky's early passion for Shakespeare's *Hamlet*, for the Socratic dialogue, and for Stanislavsky's theories about the art of acting.[34] And here we can see where Dore's observations about Emily learning to fall asleep alone mesh beautifully with Vygotsky's vision and methodology. Drama, Vygotsky intimated, is a psychologically more accurate genre label for a learning scenario than is, say, the mental test or the transcribed dialogue. This is true because drama *is* a scenario—at all times a unified event (*edinitsa*), wholly incarnated, characterized by volition, resistance, and opposition, open to interruption, and liable to fail or to triumph dependent upon how we coor-dinate *all* our senses.[35] In this connection, Yaroshevsky notes the affinity between

Vygotsky's theory of language acquisition and Bakhtin's dialogism (confirming, however, that any direct influence of one man on the other cannot be verified). But then he marks the differences. For Vygotsky, the unit of analysis is the *experience:* a fully staged and fully embodied affair, a three-way intersection of maturational level, environmental stimulus, and an emerging sense of self (*lichnost'*) expressed in social behavior. For Bakhtin, in contrast, "the center of analysis, both in matters of art and of personality, is [solely] a person's consciousness, not a person in all the fullness of his bodily and spiritual being. . . . consciousness, no matter how one might interpret it as a living and dialogic thing, is not the only 'measuring stick' for human personality."

There is a truth worth pondering in Yaroshevsky's astute remark. Bakhtin began his ruminations about the ethical self and its "non-alibi in existence" with careful attention to the body in concrete time and space. When he shifted his attention to language, however, the other human faculties and senses tended to fade away; and when the body did return in a major way to Bakhtin's value hierarchy (in his study of Rabelais and the carnival grotesque), it was at the expense of both individual personality and responsible dialogue, neither of which had much to accomplish on the saturnalian public square. Yaroshevsky appears to argue for a Vygotskian corrective to Bakhtin's human-exchange scenarios. He would claim that exchanges of the Bakhtinian sort, however full of intonation, pathos, and loopholes, nevertheless remain, under analysis, "only words." It must have occurred to Vygotsky that Hamlet, his favorite hero, would have understood that limitation. Dialogue alone won't do; the play's the thing. To secure his ends, Hamlet staged a playlet with something more concrete, emotionally satisfying, and behaviorally cumulative at stake than merely words—as Emily's parents did so lovingly with their daughter.

Our final essay, Amy Mandelker's on Bakhtin, Lotman, and the semiotics of culture, is in certain ways the most heady and cosmic in this collection. For American intellectuals, despite our recent forays into multiculturalism—most often, alas, heavily weighted against a known and naughty "us" in favor of a lesser known, virtuous "them"—do not know a professional discipline that quite accords with the Russians' "culturology." Our national tradition tends to reward the pragmatic short term, the efficient or profitable return, the inalienable rights and voices of individuals. Russian philosophy, in contrast, has had a genius for the long term, the big collective sweep, and for quasi-scientific theoretical insights into "life-modeling," which, even granted it does not "work" and turns no profit, is usually of enormous suggestive power and imaginative appeal. The late Iurii Lotman and his Tartu school have been Russia's most inspired model-builders for the last three decades.

Like so much else accomplished under the star of Saussure, the semiotic work of Lotman and his associates was initially structuralist in an almost orthodox

Formalist mode. In interdisciplinary studies of breathtaking scope and learning (covering all periods of Russian history and dozens of major authors), the Tartu school turned people's voices into texts, texts into functions or strategies, and then arranged functions into systems. But by the early 1980s one could notice a "softening," or perhaps better an "organicizing," of Lotman's approach to cultural material. That strict binary flatland into which the formal study of language and literature had been fit was abandoned—although it continued to inspire generations of French theorists—and the Russians moved beyond it. Hence the interesting paradox that serves as Mandelker's starting point: whereas our post-structuralism is often archaic (and surely logocentric) in its commitment to Saussurean concepts of language, Russian post-structuralism is genuinely *post-*, that is, increasingly suspicious of system, of mechanical parts and dehumanized "functions." But to loosen up system and to reintroduce into one's models the humanly unpredictable is not, of course, to become an empiricist or a pragmatist. Russians retain their awesome talent for thinking big. Mandelker's primary focus in her essay is the direction and implication of this intellectual shift, on the part of Iurii Lotman and his school, from binary structuralism and secondary modeling systems into multidimensionality, semiospheres, biospheres, "living membranes," and (most recently) the cultural potential of "explosion" itself.

Among Lotman's allies on this path to ever-greater organicization are the contemporary neurolinguist Nikolai Nikolaenko, the visionary Russian "biogeo-chemist" Vladimir Vernadsky (1863–1945) from an earlier generation, and Mikhail Bakhtin. In the context of the humanities, Vernadsky's name is little known in the West. In his own homeland, however, Vernadsky's concepts of biosphere and noösphere, predicated on the notion of the cosmos as living organism, have earned him a revered place as the founder of Russian ecological consciousness. The biosphere is nothing less than the "superior intelligence of the planet." Within that realm, as Mandelker portrays it, human consciousness (that is, the noösphere) is neither a divine gift nor a license to subdue the rest of nature but merely one stage in the earth's evolution toward more efficient production and retention of energy. "For Vernadsky," as one recent Russian essayist put the matter enthusiastically, "the reason for the existence of the Cosmos was a feeling that life and consciousness are eternal, as are the search for unity and wholeness. He turned the whole of his powerful intellect and his utterly unbelievable encyclopedic erudition to proving that life and its cosmic scope are not arbitrary or accidental."[36]

Vernadsky, Lotman, and Bakhtin all partake of this special predisposition in the Russian philosophical tradition for intuitivist and holistic thinking. To varying degrees, each links the most minute calculations about the microworld of the psyche or brain with speculations on that largest of macroworlds, the cosmos; and a fascination with the individuating energy of the first realm does not seem to dampen faith in the potential "wholeness" of the other. Drawing on Bakhtin's late (and little attended) writings on culture and nature, Mandelker stitches together the case for a "logosphere" in Bakhtin's conceptual world, a realm of living words that pre- and post-exist any community of embodied speakers. The existence of such an immortal or transmortal sphere accords well with Bakhtin's optimism concerning the word—which, as Mandelker points out, differs from those familiar post-structuralist models, all deeply in debt to the idea of death, that presume language to be "the site of anxiety, nostalgia, and eternal failure." But she then shows how Lotman, inspired by studies on the functional asymmetry of the brain, steals up on the cosmic logosphere, as it were, from "down under" and transcends it—the better to investigate a series of flexible, three-dimensional, organic models for information transfer and development of personality. How ancient and dry those binaries of Lotman's earlier period now appear!

Mandelker is at pains to link Lotman's research on cerebral hemispheres with Bakhtinian insights about self and language. She makes the wonderful point, for example, that the right, somatic, or "Dionysian" hemisphere, for all its access to direct experience, is helplessly inarticulate and thus "nonfecund." It cannot create. The left, language-bound hemisphere, in all its Apollonian sternness, must first establish dialogue with it. As Mandelker notes, this is the very distinction Bakhtin draws between those minimal parts of every conscious self, the "I-for-myself," private and mute, and the "I-for-others"/"others-for-me," the source of our words. While Lotman generously acknowledged Bakhtin as his inspiration, one suspects that Bakhtin, tied to the word as a cognitive, individualizing dialogic medium and so very taken by the verbal trace, would have been less than exhilarated by all these curiously pulsating membranes.

An appropriate means for summing up this introductory essay (and for summing up the volume as well) is a suggestive juxtaposition made by the Kharkov Renaissance historian Leonid Batkin, in an article published in the mid-1980s entitled "Two Means for Studying the History of Culture."[37] Batkin's essay can be read as one extended gloss on a Bakhtinian distinction invoked at the beginning of this introduction, namely, Stephen Toulmin's crucial segregation of experiences from experiments. Bakhtin's distinction is that between precision (*tochnost'*), a quality characteristic of those exact sciences that deal with a single consciousness trained on an inanimate thing, and depth (*glubina*)—the special mark of the humanities, where texts always contain a minimum of two consciousnesses. The "two methods for studying culture" that Batkin discusses in his essay are basically the approaches of Lotman and Bakhtin. Although he acknowledges their convergence in certain areas, Batkin casts their differing emphases as that between "knowledge" (*znanie*) and "understanding" (*ponimanie*).

From the early binary days of the Tartu Theses (where culture was separated from nonculture by thick lines), *knowledge* had been the special province of a semiotic-based imaging of the world. "Knowledge is always separable from nonknowledge, even if it is not always easy to draw the line between them," Batkin writes. "I don't know *that*, I *do* know this, but I cannot at one and the same time both know and not know one and the same thing in the same relation. Nonknowledge is a diminution of knowledge, and knowledge means the retreat of nonknowledge; just as water forces air out of a vessel, so do knowledge and nonknowledge ebb and flow at each other's expense. Knowledge *grows*—it can be deepened and restructured, but not abolished."

Understanding, however, works differently. Its workings became Bakhtin's abiding concern, we might even say the passion of his life. "Understanding not so much grows as *changes* (it does not so much become a greater or lesser understanding as it becomes an *other* understanding)," Batkin notes, warming to this suggestive paradox. "In place of a quantity (of precision, of volume) there is *only* the quality and potential of the transmutations. And understanding can never be separated from nonunderstanding, for it is always *simultaneously* a nonunderstanding (viewed from the perspective of an other understanding . . .). Which is to say, the more understanding there is, the less of it, in a sense (that is, the less aggressive and self-confident it becomes). For what understanding understands is precisely that which preserves its appropriate modesty, that which testifies to the nonunderstandability of the other. Knowledge exists *in spite of* nonknowledge, outside its dark territory; understanding is possible only *thanks to* nonunderstanding."

Slow going, this. And yet Batkin is on to something, it seems, that continues to distinguish Lotman's thought from Bakhtin's—for all the former's softening and organicizing of semiotic structures. Semiotics began and remains wedded to information theory. It transfers known things. Through it, people and things can be classified, stored, saved, "taught." Bakhtin had less interest in those processes. His primary purpose was not to classify, and even less was it to save. Or as Bakhtin might have put it, had it occurred to him to use the profound personal failure of Prince Myshkin in Dostoevsky's *The Idiot* as an instructive example, people don't want to be saved. They want to be considered interesting. Usually they benefit by being imperfectly understood, for this tends to keep them actively talking and listening to others. And they want to be changed.

The essays in this volume testify to an encounter between two cultures that have had a long history of imperfectly understanding one another. For this reason, I submit, across a wide number of disciplines the dialogue shows no signs of losing momentum or interest. On the far side of Russia's political night, it is fair to say that we are all being changed.

Part 1
Bakhtin and Literary Studies

Prosaic Bakhtin: Landmarks, Anti-Intelligentsialism, and the Russian Countertradition

Gary Saul Morson

Perhaps the sharpest way to formulate this situation is to insist that in our culture it is neither sexuality nor the darkest urgings to violence and domination that are repressed. Exactly these issues constitute an enormous, if not actually the major, portion of our cultural conversation about the human psyche. What is repressed, though, is the force of the prosaic, the counter-authenticity, if you will, of the texture and rhythm of our daily routines and decisions, the myriad of minute and careful adjustments that we are ready to offer in the interest of a habitable social world.
—Michael André Bernstein, *Bitter Carnival:*
"Ressentiment" and the Abject Hero

Radical Conservatism

Caryl Emerson's introduction to the present volume offers a view of Bakhtin that is at odds with reigning American interpretations. In extending the argument of our two recent volumes, *Rethinking Bakhtin* and *Mikhail Bakhtin: Creation of a Prosaics*, she suggests that American theorists have miscast Bakhtin and that, had they done otherwise, he might not have become so popular.[1]

Thus Emerson describes Bakhtin as fundamentally antirevolutionary and as a believer in what Russian intellectuals now call human values, a phrase that they oppose to what Marxism tried to inculcate: class values. By the same token, Bakhtin defended the idea of personal ethical responsibility on grounds that are doubly suspicious to a current American audience. First, he insisted that ethical responsibility is not collective but irreducibly individual. Second, he refused to identify the ethical with the political. Politicism, as this equation might be called, was for Bakhtin simply another form of reductionism fatal to a true ethical sensibility.

No less at odds with reigning American orthodoxies, Bakhtin believed without apology in the value of the Western literary tradition. Nor did he ever waver in his celebration of prerevolutionary Russian literature, including—or rather especially—Dostoevsky, who was regarded as politically suspect in the Soviet

Union. As a trained classicist, he advocated studying the sweep of Western literature, which he viewed not as a set of artifacts to be "correlated with socioeconomic
factors, as it were, behind culture's back" but as an immensely rich repository of
wisdom.[2] Bakhtin thought of literature neither as "texts" nor as cultural "products"
but as true "creations." Far from being outmoded by present values and by more recent ideological discoveries, those works and the tradition to which they belonged
had, in Bakhtin's view, barely begun to be appreciated.

He did not believe in "the death of the author," an idea that in Russia found
expression, curiously enough, in both Marxism and Formalism. Both movements,
it seems, enjoyed shocking the bourgeois by explaining works through the action
of impersonal forces, a method they recommended as a blow against individualism.
Almost all of Bakhtin's work moves in exactly the opposite direction. He argued
that great literature is unintelligible without an understanding of authors', and
characters', individual voices. Language for Bakhtin was a matter of concrete
exchanges between specific people. He would never have spoken, as some of
his current admirers do, of an impersonal "intertextuality" in which Language
apparently exchanges words with itself. And he rejected Marxist "dialectics" in
large part because it replaces living human dialogues with the interaction of impersonal categories. Although his American admirers often conflate dialectics with
dialogue, Bakhtin saw them as fundamentally opposed: "Dialogue and dialectics.
Take a dialogue and remove the voices (the partitioning of voices), remove the
intonations (emotional and individualizing ones), carve out abstract concepts and
judgments from living words and responses, then cram everything into one abstract
consciousness—and that's how you get dialectics."[3]

Dialogue allows for surprise, and the possibility of surprise is necessary for
creativity. Like his contemporary Nicholas Berdyaev, Bakhtin focused on creativity
as an alternative to all deterministic, all "causal and genetic," approaches to culture.
Such approaches make creativity the result of impersonal laws, which means they
reduce creativity to mere mechanical discovery. The centrality of creativity to
Bakhtin's thought was another reason for his reluctance to liquidate the author. He
would have seen the absence of the creative process from the current American
theoretical agenda as a shortcoming or perhaps a symptom. Least of all did Bakhtin
want to ban this topic as tainted by reactionary individualism.

Bakhtin did not refashion his theories and choice of problems to fit the
imperatives of his time. He preferred to write for the drawer, and the style of most
of his works reflects the fact that he evidently did not anticipate their publication,
at least in his lifetime. Perhaps this sort of composition is reflected in his concept of
the "superaddressee," which he defines as the image of an absent but ideal listener.
As Bakhtin describes it, the superaddressee is a constituent factor of every utterance,
however private or hidden. It is the principle of hope in even the most hopeless
circumstances. It projects value beyond present needs.

As a rule, Bakhtin chose not to adapt but to hide and, when he did publish, to risk the charge of being out of step with the times. His loyalty to a superannuated, pre-revolutionary culture may have shaped his reflections on the individual's need for tradition.

In short, I find considerable merit in Emerson's, Vitaly Makhlin's, and some other Russian critics' descriptions of Bakhtin as a radical conservative. By *radical* I mean to indicate that his theories and thought were highly unconventional and original by any standards. They were intellectually and theoretically, but not politically, radical, a judgment as true in our milieu as it was in his. His conservatism began with, but was not limited to, his efforts to forge a "new traditional consciousness." He belonged to a specific Russian tradition, which I shall describe in this essay, that endeavored to rethink, reclaim, and reassert the value of tradition itself. In our own context, too, this and similar projects make Bakhtin's conservatism "more radical than any sort of superficial revolutionism," as Emerson correctly states.

The American misreading of Bakhtin may in part be the product of accidental factors. It was not inevitable, for instance, that his works were translated so that the least characteristic, *Rabelais and His World*, should have appeared first and his early writings last. If Jakobsonians had not been so well ensconced in American Slavic departments, would we have had to contend with the exceedingly odd view of Bakhtin as a structuralist semiotician? The unnecessary, unsupported, and arbitrary ascription to him of V. N. Voloshinov's and P. N. Medvedev's books created the weird impression that he was some sort of Marxist. Bakhtin, who saw life and history as fundamentally messy, would have appreciated the way the reception of his ideas has been shaped by contingencies.

But there is also a sense in which these misappropriations were *not* entirely accidental. Behind them all is an impulse to enlist Bakhtin in our own ideological battles, to contemporize him, and to deny his otherness. Let Bakhtin be Bakhtin! In the current theoretical climate, in which otherness is ostensibly the supreme value, the real otherness of creative minds is typically transmuted into that old familiar otherness we already know.

This pattern, as Bakhtin was aware, reflects a more general impulse of the intelligentsia to turn culture into a mirror and to treat the past as a storage house conveniently raided for items of current usefulness. Bakhtin's term for this impoverishing intellectual habit was "enclosure within one's epoch," the alternative to which is the sort of "liberation" Emerson's essay mentions: the temerity to appreciate *genuine* otherness. Such temerity paradoxically demands a kind of cultural humility not usually characteristic of the intelligentsia.

One might put it this way: Bakhtin was deeply suspicious of a certain sort of complacent narrowness and self-appointed superiority that, though not inevitable for an intelligentsia, is nevertheless a recurrent temptation, almost an occupational hazard. An intelligentsia underestimates the dangers of regarding itself as culture's privileged institution for reflecting on itself. This danger is likely to increase in tandem with the intelligentsia's self-identification as a free-standing group somehow distinct from and at odds with the rest of society. That self-image has apparently taken hold among American academics to a greater and greater degree in recent decades. It was especially dominant among the Russian intelligentsia, which tended to see itself as Russia's, and the world's, savior. And it was also the object of criticism and satire among numerous other Russian thinkers, who developed their own intellectual *countertradition*. Though a minority voice, this countertradition appears to represent the most valuable (and currently applicable) legacy of Russian thought. The present essay explores some implications of viewing Bakhtin as one of these minority voices.

Liberals Choose

In 1909 seven remarkable Russian thinkers—Peter Struve, Sergei Bulgakov, Nicholas Berdyaev, A. S. Izgoev, Bogdan Kistyakovsky, Semyon Frank, and Mikhail Gershenzon—joined to publish a volume entitled *Landmarks: A Collection of Articles on the Russian Intelligentsia*. This is one case in which it is entirely justified to call a publication a scandal.[4]

With polemical power and intellectual insight, *Landmarks* dissected, and tried to bury, the intelligentsia's self-image, psychology, mores, etiquette, and unquestioned values and assumptions, most of which were described as profoundly destructive. Generally liberal in their views, the contributors attacked the intelligentsia's automatic habit of radicalism. Still more iconoclastic, they refused to consider politics as the solution to all problems, even political ones. They recommended personal moral improvement, and most of them endorsed some sort of liberal religious values. Above all, they criticized the intelligentsia for its fanaticism and advised tolerance for diverse views.

As contributors noted in subsequent editions, the very reactions of the intelligentsia to the collection confirmed a good part of its analysis, especially the parts about intolerance. The volume became the period's most widely debated—or rather, vilified—publication. It went through five editions in about a year, and the fifth included an appendix listing over two hundred books and articles written in response. Individuals, journals, even political parties published replies. The overwhelming majority were negative and betrayed (or expressed) the sense of an affront. We may appreciate how widespread this debate was when we consider that one recent historian, working on the assumption that virtually every educated person of the time had read *Landmarks*, uses its circulation figures as a first step in calculating the size of the intelligentsia.[5] Perhaps not since Chernyshevsky's *What Is to Be Done?* had a work struck a nerve to this extent.

Because of the volume's generally liberal outlook, and because Struve in particular was a leader of the Constitutional Democratic (Kadet) Party, one might have expected that *Landmarks* would at least have found support in its home base.[6] But the opposite proved to be the case. Most Kadets took pains to dissociate themselves from *Landmarks*. The party's leader, Paul Miliukov, toured Russia to denounce the book and reject its attempt to induce liberals to break from the revolutionary tradition. In effect, the volume, as Miliukov correctly understood, was directed at breaking the unthinking loyalty of liberals to the myths of the intelligentsia. It forced them to choose between their professed belief in individual liberty and their quite contrary tendency to justify the Far Left, which had contempt for liberal values; to choose, in short, between their ideals and their sense of identity as members of the intelligentsia.

And choose they did, mostly against *Landmarks*. In his memoirs, Frank explained that *Landmarks* engaged in "criticism of the basic sacred dogma of the radical intelligentsia—the 'mystique' of revolution. This was regarded as an audacious and quite intolerable betrayal of the age-old sacred testament of the Russian intelligentsia, the betrayal of the tradition handed down by the prophets and saints of Russian social thought—Belinsky, Granovsky, Chernyshevsky, Pisarev."[7] After the Bolshevik coup, Struve was to argue, as many have since, that the choice liberals made to flatter themselves by adhering to the "mystique of revolution" contributed to the eventual triumph of totalitarianism. In his remarkable meditation on the *Landmarks* controversy, Leonard Schapiro saw a more general lesson for liberals. That lesson was apparently learned by the current liberal and strongly reformist Russian weekly *Moscow News*, which welcomed the first Soviet publication of *Landmarks* in 1990.[8] By then the dangers of "revolutionism" seemed all too obvious.

Revolutionism was in fact only one of many topics in this remarkably profound collection. *Landmarks* was devoted to exploring a whole series of moral and intellectual temptations to which the authors believed the intelligentsia had yielded. Like all great satire, the book is of interest far beyond its original context, because the vices it describes, at times with unparalleled precision, are always with us. Each criticism it levels against the Russian intelligentsia also applies, at least potentially, to intelligentsias in general.

Martyrdom Sought

Inside each maximalist there is a little Napoleon of socialism or anarchism. . . . But life is an everyday affair.

—Bulgakov in *Landmarks*

A more detailed summary would be helpful. *Landmarks* faulted the intelligentsia for its addiction to abstract theorizing and for its neglect of everyday life and everyday virtues. The contributors' belief in individual self-improvement and daily decency reflects their prosaic ethos. That ethos also informs their refusal to regard all moral questions as political ones and their dismissal of the intelligentsia's claim to special insight into society's fundamental problems. The way members of the intelligentsia think—and live—does not inspire confidence.

Berdyaev in particular pointed out the danger of judging philosophical or scientific theories on the basis not of their truth but of their political utility. Of course, the wisdom of this warning was confirmed when one practitioner of such political epistemology, Vladimir Lenin, seized power. Berdyaev insisted, as Bakhtin later did, that science, art, ethics, and politics are distinct and that they cannot be reduced to each other. The world of values is forever multiple. If one regards ethics as a matter of the right politics, the results are likely to be both politically and ethically monstrous.

Rejecting politicism, the *Landmarks* contributors maintained that evil is not just a matter of external social obstacles to be removed. Individual moral self-improvement—a "person's positive labor upon himself"—is also needed (Struve 127). The idea that the right political program could somehow make up for everyday "moral slovenliness" (Izgoev 78), for a failure to take one's job seriously, and for careless treatment of others—an idea indistinguishable from a preemptive excuse—was regarded by the *Landmarks* writers as a particularly noxious, as well as dangerous, attitude of the intelligentsia.

Believing neither that laws of history were available, nor that final truths were discoverable, nor that utopian social answers were desirable, the *Landmarks* contributors denounced the intelligentsia for its maximalism, which they regarded as closely linked to its fanaticism and intolerance. Committed to political openness, to pluralism, and to the rule of law, they found Marxism distasteful. They were particularly disturbed by Plekhanov's dictum, which was later to justify Lenin's practice in dispersing the Constituent Assembly, that democratic institutions should be respected only when useful to the Party, inasmuch as "the good of the revolution is the supreme law." The very act of citing statements like this must have been particularly effective in putting Kadets on the spot.

For some contributors to *Landmarks*, pluralism was part of a positive political program—Kistyakovsky's article advocates the rule of law—and for others it shaded into a principled aversion to politics, at least insofar as politics was assumed to constitute the only, or indeed the most important, part of social life. Gershenzon, who was also the volume's editor, warned against "the tyranny of civic activism" (68). Berdyaev called for "not only political liberation but also liberation from the oppressive power of politics, an emancipation of thought which hitherto has been hard to find among our political liberationists"(15). Article after article denounced the stifling conformity of the intelligentsia, its habit of borrowing prefabricated truths, and its anti-intellectual and morally self-righteous tendency to answer criticism by calling it reactionary: "And what don't we call reactionary!"(Berdyaev 7).

The boldest of the contributors went so far as to endorse some bourgeois virtues. Daily life suffers when all effort is oriented toward humanity's utopian future and the revolutionary's defining moment, his arrest (or execution). With withering irony, Izgoev remarks that the typical *intelligent* (Russian for a member of the intelligentsia) judges theories not by their validity but by their degree of "leftness"; and he usually measures a theory's leftness by its likelihood to lead to one's arrest. Thus, "he is 'more left' who is closer to death, whose work is more dangerous—not to the social order against which he is struggling but to his own person" (Izgoev 85).

The intelligentsia seeks martyrdom, and the roseate glow of anticipated execution obscures the importance of what really makes lives good or bad and what ultimately shapes the welfare of society: the daily activity of real, individual people. But for the intelligentsia, "any concern with putting one's personal life in order . . . is declared a bourgeois affair. A man lives, marries, fathers children—what can be done! This is an unavoidable but petty detail that ought not to deflect him from his basic task. The same is true of work—the *intelligent* must work in order to eat, unless he can become a 'professional revolutionary' living at his organization's expense" (Izgoev 86–87). Of course, very few actually seek death on the scaffold. Most are content to neglect daily chores out of sheer admiration for others' martyrdom. In this way, the aura of that ideal produces the principled laziness of what Gershenzon calls "Chekhovian people" (60).

Perhaps the most widely cited passage in the anthology is Gershenzon's evocation of the intelligentsia's contempt for the prosaic:

> A handful of revolutionaries has been going from house to house and knocking on every door: "Everyone into the street! It's shameful to stay at home!" And every consciousness, the halt, the blind and the armless, poured into the square; not one stayed at home. For half a century they have been milling about, wailing and quarreling. At home there is dirt, destitution, disorder, but the master doesn't care. He is out in public, saving the people— and that is easier and more entertaining than drudgery at home. (58)

This rejection of daily life led to a peculiarly self-indulgent puritanism:

> It was a strange sort of asceticism, which renounced not personal sensual life itself, but merely all guidance over it. . . . On the whole, the intelligentsia's way of life is horrible, a true "abomination of desolation." It lacks even the slightest, most superficial discipline or consistency. A day passes, and who knows why; today things are one way, and tomorrow a

sudden fancy will turn everything upside down. In personal life, there is idleness, slovenliness, and a homeric carelessness; in work, a naive lack of conscientiousness; and in public affairs an unbridled tendency toward despotism and a total lack of respect for other people. (Gershenzon 58)

Gershenzon cites a just-published letter of Chekhov (who died five years earlier, in 1904) in support of this description: "I do not believe in our intelligentsia, which is hypocritical, false, hysterical, ill-bred, and lazy," Chekhov wrote. "I do not believe in it even when it suffers and complains, for its oppressors come from the same womb" (letter to I. I. Orlov, 22 Feb. 1889, cited in Gershenzon 58n). The idea that the mentality of the bureaucracy and secret police resembled that of the intelligentsia, and that these two types of fanatics were engaged in symbiotic terrorism, was an insight that was equally central to Joseph Conrad's *Under Western Eyes*. In his 1920 introduction to the novel, Conrad, reflecting on recent events, remarked that the moral anarchism of the autocracy and its police had provoked "the no less imbecile and atrocious answer of a purely Utopian revolutionism . . . in the strange conviction that a fundamental change of hearts must follow the downfall of any given human institutions. These people are unable to see that all they can effect is a change of names. The oppressors and the oppressed are all Russians together."[9]

The Intelligentsials versus the Intellectuals

Such citations from Chekhov are designed to illustrate another key point of *Landmarks:* generally speaking, Russia's greatest writers did not belong to the intelligentsia. For an American, such an assertion is likely to sound like a mere witticism, if not a self-contradiction. But in Russia, where the word *intelligentsia* was coined, its meaning was rather different from its English counterpart—different enough that it made perfect (if pointed) sense to exclude Tolstoy, Chekhov, and other great writers from the intelligentsia.

It is of course impossible to give a precise definition of the Russian term *intelligentsia* because it was used somewhat differently by different people, because both usage and the groups to which the term referred changed over time, and, perhaps most important of all, because debates about morals, politics, and society often took the form of describing or redescribing the allegedly authentic *intelligent.* That said, a few observations, which have struck almost everyone, can be offered.

The Russian intelligentsia in its strict sense was not equated with educated or professional people. On the one hand, many people who were barely educated at all, but who adopted a particular set of attitudes, ways of living, and political principles and had joined a radical political organization were routinely considered members of the intelligentsia, especially if they modeled themselves on such exemplary figures as Chernyshevsky. On the other hand, many educated people were not considered to be members of the intelligentsia. If they did not see the world in political terms, if they were not unalterably opposed to the autocracy, if they were not atheists, if they did not revere the persons and platforms of Chernyshevsky and Mikhailovsky, or if they held positions of authority in a government or authoritative institution, their credentials as *intelligenty* (plural for *intelligent*) would be at least dubious, if not clearly absent. A former seminarian who had become a socialist, atheist, and materialist, but had never read a novel in his life, was much more likely to be considered a member of the intelligentsia than, let us say, an apolitical university professor or a moderately liberal and highly literate mayor of Moscow.

Was Dostoevsky a member of the intelligentsia? Yes, before his exile to Siberia, and perhaps even afterward, given his credentials of Siberian punishment, in spite of his reactionary politics. His example helped make right-wing *intelligenty* possible: such figures shared the maximalism, concerns, and devotion to social issues of the intelligentsia but from a different standpoint. They were reverse *intelligenty*. Was Tolstoy an *intelligent*? In Russia at the time, the question would have sounded like a daring paradox, because it was perfectly plain that the aristocratic sage of Yasnaya Polyana, with his utter contempt for all those déclassé scribblers in the capital and his devotion to apolitical art and to religion, could not possibly be considered an *intelligent*. Were the *Landmarks* contributors themselves *intelligenty*? Yes and not in the sense that they seemed to have been regarded, and to have regarded themselves, as dissident, apostate, or renegade *intelligenty* or, as one recent historian has described them, as "self-styled ex-*intelligenty*."[10] Perhaps a good way to identify an *intelligent*—and a way that may often have been used in practice—was to assess how close the person was to acknowledged models, such as Chernyshevsky or Dobroliubov.[11]

As in accounts of any complex and evolving social group, no single criterion can be used as a definition. Rather, an evolving set of "family resemblances" offers a more accurate, because more flexible, approach. One key factor was way of living, an attitude toward manners, love, work, and daily life. That was one reason the intelligentsia was often compared to a religious order.[12] The fact that so many—and, more important, so many exemplary—figures were former seminarians was constantly stressed not only because it seemed to explain the quasi-religious fanaticism of these atheists but also because it implied a whole set of daily habits. The generation of the 1840s, that is, of the period just before the time the intelligentsia was clearly established as a distinct group and just before the term began to be circulated, never quite overcame their distaste for the bad manners of Chernyshevsky and his kind. Even Herzen made fun of the younger radicals, Turgenev coolly marked the generational difference in *Fathers and Sons*, and Dostoevsky's *Possessed* offers a savage parody on both the young terrorists and the old aristocratic "men of the forties" who resented the radicals' bad taste but fawned on them anyway.

In a curious way, the very features that the aristocrats held up to ridicule soon became badges of honor and signs of progressivity, consciously imitated by subsequent generations of would-be *intelligenty*. Bad manners were studiously copied. Indeed, at times even fictional characters were imitated. In this sense, Chernyshevsky was doubly influential. Over long periods, for example, *intelligenty* took extraordinary pains to model themselves on the characters of his "novel" *What Is to Be Done?*[13] As we shall see, attacks on the intelligentsia's style of living were central to *Landmarks*. Its contributors took on what they called the whole psychological and sociological "knot" that impoverished the intelligentsia morally as well as intellectually.

The *Landmarks* contributors were therefore anything but unique in arguing that the intelligentsia was not coterminous with "the educated classes." Where they *were* rather unconventional was in preferring the latter and in predicting (or, more accurately, advocating) the demise of the former. Russia would be considerably better off, they believed, when it had a lot more educated people and no intelligentsia (in the Russian sense) at all. Then thinkers, who would all belong to one specific class or another, would be grounded in some sort of real activity and form of life. Russia would resemble the more liberal societies of Western Europe. The *Landmarks* contributors hoped that economic modernization would rapidly anachronize the intelligentsia, and they tried to see the emergence of more and more people like themselves as signs that this change was well under way. Berdyaev put it his way: we need an *intelligentsia* (in a broad, European sense) and not our old Russian *intelligentshchina* (roughly, "intelligent-itis").

One reason that the *Landmarks* contributors took such pains to remind readers that great writers did not belong to the intelligentsia was that they wanted to establish consciously what they claimed existed in fact, a countertradition of intellectuals who were not *intelligenty*. And they wanted to claim for this countertradition the greatest cultural figures Russia had produced. Or we might put it this way: they wanted the educated young to think of themselves as heirs of Tolstoy, Chekhov, and Soloviev rather than of Chernyshevsky, Dobroliubov, and Mikhailovsky.

Struve portrays the intelligentsia as represented by its *zhurnalisty* (not quite "journalists") and critics. He recommended an alternative, the novelists and poets. This choice suggests that social identity roughly corresponds with forms of cultural activity, which may in turn be linked to whole mentalities. To Struve, "it is remarkable how our national literature remains a preserve the intelligentsia cannot capture. The great writers, Pushkin, Lermontov, Gogol, Turgenev, Dostoevsky, and Chekhov, do not have the lineaments of *intelligenty*" (121). In part, this observation is unfair, because by Struve's own criteria, the intelligentsia "in our use of the word" only began in the 1850s or 1860s, that is, after the death of the first three writers he mentions. From the standpoint of the intelligentsia, Struve's observation was contestable for a different reason. It implied a standard of greatness—of intrinsic or essential value, as we would say today—independent of utilitarian (which is to say, political) purposes. Not everyone conceded that Chekhov was greater than Chernyshevsky. Perhaps Struve was hoping that even people who had been taught to profess the standards of the intelligentsia would have tacitly sensed Chekhov's superiority and that he could appeal to this sense as the basis for conscious reformulation of values.

Gershenzon is still more polemical in distinguishing the intelligentsia from intellectuals, the politically committed from the educated, and the journalistic ethos from literary sensitivity. The reason that great literature is rarely produced by *intelligenty*, he argues, is that real creativity is incompatible with the mental conformity and the assurance that "the meaning of life was established beforehand" demanded by the intelligentsia (67). "Our great artists were free, and naturally, the more authentic their talent the more hateful they found the blinders of the intelligentsia's social-utilitarian morality" (60). Given prevailing values, the great writers required more than talent; they needed courage. One must appreciate that "public opinion . . . forbade [us] to read Fet under pain of ridicule (at the very least)" (68), which meant that in addition to government censorship a *second censorship* (as it was called) threatened artistic integrity. "Only people with an exceptionally strong spirit could resist the hypnosis of a common faith and heroic deeds. Tolstoy resisted, and so did Dostoevsky, but the average person, even if he did not believe, dared not admit it" (67). Here Gershenzon, like Struve, was answering the myth of the persecuted *intelligent* with counterimages of the *intelligent* as persecutor and of the great, nonconforming writers, standing up to a double intolerance. They, not the herd of conformist radicals, were the true heroes. A great deal of the hostility to *Landmarks* doubtless arose from such attacks on the intelligentsia's founding myths.

Gershenzon concluded that "in Russia an almost infallible gauge of the strength of an artist's genius is the extent of his hatred for the intelligentsia" (60). The Landmarks contributors repeatedly mentioned Tolstoy, for whom "what the intelligentsia lived by quite literally did not even exist. . . . at the peak of the civic movement Tolstoy was glorifying the wise 'stupidity' of Karataev and Kutuzov" (Gershenzon 60). Tolstoy's novels insist on the superiority of wisdom grounded in everyday experience to the purely theoretical knowledge of the intelligentsia. His image of virtue as always prosaic and inconspicuous, his denial that laws of history could ever be discovered, his dismissal of laws of progress as a modern superstition, his apoliticism and belief in individual self-improvement, and his repeated contrast between people like Levin, who wants ideas to be authentic, and his brothers, who wear them like a badge—all these deeply novelistic and prosaic tenets mark his anti-intelligentsialism. Struve observed that merely by turning to religion Tolstoy placed himself even further outside the intelligentsia. And the *Landmarks* contributors understood that Tolstoy's emphasis on the authenticity of beliefs, and his use of novels to measure ideologies against the lives of their advocates, constituted an attack on the intelligentsia of unprecedented power.

For their part, the intelligentsia had no difficulty in recognizing themselves in Count Tolstoy's satiric portraits. In *Resurrection*, the novel closest in time to *Landmarks*, Tolstoy focuses on the self-enclosed mind of the *intelligenty* who presume to speak for "the people" in language and concepts comprehensible, if it all, only to the intelligentsia itself.[14] This novel expresses sympathy for every criminal in every Russian prison, but the representative of the intelligentsia, whom the protagonist Nekhliudov visits in her cell, is curiously beyond help:

> Nekhliudov asked her how she came to be in prison.
> In answer she began relating all about her affairs with great animation. Her speech was intermingled with a great many long words, such as propaganda, disorganization, social groups, sections and sub-sections, about which she seemed to think everybody knew, but which Nekhliudov had never heard of.
> She told him all the secrets of the People's Will, evidently convinced that he was pleased to hear them. Nekhliudov looked at her miserable little neck, her thin, unkempt hair, and wondered why she had been doing all these strange things, and why she was now telling all this to him. He pitied her, but not as he had pitied Menshoff, the peasant, kept for no fault of his own in the stinking prison. She was pitiable because of all the confusion that filled her mind. It was clear that she considered herself a heroine, and was ready to give her life for a cause, though she could not have explained what that cause was and in what its success would lie.[15]

She presumably expects Nekhliudov to understand her because she takes her abstractions for granted. Living an intelligentsial life, she accepts its language and view of the world as natural and obvious. But if her jargon is incomprehensible to an educated nobleman like Nekhliudov, what must its effect be on the peasants for whom she is supposedly sacrificing herself? Are her ideas any more in keeping with reality than her language? *Landmarks* (like Dostoevsky) differs from Tolstoy in seeing such radicals as less pitiable than dangerous.

Destined Victims and Bourgeois Virtues

Tolstoy's attacks on the intelligentsia were often explained away, by Lenin among others, as the unavoidable consequence of his status as a nobleman. But with Chekhov, the descendant of serfs, this critical strategy was not so easy to apply.

And it must be said that Chekhov's portraits of the intelligentsia are even more savage than Tolstoy's.

Perhaps most offensive of all, Chekhov made no apologies for believing in ordinary bourgeois virtues and recommending them to "the wood lice and mollusks we call the intelligentsia" who imagine they have a higher calling (letter to Suvorin, 17 Dec. 1889, S 203).[16] Chekhov understood as well as any writer the dynamics of everyday self-excuse, and he was especially good at exposing all forms of aesthetic Raskolnikovism—the idea that superior people are at liberty to neglect middle-class virtues because they have higher goals. For Chekhov, there were no goals superior to prosaic ones. Surely culture was a sham without them.

In his view, real culture involves care in daily living and everyday responsibility. It involves self-reliance and discipline, and it demands good hygiene, good manners, and good work habits. A truly decent and cultured person pays his debts, respects property, and does not waste resources or money. Like Frank in *Landmarks*, Chekhov was particularly unsympathetic to the intelligentsia's fashionable contempt for wealth, "its inconsistent ideas—and all this on the strength of the fact that . . . money is an evil" (27 Dec. 1889, Chudakov 199). Both Chekhov and Frank were inclined to question how the materialist intelligentsia could truly help "the people" prosper while at the same time showing such contempt for material resources. Frank pointed out that equal distribution does not help if a society does not produce anything to begin with. "It is time we finally understood that our life is not simply unjust, but is primarily poor and squalid, and that the poverty-stricken cannot become rich if they devote all their attention to the equal distribution of their few pennies" (Frank 147–48). He recommended that the intelligentsia cultivate a work ethic and a respect for the production of wealth. Chekhov, too, made clear that contempt for such values represented a noxious mixture of hereditary lordliness with intelligentsial hauteur, both of which were characterized by contempt for the very bourgeois values that Chekhov respected. A great deal of the satiric energy of Chekhov's plays and stories derives from his contrariness in shocking the *anti*-bourgeois.

Perhaps Chekhov's most famous statement of his values occurs in a letter to his talented but undisciplined brother Nikolai. It may say something about our own culture that this letter, which warns against self-indulgent intelligentsial posing and recommends ordinary virtues, still possesses the shock value Chekhov intended it to have. "In my opinion," he asserted, "people of culture must fulfill the following conditions":

1. They respect the human personality and are therefore forbearing, gentle, courteous, and compliant. . . . They do not consider it a favor to a person if they live with him, and when they leave, they do not say: "It is impossible to live with you!"

2. They are sympathetic not only to beggars and cats. . . .

3. They respect the property of others and therefore pay their debts.

4. They are pure of heart and fear lying like fire. They do not lie even in small matters. . . . They don't pose. . . .

5. . . . They don't say, "I'm misunderstood!"

6. They are not vain. . . . Sincere talent always remains in obscurity. . . .

7. If they have talent, they respect it. . . .

8. They develop an aesthetic taste. They cannot bring themselves to fall asleep in their clothes, look with unconcern at a crack in the wall with bedbugs in it, breathe foul air, walk across a floor that has been spat on, or feed themselves off a kerosene stove. . . .

. . . Such are cultured people. It is not enough to have read only *Pickwick Papers* and to have memorized a monologue from *Faust*. . . .

What you need is constant work. . . . (March 1886, S 111–13)

Chekhov's plays and stories contain numerous characters to whom this letter might have been addressed, people who have never learned, or were instructed to forget, that a good life is not just enabled but in large part constituted by prosaic good behavior. Almost every statement in Chekhov's letter to his brother violated some intelligentsial taboo and consequently anticipated criticisms that were to appear in *Landmarks*. Chekhov's reference to respect for the individual personality, a prominent theme of *Landmarks*, probably alludes to the intellectually fashionable denial that a person is anything more than the product of material and social forces. The views of Bazarov in Turgenev's *Fathers and Sons* had passed from daring nonconformists to thoughtless epigones, more like that novel's shallow radicals, Sitnikov and Kukshina, who imagine that they are "continuing Bazarov's work." In appealing to aesthetics, Chekhov gave the most provocative expression possible to his denunciation of the intelligentsia's way of living, because a prime tenet of the radicals from Pisarev on was a militant anti-aestheticism. We might recall that in *The Possessed* Stepan Trofimovich's "complete fiasco" occurs when he gives a speech saying that, contrary to Pisarev, Pushkin's achievement is worth more than a pair of boots.

In its overall tone, as much as in its specific recommendations, Chekhov's letter also draws on a view of ethics as anything but service to "the cause." Even his revulsion at lying appears to have a specific as well as a general target, namely, the view that the bourgeois virtue of truth-telling may be suspended if lies contribute to the welfare of "the people." That ready justification for hypocrisy, which Chekhov subjects to withering scrutiny in *The Duel*, was attacked explicitly in *Landmarks*. Izgoev, for instance, quotes at length from the memoirs of one student who was distressed at his classmates' "lefter-than-thou" mentality, which leads to a habit of falsehood in the name of radicalism: "They lie in polemical irritation, they lie to set a new record for leftism, they lie so as not to lose popularity," the student observes (Izgoev 83). Above all, this letter of Chekhov, like many others and like his stories and plays, breathes disdain for the constant *posing* in which members of the intelligentsia engage.

Cultured people "don't say, 'I'm misunderstood!'," do not parade their sufferings as if they were a badge of honor, do not invent (still less, borrow) grand abstract oppressions that confer a spurious nobility. Perhaps Chekhov's most savage portrait of an *intelligent* of this sort is Laevsky in *The Duel*. For all his own shortcomings, Van Koren is right when he denounces the all-too-recognizable theatricality of Laevsky's shabby whining and prefabricated complaints:

> As a friend, I remonstrated with him, asked him why he drank so much, why he lived beyond his means and incurred debts, why he did nothing. . . . and in answer to all my questions he would smile bitterly and say, "I'm a failure, a superfluous man," or: "We're degenerating . . ." Or he'd start a long rigamarole about Onegin, Pechorin, Byron's Cain, Bazarov, of whom he would say: "They are our fathers in spirit and in flesh." So we are to understand that it's not he who is to blame that government packets lie unopened for weeks at a time, that he drinks and gets others drunk; it's Onegin, Pechorin, Turgenev who are to blame . . . since he is the destined victim of the age. (77)

Anyone who knows Chekhov's plays will recall how often characters engage in an unseemly competition to pass themselves off as "the destined victim of the age." The spuriousness of gaining status or claiming special respect because one is a particular type of currently fashionable victim is a recurrent theme in Russian literature, one that is all too often overlooked. It is another link between Chekhov's works and our time. For Chekhov, the self-indulgence of the alcoholic and the self-exaltation of the "misunderstood" member of the intelligentsia were part of the same complex, which is one reason that his *intelligenty* drink so much.

In making these charges, Chekhov was, as he well knew, breaking the unrelenting intelligentsial demand for group solidarity, which to Chekhov seemed like a compact among conformists to justify each other's shortcomings and praise each other for sharing the same "advanced" opinions. Invited to join one such group of *intelligenty*, Chekhov, who could spot falsity and detect conformity a mile away, angrily replied by restating his belief in prosaic, rather than intelligentsial, virtues, especially everyday decency and honesty. You don't need an intelligentsial "circle" to foster these plain virtues, he pointed out; instead, "you've got to be . . . just a plain human being. Let us be ordinary people, let us adopt the same attitude *toward all*, then an artificially overwrought solidarity will not be needed" (3 May 1888, S 165).

As this remark illustrates, Chekhov also resembled the *Landmarks* contributors in his special resentment of the intelligentsia's conformism, especially its pressure for everyone to profess the correct opinions and associate only with those who do. Because *intelligenty* also claimed to display independence of mind, and to disdain the conformism of the bourgeoisie, their own enforcement of political and behavioral correctness necessarily entailed considerable hypocrisy as well. As it happens, Chekhov was himself under pressure to break with his politically conservative friend Suvorin, whose periodical *New Times* published a good deal of Chekhov's fiction. He resented that pressure deeply. "Under the banner of science, art, and oppressed free-thinking among us in Russia, such toads and crocodiles will rule in ways not known even at the time of the Inquisition in Spain" (27 Aug. 1888, S 165). This prediction, of course, turned out to be, if anything, understated. We have already seen that the *Landmarks* contributors, who cited Chekhov a number of times, were especially impressed with his psychological comparison of Russia's current autocratic oppressors with its would-be oppressive autocrats.

The Authenticity of Beliefs

> *It serves me right because it was all false; because it was all pretense, and not from the heart. . . . Because it was all a fake! . . . I can't act except from the heart, and you act from principle.*
>
> —Kitty in Tolstoy's *Anna Karenina*

In referring to the great Russian writers, the *Landmarks* contributors were trying to discredit the intelligentsia's own myths, to challenge its professed genealogy, and, in the process, to establish their own intellectual descent. They wrote a counterhistory that served a contrary set of values. Thus they not only drew the conventional distinction between the intelligentsia and the educated class but also stressed the superior intellectual accomplishments and the lengthier traditions of the nonintelligentsial thinkers.

The intelligentsia, they maintained, began only in the 1850s or 1860s, and certainly not earlier than Bakunin, whom Struve called the first *intelligent*. Before that time, educated people were active but did not constitute a separate little world. They did not define themselves as members of a free-standing social entity, distinct from all others. They did not exhibit a common sense of "dissociation" from the state or society at large, nor did they profess an unquestioned "faith" in atheism, materialism, and socialism. Least of all did they accept what Struve calls "the basic philosopheme of socialism, its ideological axis as a world-view . . . the principle that human good and evil ultimately depend [entirely] on external conditions" (119–20). In short, the intelligentsia proper arose from the combination of two factors: a sense of separateness fused to a distinct "philosopheme." "The spiritual birth of the Russian intelligentsia, in our use of the word, took place when progressive Russian intellects accepted Western European atheistic socialism"

(Struve 120), reaccented it according to the needs and habits of the intelligentsial circles, and gave it their characteristic maximalist and salvational interpretation.

Thus it is a mistake, in Struve's view, to regard the tradition that began with Bakunin and Chernyshevsky as an organic outgrowth of earlier Russian thought. No, it was a departure from earlier intellectual tradition, which continued outside the intelligentsia. We must therefore recognize two (or more) distinct lines of development. "We need only compare Novikov, Radishchev, and Chaadaev with Bakunin and Chernyshevsky to understand the ideological gulf that separates the luminaries of the Russian educated class from the luminaries of the Russian intelligentsia." The difference between these two groups of thinkers "is not simply 'historical.' They are not links in the same chain but represent two essentially irreconcilable spiritual currents which must struggle against each other at every stage of development" (Struve 120).

Dostoevsky, Tolstoy, and Chekhov are the true heirs of Novikov and Chaadaev. Thus the greatest Russian writers do not only lie outside one tradition (the intelligentsia) but also constitute a distinct alternative tradition of their own, a separate "spiritual current." This second current also includes Russia's greatest philosopher, Vladimir Soloviev, whose very status as a religious thinker has limited his influence largely to the "educated," that is, to people like the *Landmarks* contributors.

In insisting on the length and historical groundedness of the alternative tradition, the *Landmarks* essayists were offering a sort of Slavophile argument; in calling for the replacement of the intelligentsia with the educated, they were engaging in a kind of Westernism, inasmuch as the intelligentsia "in our use of the word" was conspicuously absent from most Western countries. Thus we have the otherwise strange invocation of both the Slavophiles and Chaadaev as forerunners of the current educated class. This linkage of Chaadaev with Kireevsky is one of the most intriguing arguments of *Landmarks*.

For all their differences, what Chaadaev and the Slavophiles shared was, first, an appreciation of religion and, second, a sense that beliefs, if they are to be meaningful, need to grow out of concrete, lived experience rather than borrowed wholesale. The distinction between artificial "principles" and experientially earned wisdom was to become central to the great Russian fiction writers. In *The Possessed* Dostoevsky mocks those who adhere to what he calls "the higher liberalism," which is nothing but a uniform they don. But it is Tolstoy who developed the distinction most profoundly.

A central moment in *Anna Karenina*'s critique of the intelligentsia occurs when Levin, who has long been frustrated by opinions grounded in nothing but fashion and the desire to seem progressive, comes to appreciate even a reactionary landowner. The two disagree, but Levin appreciates that the landowner "unmistakably spoke his own individual thought—a thing that rarely happens—

and a thought to which he had been brought not by the desire of finding some exercise for an idle brain, but a thought that had grown up out of the conditions of his life, which he had brooded over in the solitude of his village, and had considered in its every aspect."[17] Tolstoy's point, that what matters is not only *what* one believes but *how* one believes and how one arrives at one's beliefs, was also Gershenzon's central thesis in his *Landmarks* essay.

Gershenzon calls the *authenticity* of belief "creative self-consciousness." In so doing he links the intelligentsia's disbelief in real creativity to its mental conformity and to the falsity with which its members hold even their valid beliefs. The intelligentsia, he contends, needs to develop a nose for falsity, for beliefs that are not grounded in one's experience and personality; For the work of the mind can be sound "only when it is a *personal* concern, a matter of the personality's self-consciousness" (Gershenzon 55).

It follows that when the intelligentsia forms groups that demand everyone profess the same correct ideas, one knows in advance that no real *thinking* is going on. That is because "nothing is more distinctive than the outlook of each living creature. All that lives lives individually" (Gershenzon 55). If ideas are not truly *assimilated* in a unique and unrepeatable way, if they are instead adopted "for some ulterior, accidental, or one-sided motive—to please accepted opinion or fashion," then they will be nothing but "a sterile twinge" of consciousness. They will not be genuine "idea-feelings" (Gershenzon 56). For Gershenzon, party-mindedness is an offense against thought itself. No one is more anti-intellectual than the intelligentsia. It is surely one of the most durable lessons of the Russian countertradition that intelligentsialism and intellectuality are anything but one and the same.

Nihilism and Creativity

The intelligentsia will not grant that the personality holds living, creative energy.
—Bulgakov in *Landmarks*

Those who know Bakhtin's emphasis on the prosaic, on the particular, on the individual personality, and on the value of great novels will recognize that his work belongs firmly to the Russian countertradition and resembles *Landmarks* in spirit.[18] Where *Landmarks* and Bakhtin's early work differ most notably is in tone and purpose.

Gershenzon's anthology on the Russian intelligentsia is above all polemical. Something between a satire and a critique, *Landmarks* is most impressive when discrediting the intelligentsia's myths. Its energy is primarily negative. Although the seven contributors tried elsewhere to work out their own positive alternatives, the effectiveness of *Landmarks* derives primarily from its power as a "warning." (So Struve described the book in his preface to its successor volume, *Out of the Depths*.)

By contrast, Bakhtin characteristically works positively, by trying to offer an alternative to received and reductive visions. His works read as if he felt that the narrowness of intelligentsial theories is best answered by offering a broader picture, whose superiority will be self-evident. To be sure, there are polemical passages in Bakhtin, and he can be quite effective when on the attack. But in most cases even his criticisms appear designed primarily as a method to clarify the difference between his position and superficially similar ones (as in the first chapter of the Dostoevsky book).

One might appreciate the ways in which Bakhtin's work resembles and departs from *Landmarks* by considering a key theme in both, creativity. The *Landmarks* contributors were disturbed by the intelligentsia's exclusive emphasis on the distribution rather than the creation (*tvorchestvo*) of material goods and cultural wealth. That is yet another reason they preferred to trace their origin to great poets and novelists—that is, to creators—rather than to journalists, mere disseminators. They were deeply disturbed by a vision of the world in which the truth was already given and the role of thinkers was consequently reduced to that of propagandists. Here, too, they were prescient in anticipating the Party's attitude to "intellectual labor." It is possible that Bakhtin was alluding to this complex of ideas in *Landmarks* when he used the charged term *tvorchestvo* in the title of his Dostoevsky book. If so, the change of title in the second edition—*Problems of Dostoevsky's Creativity* (1929) became *Problems of Dostoevsky's Poetics* (1963)—may represent the dropping of an allusion no longer current or even decipherable.[19]

For both Bakhtin and the *Landmarks* contributors, a world without creativity is a world without humanity, for creativity is essential to being human. A world that does allow for creativity, rather than mere mechanical discovery, demands freedom, entails uncertainty, and contains personal responsibility.

As the *Landmarks* contributors repeatedly point out, the radical intelligentsia rejected all these values as reactionary and as contrary to determinism, materialism, and socialism. In answering such denials, the *Landmarks* contributors use a time-honored critical tactic: they convict the intelligentsia of self-contradiction. With vigor and rhetorical power, they point to the many elements of intelligentsial thought that tacitly entail the freedom, creativity, and responsibility that are explicitly rejected in principle.

Thus *Landmarks* cites Soloviev's parody of the "syllogism" of the intelligentsia: Man is descended from the apes; *therefore*, we must sacrifice ourselves for our fellow man. Where does their moral imperative come from? How does one urge sacrifice unless both freedom and nonmaterial moral values are real?

Similar contradictions abound. Oxymoronic phrases like "scientific socialism" and "historical materialism" almost always conceal an unjustifiable combination of moral and empirical categories, and so (to use a phrase of which Bakhtin was fond) they "smuggle" values not derivable from science into a supposedly scientific doctrine. Somehow the intelligentsia manages to insist that history, which they claim is entirely governed by "blind mechanical forces, . . . will inevitably lead to the reign of reason and the building of an earthly paradise. . . . The 'scientific socialism' professed by the vast majority of the Russian intelligentsia even assumes that this metaphysical optimism is 'scientifically proven'" (Frank 142). What precisely is this scientific proof? How do they know? Where does the teleology come from? And if the forces are both blind and inevitably effective, why urge people to action?

As a rule, the *Landmarks* contributors observe, members of the intelligentsia are simultaneously nihilists (or antinomians) and moralists. It is an odd combination indeed (perhaps not unlike the more recent marriage of deconstruction with Marxism). The evident self-contradiction in this unjustified hybrid is avoided by invoking each element at distinct moments, opportunistically and on a purely ad hoc basis—standard technique when contradictory theories both offer polemical advantage. Thus nihilism justifies a plea for universal destruction (although it is unclear how the absence of norms can justify even that), while on other occasions extreme moralism justifies the demand for self-sacrifice and the hatred of opponents. Several of the *Landmarks* contributors remind us that Turgenev's great nihilist, Bazarov, eventually faced this contradiction. He at last recognized what his real-life counterparts do not: that what actually follows from nihilism is not self-sacrifice for one's neighbor but self-indulgent indifferentism. When the real consequences of nihilism became apparent to me, Bazarov tells his shocked disciple Arkady, "I felt such a hatred for this poorest peasant, this Philip or Sidor, for whom I'm to be ready to jump out of my skin, and who won't even thank me for it. . . . and what do I need his thanks for? Why, suppose he does live in a clean hut, while the nettles are growing out of me,—well, what comes after that?"[20]

Bazarov comes to this realization because he is intellectually honest (although on nihilist principle he does not believe in being so). But the real-life nihilists conveniently learned nothing from this literary portrayal. Instead, they exhibit "the fundamental antinomy of the intelligentsia's world-view: the interweaving of the irreconcilable principles of nihilism and moralism into a single whole" (Frank 149). When the contradiction is pointed out to them, they engage in a variety of tactics to "forestall this kind of acute perplexity" (Frank 136): they resort to fixed phrases, denounce their opponents as reactionary, apply forms of censorship, or trace the class origins of those who point out the contradiction.

In passages like these, Frank and his fellow contributors allude to or cite Dostoevsky's legend of the Grand Inquisitor, which bases a social order on various sorts of "preventive epistemology." Perplexing questions are not answered; they are avoided or ideally never asked at all. This insight looks forward to Eugene Zamyatin's early response to the Bolshevik coup, the anti-utopian novel *We*. If thought control fails, the unfortunate hero discovers, then lobotomy becomes the surest preventive medicine for skepticism. Zamyatin's novel in turn lent this insight about the age-old problem of knowledge to the dystopian novel as a genre, both Russian (*Lyubimov*) and Western (*1984*). (Actual Soviet practice must have been no less important as a source.)

The title *We* of course alludes to the collectivist denial of the self, a denial in which the *Landmarks* contributors also discovered contradiction. If individuals do not exist, why does the intelligentsia construct its own "calendar of saints" and engage in the most extraordinary self-deification of its leaders? (This is a particularly interesting charge in light of Stalin's later "cult of personality.") If the laws of history produce everything and individual creativity is a myth, then on what basis are extraordinary members of the intelligentsia praised for their contributions and set up as models? Why should we care so much about Chernyshevsky? Bulgakov put his finger on the contradiction that seems to have been most important for Bakhtin: "The intelligentsia asserts that the personality is wholly a product of the environment, and at the same time suggests to it that it improve its surroundings, like Baron Münchausen pulling himself out of the swamp by his own hair" (Bulgakov 36). Bakhtin was to make the same point and twice used the same striking allusion.[21]

The *Landmarks* contributors go on to examine the "psychological knot" capable of tying together such incompatible assertions and the sociological factors that have allowed this knot to be tied. That is, they do to the intelligentsia what the intelligentsia loves to do to others: treat opponents' beliefs as the product of unconscious drives rather than of reasons, and reveal their principles to be so many products of false consciousness or psychic illness. As if parodying the intelligentsia's own ploys, they seem to ask: What else is one to expect from a group so many of whose influential members were seminarians or priests' sons? What else but an irrational cult of victimhood would emerge from people suffused with bitterness, with a combination of megalomania and self-contempt, with *ressentiment*? A nineteenth-century saw about the German love of abstractions had it that while the French control the land and the British rule the sea, the Germans have dominion of the air; to this Dostoevsky's heirs seem to add, "and the Russians reside in the underground." The very attempt to turn the intelligentsia's favorite tactic— answering objections by discrediting their supposed origin—on the intelligentsia itself must have been an important reason for the unprecedented hostility evoked by *Landmarks*.

Denying the Surplus

Landmarks, in short, displays impressive power in criticizing the intelligentsia's mentality and locating the contradictions among its tenets. But its articles are less memorable if one is looking for fleshed-out, viable alternatives. It is one thing to show that no one can be a true determinist and quite another to persuade people that a different vision of the world is tenable or even imaginable.

What would a nondeterminist world look like? We are so used to imagining events as the results of blind forces and causal chains that it is hard to picture a world in which such chains are only one element. For Bakhtin the real goal, to which he devoted the better part of his life, was to sketch out such an alternative picture. Not quite at the beginning of his career, he hit upon the idea that we already know such alternatives but do not recognize them as such. They are so familiar that we do not see them. They are to be found in the great novels— especially Dostoevsky—if we could only read them from the proper perspective. Hence a key purpose of Bakhtinian criticism is to help us become aware of the wisdom we already have but neither notice nor value nor act upon.

Above all, Bakhtin wanted to give body and weight to an understanding of the world in which real selves create, exercise choice, take responsibility, and develop unexpectedly while interacting with a social world that is also uncertain. He never lost his interest in the problem of creativity, which he realized necessitated describing a sort of world in which creativity is conceivable.

Some of Bakhtin's work reads as if he had taken his cue from a concept developed by Gershenzon, among others: "the ready-made" (*gotovyi*). The editor of *Landmarks* used this term to describe the apriority and intellectual conformity of the intelligentsia. One joined that social group by adopting someone else's theory with proper deference, fanaticism, and intolerance: "Thus, a young man did not have to take the risk of defining the purpose of life for himself; he found it ready-made" (Gershenzon 67). Bakhtin extends this term's range far beyond borrowed ideas. He uses it to describe what he finds objectionable in theories as diverse as Freudianism, Marxism, Formalism, and structuralism. The term in fact plays an important role in his polemic with the dominant line of Western philosophical thought per se.

Bakhtin's point is that, if one has the wrong picture of the world, *everything* sooner or later turns out to be ready-made:

> An object is ready-made, the linguistic means for its depiction are ready-made, the artist himself is ready-made, and his world view is ready-made. And here with ready-made means, in light of a ready-made world view, the ready-made poet reflects a ready-made object. But in fact the object is created in the process of creativity, as are the poet himself, his world view, and his means of expression.[22]

For Bakhtin, the object of human effort is created in the eventful process of creativity, action cannot be exhaustively described by referring to the conditions in which it arose, people are not just the product of their biology and biography, the world allows for real surprise, and we human beings are always turning what is "given" to us into something that is in part "created" (*sozdan*) by us. The wrong sort of scholarship "amounts to a disclosure of everything that has been given, already at hand, and ready-made before the work has existed (that which is found by the artist and not created by him)," but the right sort recognizes that "everything given is created anew in what is created, transformed in it."[23] It explores the *gap* between the given and the created. That gap, in which real *eventness* happens, defines human effort, human creativity, ultimately human life itself. Indeed, Bakhtin goes on, even what is "given" is itself largely the "sclerotic deposits" of earlier creative acts.

In short, those who reduce the human world to ready-made elements overlook what we *add* to what we find; they disregard what Bakhtin calls the "surplus" (*izbytok*). The surplus makes real creativity possible (and vice versa). And because our actions, from our most prosaic daily decisions to our greatest works of art, cannot be reduced to preexisting conditions, ethical responsibility is also real. We may meaningfully add what Bakhtin calls our "signature" to what we do or make, and so take responsibility for it.

It is therefore understandable why Bakhtin reacted with such antipathy to Russian Formalism, which he regarded, interestingly enough, as an odd form of materialism. He in fact referred to Formalist thinking as "material aesthetics" because it reduced literature to the raw material from which it was made by the mechanical application of "devices." In this quasi-industrial model, so to speak, technique is applied by rule to raw material in order to yield art. This is the "ready-made" view with a vengeance. And of course the reference to Formalism as a type of materialism implicitly links it to its ostensible opposite, Marxism.

It is their impoverished understanding of creativity that, in Bakhtin's view, necessarily leads to their radical elimination of the individual author. The poet, too, is ready-made. Since for Bakhtin authorship and creativity are defining attributes of humanity, the liquidation of the author destroys the human.

With their characteristic extremism and insouciance, with all the maximalism that marked them as true *intelligenty*, the Formalists boldly took this position to its logical end and so revealed its defects with special clarity. To translate their idea into Bakhtin's terms, the Formalists describe writers as interchangeable and essentially mechanical artificers. They see the great artist as Salieri, who "checked harmony by algebra." Working on ready-made material with ready-made means, the Formalists' poet serves only as history's executor of a ready-made plan. One Formalist spokesman put it this way: "OPOIAZ [the Formalists' Society for the Study of Poetic Language] presumes that there are no poets and writers, there are only poetry and literature. . . . If there were no Pushkin, *Eugene Onegin* would have been written all the same. America would have been discovered even without Columbus."[24] For Bakhtin, the absurdity of this position indicates what is wrong with "material aesthetics" or any other position that eliminates the agency and the real creative work of the author.

When he had a chance to publish a second edition of his book on Dostoevsky, Bakhtin made essentially the same point about Marxist aesthetics, which, when consistently applied, leads to the same result by a different route. In a review of the book's first edition, the commissar of education Anatoly Lunacharsky had suggested that Bakhtin could link his thesis to Marxism by describing polyphony as a symptom of the capitalist era. As the product of capitalism, Lunacharsky reasoned, Dostoevsky's novels are of interest only as a document of that era. Bakhtin cites the following sentence from Lunacharsky's review: "Dostoevsky has not yet died, neither here nor in the West, because capitalism has not yet died, and even less the vestiges of capitalism."[25]

Bakhtin decisively rejected Lunacharsky's "favor" of linking the Dostoevsky book to Marxism. For one thing, Bakhtin argued, the material with which Dostoevsky worked was not developed "under capitalism" but was the product of countless authors working over millennia. For another, neither capitalism nor any other economic system is ever sufficient to account for the creative acts that occur in its time.

The epoch is given, but "a given epoch can do more than create optimal conditions" for the creation of a new form (PDP 36). The creative act need not happen, and if it does, it may have various outcomes. Regardless of economic conditions, if there had been no Dostoevsky, there may well have been no polyphonic novel. Dostoevsky himself might well have created some other form. To be sure, capitalism (and many other factors) may have contributed to Dostoevsky's work, but it is a mistake to reduce an action to its enabling conditions. "A poetics cannot, of course, be divorced from social and historical analyses, but neither can it be dissolved in them" (PDP 36).

For these reasons, Dostoevsky's novels cannot be treated as a mere document of a given socioeconomic period. Dostoevsky and his epoch "have long since faded into the past—but the new structural principle of polyphony, *discovered* under these conditions, retains and will continue to retain its artistic significance under the completely different conditions of subsequent epochs. Great discoveries of human genius are made possible by the specific conditions of specific epochs, but they never die or lose their value along with the epochs that gave them birth" (PDP 35).

Scientism and Noncoincidence

The possibility of real creativity, of something genuinely new and valuable, remained for Bakhtin an acid test of worldviews. In Freudianism, Marxism, and Formalism he detected an impulse that represented itself as scientific but in fact was scientistic, a naive misapplication of scientific models to the humanities.

One sign of scientism is that tone of special pride taken when yet another way to deny human agency is announced. Culture, history, and the individual mind are "discovered" to be either the consequence or the mechanical instantiation of pregiven laws. Everything on which we expend such effort—moral choice, daily decisions, acts of creation—turns out to be mere epiphenomena, subjectively experienced as our own but objectively the product of purely impersonal forces. Or as the underground man puts it, creativity turns into "the extraction of square roots." Inasmuch as determinism guarantees this conclusion in advance, each new discovery (or rather, application) is hardly unexpected. Bakhtin saw Dostoevsky's rejection of one version of scientistic reductionism—psychologism—as more generally applicable.

Bakhtin dwells on Dostoevsky's most surprising self-characterization, "I am not a psychologist." If Dostoevsky is not a psychologist, we may ask, then who is? As Bakhtin understands this gnomic statement, Dostoevsky meant to reject the *wrong sort* of psychology, which treats people as the "ready-made" product of pregiven psychic drives. For all their similarity in some respects, Freud and Dostoevsky part company on this fundamental issue. For Dostoevsky, to understand people is to comprehend not their predetermination but their freedom. As Bakhtin describes him, Dostoevsky has never been equaled in his ability to represent a character's ongoing process of choosing, the throb of the "real present moment," when the next moment is uncertain *even for the author.* Such authorial uncertainty, which is sensed as one reads, is what endows Dostoevsky's novels with their special immediacy, that palpable "momentousness" so thrilling to his readers. It is also what defines Bakhtin's concept of polyphony and establishes it as the best way ever devised to convey the feel of human freedom. The quiddity of Dostoevsky's work—what makes it truly Dostoevskian—is its palpable sense of what it is like to be making a choice and taking responsibility.

Polyphony allowed Dostoevsky to convey his sense that the "living core" of human personality is essentially and irreducibly surprising, something that no imaginable laws or knowledge could entirely explain away. By contrast, "psychologists" give us a world without "surprisingness." "In place of this living core, bursting with new life, they substitute a sort of *ready-made definitiveness,* 'naturally' and 'normally' *predetermined* in all its words and acts by 'psychological laws'" (*PDP* 62).

Bakhtin's term for the source of surprisingness in people is *noncoincidence.* This neologism names the quality that gives life a "loophole" to other possibilities, without which we would be what the underground man calls "a piano key or an organ stop."

As long as a person is alive he lives by the fact that he is not yet finalized, that he has not yet uttered his ultimate word. . . . man is free, and can therefore violate any regulating norms which might be thrust upon him. . . .

A man never coincides with himself. One cannot apply to him the formula of identity A ≡ A. In Dostoevsky's artistic thinking, the genuine life of the personality takes place at the point of non-coincidence between a man and himself, at his point of departure beyond the limits of all that he is as a material being, a being that can be spied on, defined, predicted apart from his own will, "at second hand." (*PDP* 59)

Like the *Landmarks* contributors, Bakhtin never tired of rejecting the "causal or genetic" approach to people or culture and was unremitting in placing the highest value on the individual personality. He provided an image of people and of "the world as an event (and not as existence in ready-made form)."[26]

Theoretism and the Nonalibi

Landmarks maintains that the radical intelligentsia made a fundamental theoretical error in its understanding of theory itself. Like Pierre in *War and Peace* and the "gentlemen in the crystal palace" mocked by Dostoevsky's underground man, the intelligentsia regarded theory as a kind of Revelation. Theory was supposed— at least in principle—to be capable of explaining everything of significance. To possess the right theory was to understand the world or, at least, to be in a position to do so in the near future. Of course, Soviet Marxism was to advance just such a claim of infallibility. Perfect understanding was in turn supposed to offer a key to a perfect world, and so semiotic (or epistemic) totalism was closely linked to political totalism (or utopianism). This supreme confidence in the power of the right theory was also inherited by the Bolsheviks.

Behind this assumption about theory lay another about its object. Theory's power depends on the belief that the world is fundamentally *simple and ordered* rather than irretrievably *complex and messy*, as the great Russian writers believed. Examined by the theoretical eye, the world fits perfectly together, and what does not fit does not matter. Examined in the great novels, theories fail miserably and dangerously to capture and contain life's myriad and elusive mutabilities. One might say that the basic plot of that special Russian literary achievement, the novel of ideas, is the encounter of the ideologue with daily life, whose unsuspected and unappreciated particularities overturn theoretical symmetries. In Turgenev, Dostoevsky, Tolstoy, and others theoretical hubris is overwhelmed by contingency, disorder, and choice—in short, by life—in a revision of satiric traditions extending back to *The Clouds* and *The Dialogues of the Dead*. Perhaps more powerfully than ever before, the Russian novels and the Russian intelligentsia restaged a timeless debate. Taking sides in that argument, the *Landmarks* contributors stressed the superiority of the writers who possessed "vital understanding" to the journalists who could not see the forest for the textbook.

"The history of our journalism, from Belinsky onward, is a sheer nightmare, as far as vital understanding is concerned," Gershenzon insisted (59).

> Absurd and alarming as it may be, the journalists made all their calculations on the assumption that the whole world, all things and all human souls, were created and are governed by the rules of human logic—only not consistently enough; hence, with our reason we can perfectly comprehend the laws of universal life, we can set provisional goals for the universe . . . we can truly change the nature of things, etc. It seems incomprehensible that entire generations could live under such a monstrous delusion. Indeed, they [the intelligentsia] too had irrational feelings, they saw the miracle of life before them, saw death and expected it themselves. But they neither thought about their feelings nor looked at God's universe; and their thought lived a self-sufficient life playing with its anemic ideas. (Gershenzon 59–60)

Prosaic facts remain invisible to the theoretical eye. Although the intelligentsia claims to demystify the world, it mystifies theory itself. It claims to base its ideas on science, but it treats science religiously. Science becomes a body of dogma, and its discoveries are integrated into a catechism. And what this means is that the intelligentsia does not understand the most important, and most scientific, aspect of science, namely its critical and investigatory spirit. Nor does the failure of one aspiration to perfect knowledge ever lead to greater caution when claims are made for the next. And so the intelligentsia lurches from dogma to dogma, and its intellectual history—traced ironically by several *Landmarks* contributors—records a succession of jury-rigged and hastily abandoned infallibilities.

Somehow disconfirmation never seems to count. The psychological mechanisms to ward off disturbing conclusions about the theoretical enterprise also constitute a key theme in Russian novels of ideas. They tell the story of how, at all costs, the *intelligent* tries to "forestall complexity" at least until the very end of the story, when—this is the hopeful if not always the most convincing part—the need to think differently sometimes becomes evident to a Bazarov or a Raskolnikov.

One exemplary way to block recognition is to regard embarrassing failures or disconfirming facts as unimportant because the theory, or at the very least Theory, remains valid "in principle": "No other word seems to fly so often from the *intelligent's* lips: he judges everything first 'in principle,' which in fact means abstractly, without trying to grasp the complexity of reality, and thereby he often frees himself from the difficulty of evaluating a situation properly. Anyone who has ever worked with *intelligenty* knows the high cost of this 'principled' impracticality, which sometimes leads to 'straining at a gnat and swallowing a camel'" (Bulgakov 29). The reference to principled impracticality is echoed in the description of the intelligentsia as "Chekhovian people." It is also linked to the charge that intelligentsial theory is ill-matched to its own ostensible subject matter—people—which it wishes to change but cannot comprehend.

For the *Landmarks* contributors, as for the Russian countertradition as a whole, there neither is nor could be any magic formula for explaining everything. What we can do, however, is pay close attention to the world immediately around us, to the people we encounter daily, and to the small opportunities of each moment. From the countertraditional perspective, Chekhov's Elena Andreevna is entirely correct when she tells Uncle Vanya: "Ivan Petrovich, you are an educated, intelligent man, and I should think you would understand that the world is being destroyed not by crime and fire, but by . . . all these petty squabbles."[27] What makes a life good or bad is not its heroics but its prosaics.

That is precisely what the intelligentsia has consistently refused to believe. Instead, at every turn

> it managed to give even the most practical social concerns a philosophical character: it transformed the concrete and the particular into the abstract and the general; it saw the agrarian and labor problems as problems of universal salvation, and it gave sociological doctrines an almost theological color. Our journalism reflected this tendency, for it taught the meaning of life and tended to be abstract and philosophical rather than concrete and practical, even when examining economic issues. . . . The Russian intelligentsia wished to live and to determine its attitude to the most practical and most prosaic aspects of social life on the basis of a materialist catechism and metaphysics. (Berdyaev 3)

The better part of Bakhtin's intellectual career was devoted to developing this contrast of theory and daily life, of abstractions and particulars, of philosophical systems and what he called prosaic intelligence. One might regard him as reviving the sense that "practical wisdom"—*phronesis*—is more than applied theory and as ascribing the richest understanding of practical wisdom to great fiction. Because so many of the world's great novels are Russian, Russia emerges—its own intelligentsia notwithstanding—as a place of special importance in the history of practical and prosaic thought. The Russian countertradition is closer to George Eliot than to Karl Marx. For some reason, the irony of such a view of Russian culture emerging from the greatest literary scholar of the Union of Soviet Socialist Republics has been lost on most of Bakhtin's American admirers.

In his earliest work, Bakhtin mounts an attack on what he called *theoretism*. (Later he would speak of "monologism" or "dogmatism.") This term, which refers to an error common to numerous influential *isms*, appears in his unfinished manuscript "Toward a Philosophy of the Act" and figures in his redefinition of ethical thought.

Theoretism names the widespread tendency to assume that the world is adequately and in principle exhaustively describable by a set of norms and rules. The world according to theoretism is imagined as consisting of three sorts of elements: the rules themselves, which is what real knowledge seeks to identify; empirical events, which are regarded as mere exemplifications or instantiations of the rules; and, perhaps, some residue of phenomena that are thought to be either subject to future formalization or too insignificant to bother with. When Bakhtin turned his attention to language, Saussurean linguistics—with its division of *langage* into *langue* (the rules), *parole* (the concrete speech acts instantiating *langue*), and perhaps some uninteresting residue of accidents—provided a convenient illustration of this sort of thinking. In "Toward a Philosophy of the Act" he directs his fire at the view of Kantians and others that ethics is a matter of knowing and applying the right abstract and universal norms.

A fatal flaw of this view is to be found in the presumption that the ethical world is "transcribable," that is, that it is possible to offer a theoretical description of a particular situation so that the features relevant to a proper ethical decision are preserved. Theoretist ethics glosses over the problem of transcription, which is understood to be minor and technical. But upon proper reflection it is much more, and the whole approach falls once we recognize that the fundamental principle of theoretist ethics is "in no sense the principle of the [concrete] act, but the principle of possible generalizations from already completed acts in their theoretical transcription."28

What if ethical situations cannot be adequately transcribed? What if transcriptions can never come closer to the concrete act than a map comes to a battlefield, as Tolstoy suggests in *War and Peace?* In short, what if too many particulars unimaginable in advance by any transcription system are essential to making the right ethical decision? In that case there would be no substitute for real presence at the situation and an experienced ethical sensitivity not reducible to rules. Bakhtin would later illustrate his point by evoking the dense and thick description of ethical situations in the great novels and by asking us to compare the rich ethical sense they evoke with alternatives produced by some generalized description. Characters in novels who apply some prefabricated set of rules to the rich world around them make colossal ethical mistakes. In offering this contrast, Bakhtin was once again working less by direct polemic than by reminders of what we already know but have not appreciated precisely because it is so familiar.

Our experience tells us that generalized descriptions fall short, which means that for some purposes we need to develop better transcriptions and for others to rely on something quite different, a rich sensitivity to the role played by unrepeatable actions and apparently trivial facts.

In Bakhtin's terms, morality is a matter of "the historical concreteness of the individual fact, and not . . . the theoretical truth of a proposition." One needs to understand the particular context of the particular act, which usually "cannot be transcribed in such a way that it will not lose the very sense of its eventness, that precise thing that it knows responsibly and toward which the act is oriented" (KFP 104). Like Tolstoy, Bakhtin is best described as a casuist in the root sense of the word, that is, one who believes in the irreducibility of particular cases.[29]

In Bakhtin's view, as for casuistry in general, norms are not worthless. They can be helpful to the ethical agent as a set of reminders. And to the pedagogue they may serve as a useful starting point in ethical education, much as one may teach effective style by beginning with principles outlined in a textbook. But ultimately, good style and ethical responsibility are unformalizable, for they are ultimately not a matter of applying rules but of responding sensitively to specific people and situations. It is a mistake, characteristic of theoretist minds, to imagine the sensitivity of ethical people as the sign of rules mastered or norms intuitively known. No, such sensitivity is itself what a good ethical sense is. That is what Bakhtin means when he concludes: "There are no moral norms signifying in themselves, but there is a moral subject . . . on which one must rely" (KFP 85).

An ethically sensitive person, in short, does not know by *applying* the right rules what *one* must do in *a situation of this sort*. No, he—I—know from experience what I must do in this situation at this moment. And I also understand that my responsibility is neither transferable nor replaceable: "That which can be accomplished by me cannot be accomplished by anyone else, ever" (KFP 112). The simultaneous uniqueness and ineluctability of responsibility is what Bakhtin means to capture when he repeats: "There is no alibi for being." Theoretism can never appreciate the "nonalibi" (*ne-alibi*).

The impulse of theoretism, and of Western thinkers generally, is to bypass or deny this nonalibi. Among the most interesting parts of Bakhtin's essay are his discussions of these avoidance mechanisms. One that he finds particularly disturbing effectively eliminates ethics by subsuming it in something else—for example, in politics. Political rectitude—politic*ism* as a form of reductionism—is assumed to be what ethics is, and so the very possibility of criticizing a political mentality from an ethical standpoint is eliminated.[30] Here again, Bakhtin echoes the concerns of *Landmarks*, which must have seemed still more pressing in the early years of Soviet rule.

When theoretists do arrive at an understanding of particularity, they typically generalize it. That is, they try to overcome the limitations of positive theory in a higher-order negative theory. We are given abstract general statements refuting abstractions—pirouettes of deconstruction, as we might say today—but no real movement toward understanding concrete acts. This is a depressingly familiar habit of intellectuals. Typically, at moments like these they resort to one or another type of extreme relativism, which for Bakhtin was simply another form of theoretism. Extreme relativism makes examination of particular circumstances as pointless as the most absolute dogmatism. If everything is relative, or subjective, or a matter of power, or morally indifferent, why train oneself to attend with sensitivity to specific people in subtly different circumstances? Such a perspective does not foster the real ethical sense or an awareness of the nonalibi. Relativism is dogmatism in reverse.

Alternatively, a theoretist confronted with his own singularity might try to formulate exhaustive rules to account for *singularity in general*. This move too is depressingly familiar. Of course, "as soon as I think my singularity as an aspect of existence, shared by all existence, I have already exited from my singular singularity" (KFP 112). Bakhtin concludes that "all attempts to overcome the dualism of cognition and life, of thought and singular concrete reality from inside theoretical cognition are absolutely hopeless. . . . It is just like trying to lift oneself up by one's own hair" (KFP 86).

But what is hopeless in fact may be fostered as an illusion. It is indeed quite common for people in possession of a theory to behave as if it gave them an airtight ethical alibi. In such cases, one imagines oneself as the replaceable element of some perfect system, to which all responsibility is transferred. Life ceases to be truly lived but is instead falsely "ritualized" or "represented." Giving up one's singular responsibility, one behaves as if one had a "double" or "pretender" performing acts in one's stead (as one's representative) according to some perfect rule laid down by an infallible authority. Such thinking, Bakhtin observes acidly, "is especially common in political responsibility" in which one acts as "the representative of some larger whole" (KFP 121). In the context of the times, the allusion to the Leninist doctrine of *partiinost'* is almost unmistakable. This form of thinking, as we have seen, was also a special concern of the *Landmarks* contributors. (In the period between the publication of *Landmarks* and the revolution it was a common topic of debate.[31]) They too dwelled on the danger of ideological conformity, of reducing ethics to political correctness, and of allowing an organization armed with a theory to assume one's responsibility.

Objects of Salvation

Endowed with a sense that they are a distinct and special group, and possessing what they believe to be an infallible theory for the solution of all problems, the intelligentsia tends to adopt what Bulgakov calls "a special spiritual hauteur, a certified heroism, so to speak" (27). Indeed, it would seem that such a sense of group identity and special knowledge are likely to produce this mentality in any intelligentsia. This is another occupational hazard, and one reason to study the Russian case, which was particularly extreme, is as an object lesson. For this reason, countertraditional diagnoses and warnings constitute an important legacy of Russian thought.

"*Heroism*—for me, this word expresses the fundamental essence of the intelligentsia's world-view and ideal, and it is the heroism of self-worship," wrote Bulgakov (26–27). Combining self-worship with a psychology of persecution, which was also felt to confer a special moral authority, the intelligentsia was suffused with both *ressentiment* and a sense of historical chosenness. The *intelligent* would therefore "periodically fall into an heroic ecstasy, with a patently hysterical overtone."[32] Like other *Landmarks* contributors, Bulgakov has in mind the mentality of humiliated megalomania and insulted self-deification associated with the revolutionary *intelligenty* in Dostoevsky's fiction.

Bulgakov apparently takes a page from Chekhov, as well as from Dostoevsky, when he describes the intelligentsia's theatricality. Intelligentsial heroism, unlike the real thing, is a role that can be acquired with ease, Bulgakov observes; and if the aspiring *intelligent* should have any doubt of his worthiness and threat to society, the tsarist police are likely to help out by arresting him even before he has done anything in particular. All doubts "disappear when he finds that his maturity is acknowledged by the Ministry of Internal Affairs" (Bulgakov 27). Here again *Landmarks* describes the relationship between the secret police and their conspiratorial opponents as symbiotic.

Until the happy day when his heroism is certified, the *intelligent* can prepare by memorizing his lines. "Once he masters a few dogmas of the religion of man-Godhood and the quasi-scientific 'program' of some party, there is a corresponding change in his self-image, and the buskins of heroism sprout of their own accord" (Bulgakov 27–28).

The intelligentsia's dream is always to "save the people," but unfortunately, the people usually accept neither the intelligentsia's self-appointed role nor the jargon-ridden dogmas that allegedly constitute "enlightenment." Least of all are they willing to adopt the intelligentsia's rather demeaning image of the people themselves. In *Anna Karenina* Levin refuses to characterize "the people" either positively or negatively because, living among them, he knows that they are as varied as the rest of humanity, but this very refusal to generalize is itself enough to exclude him from the intelligentsia. "That word 'the people' is so vague," Levin remarks, in violation of a fundamental taboo (*AK* 841).

Levin has learned that peasants cannot be treated as objects and that there is a thin line between doing so to exploit them and doing so to save them. Perhaps there is no line at all. The "agricultural" sections of *Anna Karenina* are in this way closely connected with its polemic against the intelligentsia's self-appointed role. And that role is what persists, according to Bulgakov. The favored theory changes with utopian abandon, but each one preserves the intelligentsia's mission of saving "the people." Like folktales as described by Propp, intelligentsial myths tolerate varying ideological content so long as the basic functions remain.

Bulgakov contends that all these myths reflect "an arrogant view of the people as an object of salvation, as a minor, unenlightened in the intelligentsia's sense of the word and in need of a nursemaid to develop its 'consciousness'" (Bulgakov 43). This arrogance persists longer than any of the platforms or dogmas because it is the source of all of them. "The very essence of heroism presupposes a passive object of activity, the nation or people that is being saved" (Bulgakov 29).

The people are not allowed their own opinions, desires, needs, values, and worldviews; they are, instead, *allowed to be saved*. In case they resist, doctrines like "false consciousness" are helpful. The *Landmarks* contributors deftly describe the way in which the intelligentsia's need for self-justification feeds its vanity, colors its perceptions, and prefabricates its theories.

But they were even more concerned to point out the fundamental immorality in treating other people with such contempt. For all its striving for democracy, the intelligentsia is only a special kind of aristocratic class, arrogantly contrasting itself to 'common people'" (Bulgakov 29). Berdyaev concludes that the intelligentsia's supposed love of the people is necessarily "a false love because it was not based on true respect for men as equals and kinsmen. . . . Genuine love for the people . . . is not pity, which denies a person's dignity, but recognition of God's own image in every human being" (6). Real respect for people, and for the people, entails recognition of the value and distinctiveness of their own experience. Above all, it involves acknowledging their capacity and right to *respond*. Here we are on the verge of Bakhtin's approach to ethics.

For Bakhtin, as we have seen, an ethical approach to other people necessarily involves a recognition of their "noncoincidence" and "unfinalizability," that is, "their capacity to outgrow, as it were, from within and to render *untrue* any externalizing and finalizing definition of them. As long as a person is alive he lives by the fact that he is not yet finalized, that he has not yet uttered his ultimate word." Bakhtin reminds us that one of the underground man's "basic ideas, which he advances in his polemic with the socialists, is precisely the idea that man is not a final and defined quantity upon which firm calculations can be made; man is free, and can therefore violate any regulating norms which might be thrust upon him" (*PDP* 59). This was also a basic idea of Bakhtin himself.

Freedom so conceived is expressed above all in the right and ability to say something surprising and to change oneself in the course of saying it. That is why ethics, in recognizing unfinalizability, must also take its cue from dialogue. One must truly *address* another, treat him or her as a partner in an open-ended conversation, and come to know his personality "only through a *dialogic* penetration of that personality, during which it freely and reciprocally reveals itself" (*PDP* 59). Bakhtin's image of freedom is the freewheeling conversation, not the pedagogical session of an *intelligent* teaching "the people."

Bakhtin was unremitting in his attacks on all belief systems that authorize the believer to treat others as mere objects, as definable "at second hand," or as laboring under delusions that the believer understands better than the others do. That is the lesson Bakhtin draws from Alyosha Karamazov's conversation with Lise. The two well-intentioned young people, who are overly impressed with their own psychological insight, conclude that Captain Snegiryov, who has already saved his dignity by rejecting charity, will certainly take it the next time it is offered. At last Lise is disturbed by the sense that this analysis in effect treats the captain's responses as predetermined and that the whole discussion is therefore even more insulting to his dignity than the offer of charity: "Listen, Alexey Fyodorvich. Isn't there in all our analysis—I mean your analysis . . . no, better call it ours—aren't we showing *contempt* for him, for that poor man—*in analyzing his soul like this*, as it were, *from above*, eh? In deciding so *certainly* that he will take the money?" (cited in *PDP* 60; italics Bakhtin's)

To save people by taking away the freedom and unfinalizability that makes them human: this was for Bakhtin, as for Bulgakov and Berdyaev, to accept the bargain offered by Dostoevsky's Grand Inquisitor. As Dostoevsky stressed, this was the bargain of intelligentsial socialism. In Bakhtin's case, it was also implicit both in sentimental views of the unfortunate and in Freudianism. These approaches turn people into children. Whether political or therapeutic, the schools of theoretism hand agency over to

> forces that lie outside consciousness, externally (mechanically) defining it, from environment and violence to miracle, mystery, and authority. Consciousness under the influence of these forces loses its authentic freedom, and personality is destroyed. There, among these forces, must one also consign the unconscious (the "id").
>
> The sentimental-humanistic dematerialization of man, which remains objectified, pity, the lower forms of love (for children, for everything weak and small). A person ceases to be a thing, but does not become a personality, that is, remains an object lying in the zone of *another*, experienced in the pure form of *another*, distanced from the zone of *I*.[33]

"Miracle, mystery, and authority" is of course the Grand Inquisitor's phrase for the various temptations to surrender freedom. For Bakhtin, and for the *Landmarks* contributors, all definitions of humanity based on political pity, scientific therapy, or condescending salvationism were themselves such temptations. All of them are the disease they purport to cure.[34]

Urgency

Then there will be a new life, a new man; everything will be new . . . then they will divide history into two parts: from the gorilla to the annihilation of God and from the annihilation of God to . . ."
    "To the gorilla?"
    "To the transformation of the earth, and of man physically."
. . . .
    He looked as though he were expecting the destruction of the world, and not at some indefinite time in accordance with prophecies, which might never be fulfilled, but quite definitely, as though it were to be the day after tomorrow at twenty-five minutes past ten.
                           — Dostoevsky, *The Possessed*

Bakhtin also echoes a closely related argument about the intelligentsia's mentality of superiority. Bulgakov and others insist that the intelligentsia treats not only "the people" but also all of culture as mere raw material. Everyone and everything are measured by their potential for apocalyptic destruction or utopian transformation.

This attitude leads above all to contempt for tradition and for inherited social practices. Thus, *Landmarks* argues, the intelligentsia cherished a special animus for the family and repeatedly exemplified especially loathsome forms of conflict between "fathers and children." Continuity with previous generations was taken as a sign of insufficient revolutionary fervor. So was respect for the heritage of high culture, except insofar as it could be used to serve rigid and limited propagandistic purposes. Bazarov's contempt for art proved exemplary, and Pisarev's famous statement that boots are more important than Shakespeare established a long tradition of hostility to tradition.

In this typical intelligentsial view, the past becomes either so much debris to be carted away or so many tools for destruction. Their attitude, as Razumihin observes in *Crime and Punishment*, is that history is all so much nonsense; they want just to start all over. Bulgakov observes that "the hero creates history according to his own plan—he starts history off, as it were, and he regards everything around him as material or a passive object on which he can act. Hence he inevitably loses either feeling or desire for historical continuity" (39).

A special fallacy about time operates here in a way that was to fascinate the author of the chronotope essay. That fallacy involves, first of all, a sense that the present moment enjoys a special privilege and that the people who understand it are in a unique position to remake the universe. This is the time that could split history in half. Time as it has been "shall be no longer," and we shall leap from the kingdom of necessity to the kingdom of freedom— provided that we act correctly now. That is another reason that anything less than perfect vigilance "at such a moment" (to use Dostoevsky's phrase) cannot be tolerated.

How this extraordinary sense of present freedom squares with intelligentsial determinism was never adequately explained. Nevertheless, intelligentsial maximalism and totalism were combined with extreme *urgency* (in both meanings of the word). "The time is at hand," and we must immediately persuade people to take advantage of it. Unprecedented agency and special power for transformation are available for the first and only time.

According to the *Landmarks* contributors, this eschatological mentality represents another quality distinguishing the intelligentsial journalists from most of the great writers. The writers were sensitive to historical continuity, valued the past, and did not imagine that political rectitude could substitute for a sense of tradition. Their vision of time and history was complex. On the palette of the intelligentsia, however,

> two colors predominate, black for the past and rosy pink for the future. (The spiritual stature and acute vision of our great writers, who plumbed the depths of Russian history and drew from it *Boris Godunov, Song of the Merchant Kalashnikov*, and *War and Peace*, appear all the more vividly by contrast.) The intelligentsia generally uses history as material for the application of the theoretical formulas which hold given time (such as the theory of class struggle), or for journalistic and agitational purposes. (Bulgakov 43)

For the radical journalists and critics, the past exists to illustrate salvational theories, and the present exists to put those theories into practice. But authors of historical fiction (or, as Bakhtin would say, the genre itself) understand that our present moment is not special in the way the intelligentsia imagines. After all, each past moment was experienced as present. The author of *War and Peace* was quite clear about that when he replied to intelligentsial critics. He stressed that the past consists of present moments gone by. When experienced, they had just as much (or as little) openness and potential for change as the present moment currently going by.

But the intelligentsia as Bulgakov describes it has yielded with special abandon to the contrary belief. Their views confer a heady but spurious sanctity on their own time, their own generation. Izgoev observes that each generation of the intelligentsia imagines that it is chosen by time itself. This has been going on for generations.

Time and Choice

History not Theory.
Patriotism not Internationalism.
Evolution not Revolution.
Direction not Destruction.
Unity not Disruption.
—Razumov's notes in Conrad's *Under Western Eyes*

The idea that one has the right to remake the world turns out to be rather unfortunate for those who happen to live in it. Whether or not they are consciously alluding to the revolutionaries in *The Possessed*, who foresee the necessity of cutting off "a hundred million heads" in order to "solve the social problem," the *Landmarks* contributors are certainly prescient when they caution against underestimating what people like Lenin and his Bolsheviks would do if ever in power. This warning pertains to another set of intelligentsial fallacies concerning time and the intelligentsia's specially privileged role.

The root fallacy, as *Landmarks* describes it, is this: the intelligentsia is concerned to save humanity. However, they mean not the people around them but at best their descendants, "future humanity." But future humanity recedes like the horizon, and so salvational schemes condemn all real people to a new, politicist version of the myth of Sisyphus.

Bulgakov summarizes the argument by referring to the blood and pointless sacrifice it entails. For the intelligentsia, the object of salvation is not "mankind" but "more precisely, its future portion" (Bulgakov 39). And the goal of history "is the happiness of the last generations, who will triumph on the bones and blood of their forebears" (Bulgakov 37). Each generation is sacrificed for later ones, who are sacrificed in turn for still later ones. Thus does a salvational mentality ruin the lives of real people forevermore.

This sense of time leads to a remarkable carelessness with human life. "You can't make an omelette without breaking a few eggs." The world and the people in it exist to be remade. And "since he [the member of the intelligentsia] is sacrificing himself to this idea, he does not hesitate to sacrifice others as well" (Frank 143). When viewed from the perspective of a salvational political system, of an infallible theory, and of the most privileged historical moment, the intelligentsia's contemporaries cease to have any value. Typically classifying them in two groups, the *intelligent*

> can see his contemporaries only as victims of the world's evil that he dreams of eradicating or as perpetrators of that evil. He pities the former but can provide them with no direct aid, since his activity will benefit only their

remote descendants; consequently, there is no *genuine* feeling in his attitude toward them. The others he hates, and he regards the struggle against them as his immediate task and the fundamental means of achieving his ideal. It is this feeling of hatred for the enemies of the people that forms the concrete, active psychological foundation of his life. Thus, great love for future humanity engenders great hatred for people, the passion for building the earthly paradise becomes a passion for destruction, and the faithful populist-socialist becomes a *revolutionary*. (Frank 143)

In opposing this revolutionary ardor, Frank advocates everyday prosaic virtues. Like Chekhov, he dwells on a different sort of social responsibility: decent treatment of the people among whom one actually lives. From this perspective, Frank contrasts the prosaic love of one's neighbor with the revolutionary's love of those "far away," that is, humanity in the abstract.

This contrast of the near and far in fact echoes a number of thinkers in the Russian countertradition, which is perhaps one reason that it resonates so powerfully. Readers would probably have recalled Ivan Karamazov's taunt to Alyosha: "I could never understand how one can love one's neighbors. It's just one's neighbors, to my mind, that one cannot love, though one might love those at a distance."[35] Ivan's argument, which he develops at length, is designed by Dostoevsky to expose the cruel underpinnings of salvational schemes. As Ivan himself suspects, it is also a sign of his moral illness and of his unwilling resemblance to his vicious father, whose abstract sentimentality masks quite specific and quite horrendous cruelty. In Dostoevsky, generalized love and the tyrannical "benefactor" usually contribute to the most unimaginable and imaginative torture. The maudlin is cousin to murder. But Alyosha reminds Ivan that Father Zossima insists on kindness to one's neighbors as the true expression of love.

Readers of *Landmarks* might also have recalled Konstantin Levin's assertion, and Tolstoy's deep belief, that morality is fundamentally a matter of goodness to one's family and neighbors. It begins at home. We know that Levin has learned his lesson in prosaics when he stops defending even ordinary virtue to his brother: "One thing could be seen beyond doubt—that at the actual moment the discussion was irritating Sergei Ivanovich, and so it was wrong to continue it" (*AK* 844). Morality is usually a matter of "the actual moment."

Most famously, that is also what Alexander Herzen concludes in a frequently cited critique of revolutionary thinking in *From the Other Shore:*

If progress is the end, for whom are we working? Who is this Moloch who, as the toilers approach him, instead of rewarding them, only recedes, and as a consolation to the exhausted, doomed multitudes . . . can give back only the mocking answer that after their death all will be beautiful on earth. Do you truly wish to condemn all human beings alive today to the sad role . . . of wretched galley slaves, up to their knees in mud, dragging a barge filled with some mysterious treasure and with the words "progress in the future" inscribed on its bows? . . . This alone should serve as a warning to people: an end that is infinitely remote is not an end, but, if you like, a trap; an end must be nearer—it ought to be, at the very least, the laborer's wage, or pleasure in the work done.[36]

It is easy to multiply citations of this sort because the contrasts on which they rely are central to countertraditional thinking. Prosaic morality is opposed to grand schemes, the moment's small opportunities to history's ultimate transfiguration, kindness to socialism, bourgeois virtues to revolutionary élan, daily work to theory, individual decency to political correctness, and specific people to "the people." According to the Russian countertradition, systems at best mislead and at worst justify cruelty in the name of a higher ideal. Life is first and foremost a matter of our own actions to each other at each present moment. The real "accursed question" is the question of "petty squabbles."

That is how Bakhtin saw morality. In his view, our responsibility is neither generalizable nor deferrable. It can hide behind no theories, it can exhaust itself in no religious "rituals" or political programs, and it allows for no alibis. One can appreciate how specific responsibility is to Bakhtin when one understands its link to a certain kind of love—love whose object is necessarily a specific person, appreciated in all his or her particularity. For Bakhtin, love is a special way of concentrating attention so as to dwell, as we usually do not, on each contingent crevice, each unrepeatable experience reflected in another's face. Love is a prosaic way of knowing the specific. One does not love the instantiation of a principle. Love allows us to learn and to appreciate things inaccessible to the theoretist mind. That is because love alone "can muster enough intense force to grasp and retain the concrete multiplicity of existence without impoverishing or schematizing it" (KFP 130).[37]

In *Landmarks*, Frank offers a compendium of countertraditional truths when he characterizes the antiprosaic faith of the intelligentsia:

Once a person has been seduced by this optimistic faith, he can no longer be satisfied with direct, altruistic, day-to-day service to the people's immediate needs. He is intoxicated by the ideal of the radical, universal achievement of the people's happiness. In comparison with this ideal, simple, individual, person-to-person aid, mere relief of current sorrows and anxieties, not only pales and loses its moral attractiveness but even seems a waste of time and energy on petty, useless concerns, a betrayal of all mankind and its eternal salvation for the sake of a few individuals close at hand. And in fact, militant socialist populism not only displaced altruistic populism but morally slandered it as well, branding it as cheap and trivial "philanthropy." Holding as it does the simple and true key to the universal salvation of mankind, socialist populism cannot help but scorn and condemn prosaic, unending activity of the kind that is guided by direct altruistic sentiment. . . .

In theory, the same utilitarian altruism—the striving for the well-being of one's neighbor—lies at the basis of the socialist faith. But the abstract ideal of absolute happiness in the remote future destroys the concrete moral relationship of one individual to another and the vital sensation of love for one's neighbor, one's contemporaries and their concrete needs. The socialist is not an altruist. True, he too is striving for human happiness, but he does not love living people, only his *idea*, the idea of universal happiness. (Frank 142–43)

Concepts like theoretism, the nonalibi, and pretendership mark "Toward a Philosophy of the Act" as a characteristically countertraditional essay. According to Bakhtin's linguistic studies, dialogue is not intertextual but interpersonal; in his early ethical writings, responsibility obligates particular people. We are responsible to each other and not to "humanity," to the near future and not to "history." Marxism or revolutionism notwithstanding, "there is no person in general, there is me, there is a definite concrete other: my close friend, my contemporary (social humanity), the past and future of real people (of real historical humanity)" (KFP 117). By now it should be clear that in the Russian context this insistence on responsibility to one's contemporaries is highly charged. It evokes the basic themes and values of the countertradition. Written during the years of the early Bolshevik Red Terror in the name of a utopian future, it also conveys a political message that is anything but "party-minded."

Clearly, Bakhtin linked a good ethical sensibility to a proper sense of time. This is one way in which the Dostoevsky book, with its emphasis on the present moment of choice, grew out of his early ethical writings. "Forms of Time and of the Chronotope in the Novel" further deepens the connection between temporality and responsibility. Basically, this essay describes Western narrative genres as concrete conceptualizations of the *field* of ethical action. In some genres, people are sports of fate or chance, and so lack ethical initiative, but in others they have different degrees and kinds of agency. Choice, creativity, and responsibility become possible. From genre to genre, it means something different to be human.

To use Bakhtin's phrase, "the image of a person" derives in part from what a person *can do*, and so it is intimately related to the openness of time, the nature of choice, the relation of the private to the public world, and the possibility of genuine, unforeseen development of each personality and each society. Bakhtin's impassioned defense of the novel's "prosaic wisdom" reflects his sense that it offers the subtlest and most accurate "image of a person," which means that it also comprehends history and society, time and place, better than all other genres. It is suffused with an unsurpassed "chronotopicity." As we attend to the greatest novels, to Dostoevsky and Tolstoy, Balzac, James, and George Eliot, we experience a world in which responsibility is so concretely realized that it cannot be doubted. When the gentlemen in their crystal palace say that choice is unreal and creativity is inconceivable, we might best reply by recommending a course of reading. What has been conceived is manifestly conceivable.

The simplistic world of the theoretists resembles the more primitive genres, with their elementary chronotopes. Thus we have the interesting and common phenomenon of intellectuals who disdain adventure stories or romances but nevertheless endorse philosophies rather similar in their image of a person and the world. The chronotope essay offers a catalog of simplicities that can help us identify the shortcomings of the latest intellectual fad.

Among those genres that desiccate responsibility, Bakhtin locates various utopian and eschatological visions. Whether they place perfection in a remote past, in a contemporary but inaccessible country, or in a communist or millennarian future, such visions weaken real ethical choice. That is because they redirect energy, significance, and attention from the *immediate future*, from the next moment and, when that moment arrives, from the moment right after that. Like Herzen's mirage of perfection, significant time is always remote and ever receding. Like characters in Chekhov, utopians neglect or destroy the immediate world while wondering what "life will be like two or three hundred years from now." As a rule, they regard the only time that counts as insignificant. But for Bakhtin, meaningful acts are made and revised with the moment to come in mind. Responsibility must not be indefinitely deferred. Least of all can it be abdicated to transcendent forces guaranteed to provide universal answers apart from our daily participation.

Bakhtin observes that, "in its own way, each of these forms [of utopianism] empties out the future, dissects and bleeds it white, as it were."[38] When utopia is located in the past, the immediate future "is denied a basic concreteness, it is somehow empty and fragmented—since everything affirmative, ideal, obligatory, desired has been shifted . . . into the past" (FTC 147). Preexisting perfection renders creativity and present responsibility relatively trivial, because everything important is already over. (In a different way, that is also true of epic.) When utopia is imagined as coming, then the immediate future is "emptied out in another way," by devaluing the present moment for the sake of the End. Such thinking "always sees the segment of a future separating the present from the end as lacking value; this separating segment of time loses its significance and interest, it is merely an unnecessary continuation of an indefinitely prolonged present" (FTC 148).[39]

By contrast, Bakhtin's favorite genre, the realist novel, places the weight of ethical significance where it belongs, on the immediate future. It is suffused with the sense that the ones who matter are our neighbors and our contemporaries. Bakhtin develops the themes and motifs of the Russian countertradition not only in his explicit attacks on Marxism and utopianism but also in his entire project of exalting the novel's prosaic wisdom.

Critical Presumptions

Bakhtin's devotion to the novel extends the argument of *Landmarks* in yet another interesting way. We have seen that the *Landmarks* contributors contrasted the spirit of Russian literature with that of intelligentsial journalism. The novel, after all, was the greatest achievement of Russian literature. In exalting it, Bakhtin was affirming the irreplaceable value of literature per se.

In Bakhtin's work, the opposition of literature to journalism reappears as a defense of literature from presumptuous forms of criticism. In both Formalism and Marxism he apparently detected the impoverishing notion that the critic wielding a Method was somehow wiser than the writers he analyzed. If method is inadequate even with respect to the dialogues of daily life, then surely its presumptions are still more absurd when the recently certified academician gives lessons to Shakespeare. Bakhtin, I think, would have had no sympathy with modern American critical schools that treat the treasures of the past as mere "raw material" to illustrate current theoretical truisms. Neither would he have been sympathetic to those theoretical approaches that measure literature against the political prejudices of the day.

A character in one of Solzhenitsyn's novels wonders why she has to read Turgenev and Pushkin when they made errors that today any fifth grader could identify. If critics could efficiently extract the content of a literary work and assess it from the superior standpoint of present knowledge and values, then this character's question would be a fair one. Great literature would turn into mere documents, of no more interest than outmoded scientific theories. I like to think of this approach as the "phlogiston theory of Shakespeare." If its basic presumptions are accepted, then both official Soviet criticism and spiritually similar American schools become tenable. But they are not, and a good deal of Bakhtin's thinking was devoted to explaining why.

Bakhtin detects in this approach a number of related errors pertaining to time, knowledge, and theory. Most obviously, its adherents commit the error of theoretism when, overestimating the power of their favorite theory, they proceed as if transcription of a work's content is possible without significant loss. The only works for which that might be the case are works written to formula (such as socialist realist fiction), which is to say, transcribability is inversely proportional to quality. Bakhtin, it might be guessed, was anything but an axiological relativist. He believed that theoretism takes the weakest works and genres and proceeds as if they were representative of all literature. But great literature is not transcribable, and the presumption that it is impoverishes it.

It is in this context that we may appreciate the importance of genres to Bakhtin's thought. Most of them, and all the great ones, embody untranscribable wisdom. For Bakhtin, genres are neither sets of conventions nor templates for the production of works nor inherited combinations of themes and devices, as various schools have proposed. Rather, they are historically laden "forms of thinking" and experientially layered "ways of seeing" or conceptualizing the world.

A "way of seeing" is not a set of optical rules. Rather, it is better compared to a kind of energy, a "living impulse" of a specific sort. The works belonging to a genre do not constitute or comprise it, but are rather the record of its activity to date. It is a mistake to think of genres as tools for cataloging or to model genre theory on census taking. Such approaches overlook what is most important about great genres, namely, the special intelligence that has developed over centuries of "great time" and is "remembered" in the very form of works. For Bakhtin, received forms are a great writer's avenue to the genre's wisdom, which can, with suitable sensitivity, be more or less intuited from the record of its products. One might say that Bakhtin objected to Formalism because it *undervalued* the significance of form.

Great writers do not deploy devices or instantiate rules; rather, they learn to see the world with the eyes of the genre. They draw on, and contribute to, its wisdom. Their creative process involves a dialogue between the writer's own vision and the genre's way of seeing. In that dialogue, two forms of wisdom develop unforeseen potential in each other. Should the writer try to insist on his point of view, or dictate a party line to his characters, he will feel the genre's resistance and sense a flaw or a falsity in his composition. If he is a good writer, he will adjust his choices accordingly and sequentially. Over time, this process may teach him truths he did not know. Or it may suggest the possibility of taking the genre in a direction it had not gone before, as Dostoevsky extended the possibilities of the novel. For Bakhtin, the greatest writers are those who enrich generic wisdom in this way, rather than just skillfully exploit it (his example of this lesser accomplishment is Turgenev).

Over time, the genre accumulates wisdom and possibilities, becomes adaptable to diverse contexts, and extends its range over various kinds of experience. In this way, ongoing experience shapes the history of a genre, which is at base the evolution of perceptual habits of a certain sort. The writer's creative process is therefore of immense importance, for it serves as a conduit from daily experience to the wisdom of genres. Thus, creativity must be understood as the dialogue of individuality with tradition, which means that any worldview that does not give a rich meaning to each of these terms—dialogue, individuality, and tradition—will be to that extent unable to comprehend creativity.

In short, Bakhtin viewed literary creation as a special kind of thinking, no less valuable than discursive philosophy or criticism. It makes discoveries available in no other way. And yet, almost in spite of ourselves, we still tend to reduce art to mere exemplification of ideas originating elsewhere. So long as we do, we contribute to the excesses of critical presumptuousness.

Bakhtin elaborated on this insight in his essay on the *Bildungsroman*. He takes issue with the commonplace view that eighteenth-century thought lacked a real historical sense. This judgment can be sustained only if one overlooks the primary mode and locale of real historical thinking, the new narrative forms that were being developed by the great fiction writers. In fact, eighteenth-century fiction created the most profound conceptualizations of experienced temporality yet developed in the West. For the first time, individuality and social context were understood as shaped by genuine "becoming" and as interacting with each other. Without these discoveries, the still richer chronotopes of the nineteenth-century novel would not have been possible. It is clear to Bakhtin that "this process of preparing for the disclosure of historical time took place more rapidly, completely, and profoundly in *literary creativity* than in the abstract philosophical and strictly historical, ideological views of Enlightenment thinkers."[40] The contrary view results not from the historical facts but from mistaken parameters of research.

In saying that literary creativity makes cognitive discoveries, Bakhtin was not only rejecting the view of great novels as watered-down or sugar-coated philosophy—the view of *Anna Karenina* as applied Schopenhauer or *Remembrance of Things Past* as Bergson with examples. He was also trying to explore the reasons that might account for a genre's untranscribability. As transcription loses the "eventness" of ethical events, it also dissipates the "density and concreteness" of complex literary chronotopes. What is it about chronotopes that resists theoretical probing?

For one thing, a genre's chronotope is not actually an element in a work. That is one reason it is especially hard to grasp. Strictly speaking, it is not "represented" but is itself "the ground essential for . . . the representability of events" (FTC 250). It informs the work as a whole by creating the field of *possible* actions. The actions described, like the choices we make in our lives, do not define the whole field from which they arise. Bakhtin was to make much the same point when he approached genres via discourse. A given "language consciousness" does not "express itself" but renders a particular field of expression possible. In neither case is the genre's special wisdom anything analogous in kind or form to a set of concealed propositions.

It is also not closed. Much as the ethical sense of a morally experienced person continues to grow in unpredictable ways, so the wisdom of a complex genre is always unfinalized. To use Bakhtin's terminology, genres, as "living impulses," contain rich "potentials." The failure of his Western admirers to recognize the importance Bakhtin ascribed to potentials is perhaps the most notable indication that he has been read inattentively. Among other things, this omission makes it difficult to appreciate his view of criticism's proper role.

"Semantic phenomena can exist in concealed form, potentially," Bakhtin writes in his last published essay. "Shakespeare took advantage of and included in his works immense treasures of potential meaning that could not be fully realized or recognized in his epoch."[41] One task of criticism is to help "liberate" these potentials by engaging them in a dialogue. This formulation makes criticism important but still unmistakably subservient to literature and tradition. It also makes clear why dictating criticism's current truisms to a work keeps it in captivity.

Potentials are by definition not wholly accountable. If they were, they would be not potential but actual. Therefore, they are not extractable, though their presence *as potentials* may be sensed. Good readers develop such a sense, and great writers, who have experience as readers of earlier masterpieces, assess the potentials of their own works as they are in the process of creation. Writers are keenly aware of the difference between just saying what they want to say and creating something that also has rich potential that cannot be precisely specified. Shakespeare knew when a line resonated with unspecified richness and potential development by future generations, and he strove for this power, which he presumably appreciated in earlier poets. Having engaged them in dialogue, he listened to his own evolving works for the premonitory echo of dialogues to come.

To put the point paradoxically, great writers intend to say more than they intend (in the narrow sense). They seek not just to convey a message but to plant what Bakhtin calls "intentional potentials."[42] One objection Bakhtin raised against the usual sort of intentionalism is that it is not intentional *enough*, because it recognizes only the narrow sort of intention.

A work's potentials are open and amenable to development in diverse ways. In different circumstances, when activated in varying dialogues, they may not only yield quite surprising insights but also give birth to new potentials. Like time itself, a genre's sense of the world is open. That is part of what Bakhtin means by referring to a genre as a *living* impulse.

Respectful of potentials, good criticism never descends upon a work from a cognitively superior position. It presumes neither to understand all of a great work's "semantic treasures" (still less its potential treasures) nor to transcribe without meaningful loss what is indeed apprehended by the sensitive reader. The proper role of critical transcription and formal interpretation is, first, to capture, so far as possible, the wisdom of the work or genre, and then to point in the direction of further insights. It never offers itself as definitive, but as evocative of insights still taking shape and ways of seeing still not exhausted. In his own criticism, Bakhtin never claims to be doing anything more, and he reminds his readers (or, in his notes, himself) not to mistake his transcription for the real thing.

The wisdom and potential of genres derive from human experience across "great time." Tradition liberates. Historically saturated material enables real originality. The past is not a burden but an inexhaustible source of creative possibilities:

The semantic treasures Shakespeare embedded in his works were created and collected through the centuries and even millennia: they lay hidden in the language, and not only in the literary language . . . in plots whose roots go back to prehistoric antiquity, and, finally, in forms of thinking. Shakespeare, like any artist, constructed his works not out of inanimate elements, not out of bricks, but out of forms that were already heavily laden with meaning, filled with it. . . .

Genres are of special significance. Genres (of literature and speech) throughout the centuries of their life accumulate forms of seeing and inter- preting particular aspects of the world. For the writer-craftsman, the genre serves [merely] as an external template, but the great artist awakens the semantic possibilities that lie within it. Shakespeare took advantage of and included in his works immense treasures of potential meaning.[43]

Genres embody and serve to ensure historical continuity. Through them, the resources of the past open possibilities for the future.

In this distinctly anti-utopian view of history, the present moment is never in a position to sum up the past. The critic's sense of privilege, like the intelligentsia's belief in the special importance of present historical assessments, is entirely unfounded. Criticism does not possess and never will possess a scientific or infallible method. Methodologies purporting to offer a key to the mysteries of history and literature are Potemkin disciplines.

Another Russian anti-utopian thinker, Zamyatin, compared the notion of a final truth to the chimera of a final number. In much the same spirit, Bakhtin continued to believe in the endless and unfinalizable potential of free dialogues. Dialogues must never be closed down in the name of a political, religious, or philosophical doctrine. For Bakhtin, life, ethics, and creativity are always "risk- laden," "unfinalizable," and "surprising."

As intellectuals, we are subject to the recurrent and flattering temptation to think otherwise, and as members of the present generation we are ever lured to treat our own time as unprecedented in its insight. Shakespeare and Dostoevsky saw as through a glass darkly, but we see face to face. Our parents and teachers thought the same thing about themselves, but we are correct.

As much or more than anybody, intelligentsials yield to the fallacy of present privilege and their own special role. But every generation knows that it is more "up-to-date" than its predecessors, and at each moment thinkers judge dead sages who cannot answer back. We notice the datedness of others and imagine ourselves exempt from superannuation. The education of our generation was a historical milestone. But in fact not just our present but every present has been and will be a landmark toward an open future. This is Bakhtin's credo: "Nothing conclusive has yet taken place in the world, the ultimate word of the world and about the world has not yet been spoken, the world is open and free, everything is still in the future and will always be in the future" (PDP 166).[44]

Inventing the Novel

R. Bracht Branham

The purpose of this essay is threefold: to offer a brief account of the conception of the ancient novel developed by Mikhail Bakhtin in a series of idiosyncratic studies written in the 1930s and to ask, first, whether his work provides a theoretical basis for a genuinely historical approach to the genre and, second, given this approach, what a coherent picture of the evolution of narrative in antiquity would look like. While they were written more than fifty years ago, Bakhtin's essays on ancient literary history were not readily available in English until they were translated and collected into the volume entitled *The Dialogic Imagination* published in 1981.[1] Although they are not new, their content is novel to many students of fiction precisely because Bakhtin focuses his discussion on antiquity—the significance of which for the novel, he argues, has been "greatly underestimated" (39)—and to classicists because they are less likely to know the remarkable studies of Dostoevsky and Rabelais by which Bakhtin first became known in the West.

It is not, however, the novelty of Bakhtin's reflections that interests me but their power to provoke us into reconceiving some of the most basic questions of ancient literary history, such as the origin and character of the postclassical genres. Bakhtin's work on the place of the novel in the ancient hierarchy of genres is firmly based on a series of pioneering theoretical studies produced by the Bakhtin circle in the 1920s in direct response to the emergence of Russian Formalism on the one hand, and to the prevailing schools of official Marxist thought on the other.[2] In these polemical works Bakhtin and his collaborators strive to develop an approach to literary studies that avoids the Scylla and Charybdis of intrinsic or extrinsic reductivism—that is, the Formalist reduction of a text to its linguistic form or the historicist reduction of a text to the ideological context of its origins. Bakhtin's path between the two is based on his theory of speech genres: it is genre—both oral and literary—he argues, that mediates between social reality—the bedrock of ordinary usage (or "ideological behavior")—and the formal specifics of literary practice. And it is the mediating function of genre that both the Formalists and the Marxists had failed, in their different ways, to appreciate. At the center of Bakhtin's understanding of genre in general is his distinctive conception of the novel as fundamentally different from the older classical kinds—epic, lyric, and drama. Thus in reconstructing Bakhtin's understanding of the ancient novel, we are specifying one of the cornerstones of his approach to literary history generally and to that of classical antiquity in particular.

If we want to understand the place of prose fiction in ancient literary culture, it would seem unavoidable that we situate it in relation to the dominant form of narrative in ancient traditions, namely, epic, the most influential and prestigious genre in antiquity. It is not surprising that Bakhtin, following Lukács and other critics back to Hegel and Blankenburg, thinks it worthwhile to distinguish these two types of narrative in general terms. What I would like to do here in examining this central contrast is to argue that it applies much more neatly if for "novel" we read "Roman novel," or Petronius. This, consequently, implies that a third generic concept is needed both to account for the salient differences between Greek and Roman traditions of fiction and as a means of understanding the process of change that takes us from heroic verse to comic prose.

In his influential study of Bakhtin, Tzvetan Todorov recognizes the centrality of the novel to Bakhtin's thinking about literature but criticizes his conception of the genre as derivative—from Romantic criticism—and, more important, as insufficiently specific. Bakhtin has confused, he says, the "properties of a discourse" with the definition of a genre.[3] While there are problems with Bakhtin's terminology—he is not a systematic thinker, and his essays, culled from notebooks, always have an unfinished quality—what Todorov describes as problems are actually essential aspects of Bakhtin's thesis and explicitly acknowledged as such. Conceding that the contrast of novel and epic developed by Hegel and Blankenburg "is but one moment in the criticism of other literary genres," Bakhtin stresses its importance as part of an emerging apologia for the novel as "the dominant genre in contemporary literature," bearing the same relationship to the modern world as epic did to the ancient. This comparison, he argues, is "one of the high-points in the novel's coming to self-consciousness": "I am not constructing here a functional definition of the novelistic canon in literary history, that is, a definition that would make of it a system of fixed generic characteristics. Rather, I am trying to grope my way toward the basic structural characteristics of this most fluid of genres, characteristics that might determine the direction of its peculiar capacity for change and of its influence and effect on the rest of literature" (11).

This position follows logically from the premises set forth in the opening section of "Epic and Novel: Toward a Methodology for the Study of the Novel," where the peculiar status of the novel as a genre is attributed to its youth:

We know other genres, as genres, in their completed aspect, that is, as more or less fixed pre-existing forms into which one may then pour artistic experience. The primordial process of their formation lies outside historically documented observation. We encounter the epic as a genre that has not only long since completed its development, but one that is already antiquated. With certain reservations we can say the same for the other major genres, even for tragedy. The life they have in history, the life with which we are familiar, is the life they have lived as already completed genres, with a hardened and no longer flexible skeleton. Each of them has developed its own canon that operates in literature as an authentic historical force.

All these genres, or in any case their defining features, are considerably older than written language and the book, and to the present day they retain their ancient oral and auditory characteristics. Of all the major genres only the novel is younger than writing and the book; it alone is organically receptive to new forms of mute perception, that is, to reading. But of critical importance here is the fact that the novel has no canon of its own, as do other genres; only individual examples of the novel are historically active, not a generic canon as such. (3)

The novel is thus the sole major genre whose identity continues to develop, that is as yet "uncompleted." Consequently, the novel differs from the first genera-tion of genres—the Titans, epic, lyric, and drama—in that it does not complement them and hence does not fit neatly into a generic hierarchy. As a form of long narrative, it necessarily imitates and remodels what is, perhaps, the oldest genre and, hence, assumes the position of a younger rival. The idea that genres develop continually in a complex process of imitation and rivalry, which mediates their response to extraliterary historical pressures, underlies the idea of "novelization," Bakhtin's account of the mechanism of literary change. Hence the older genres, while already mature when we first meet them, nonetheless continue to adapt— "some better, some worse"—to the "new conditions of their existence" (4) created by the rise of literacy. Bakhtin would have agreed with the Formalist Iurii Tynianov that "it is only in the context of changing generic paradigms that a single genre's function can be grasped."[4]

Bakhtin charts the course of narrative's evolution along three axes of change, all of which reflect his abiding interest in the author-character-audience triangle: they are language, time or "the temporal coordinates of the literary image," and space or "the zone of maximal contact with . . . reality." Each of these nodal points is developed in several overlapping directions as Bakhtin contrasts the homogeneity of traditional epic language with the novel's linguistic "three-dimensionality"; the epic's "past perfect" temporal frame with the novel's contemporaneity; and, most important, the "distanced plane" of epic representation with the novel's "zone of maximal contact with the present . . . in all its openendedness" (11). If the last two categories sound like different aspects of the same thing, that is because Bakhtin is here applying his concept of the "chronotope," which he develops in another essay in the same volume—namely, the idea, freely adapted from Einstein, that the temporal and spatial relationships articulated in literature are intrinsically related and that their articulation is generically significant—"a formally constitutive category of literature" (84). It is the change in the "chronotope" of narrative from oral epic to the novel that makes possible a reconceptualization of the hero, and it is this "re-structuring of the image of the individual . . . in literature" (35) that makes the novel's emergence historically significant for Bakhtin.

Beginning, then, with the category of language, what Bakhtin means by the "three-dimensionality" or heterogeneity of the novel's linguistic style is not just that the genre is open to linguistic diversity, but that the diachronic sedimentation of natural language and the synchronic diversity of social and cultural languages is of central thematic importance in the novel; only the novel is concerned with creating this "distinctive social dialogue among languages" (263). In epic, on the other hand, the poet narrator shares with all his characters, mortal and immortal, a single language and ideology given by tradition. There is, of course, linguistic characterization of individual voices in epic; the speeches of Achilles, for example, exhibit distinctive kinds of imagery, but such distinctions can only be registered against the monumental consistency of Homeric style, a kind of consistency entailed by the nature of oral traditions. Such variations as there are appear within this style and do not represent divergences from it or violations of its norms. Thus Achilles and Hector speak the same language in a way in which Eumolpus and Trimalchio do not. (The use of linguistic diversity in the novel is comically evident in Petronius's *Cena*, where the narrator and his companions are accused of laughing under their breath at the conversations of the other, less cultured guests, or, more outrageously, when Eumolpus launches into hundreds of heroic hexameters to illustrate his opinions on epic.) It is true, of course, that Homer's traditional language draws on several dialects, but these dialects are not represented in the poem as such. No character speaks a dialect or the language of a class or profession. The swineherd Eumaios's speech is stylistically continuous with that of the gods and heroes.

Just as the relative homogeneity of epic language is closely tied to its origins in oral traditions, so its spatiotemporal frames of reference are also distinctly expressive of epic traditionality and essential to Bakhtin's generic dichotomy. Epic, he argues, treats a past that is "absolute" in that it is in principle remote from the historical present—the world of the singer and his audience—and does so by means of a public and, thereby, impersonal tradition that creates the sense of epic distance from a world as finished and complete as it is heroically elevated and inaccessible. These three constitutive features—the impersonal character of oral traditions, the absolute nature of the epic past, and the valorization of that past by means of epic distance—characterize the genre of epic for Bakhtin. The gap that separates the epic narrator and his audience from the world he relates places them not simply in different times or places but on different planes of value, between which no commerce is possible. Epic aestheticizes the past by transferring "the world it describes" to a "sublime and distant horizon" of memory—of beginnings, firsts, founders, ancestors, and gods (25–26). No purely temporal progressions connect it with the present. Its value is a given and is not relative to context, that is, to what preceded or followed it. Hence Bakhtin uses the term *absolute* for this distinctly epic conception of a world remembered. Its asymmetry with the "merely transitory present"—its implicit devaluation of the contemporary—is comically inverted in Eumolpus's performance as a rhapsode; epic can enter the novel, but when it does so, it ceases to be itself and becomes a comic image of epic, just as neither the epic narrator nor any member of his audience could conceivably enter heroic narrative without comic results. Similarly, the source of the story we are told in epic is not in the experience of its narrators, as it is in the Roman novel, but rather in a Panhellenic tradition, the cultural memory personified by the Muses. Thus, whereas epic is public, impersonal, and set in a spatiotemporally remote heroic past, the novel is personal, that is, told by first-person actor-narrators, who in speaking to and about their contemporaries open up a new and linguistically variegated world (or "zone of contact with reality").

Thus the novel can be seen as the obverse of epic in its orientation to language—it cultivates variety, the epic unity—and in its spatiotemporal frames of reference. What both types of narrative would seem to share is a paramount interest in a hero with all that implies for organizing a story. But of course, the conception of the hero is where the significance of the other differences is most clearly registered: "The changes that take place in temporal orientation, and in the zone where images are constructed, appear nowhere more profoundly and inevitably than in the process of re-structuring the image of the individual in literature" (33–34). It is indicative of the nature of epic that its hero appears "fully finished" and "completed." As Bakhtin argues, "Outside his destiny, the epic and tragic hero is nothing; he is, therefore, a function of the plot fate assigns him; he cannot become the hero of another destiny of another plot" (36). Because his fate is predetermined, he seems "ready-made," by which Bakhtin means that the hero's identity is a given: "He has already become everything that he could become, and he could become only that which he has already become. He is entirely externalized [in an] almost literal sense: everything in him is exposed and loudly expressed: his internal world and all his external characteristics . . . lie on a single plane." Hence "his view of himself coincides completely with others' views of him—the view of his society (his community), the epic singer and the audience also coincide" (34). In epic "characters are . . . individualized by their various situations and destinies, but not by varying 'truths'" or any "ideological initiative": "Not even the gods are separated from men by a special truth." "These traits," observes Bakhtin, are "shared by and large with other highly distanced genres" and "are responsible for the exclusive beauty, wholeness, crystal clarity and artistic completedness of this image of man" (35).

Unlike Lukács, who saw the novel as kind of epic manqué—totalizing narrative without immanent meaning[5]—Bakhtin sees the novel as, above all, a countergenre that responds dialogically to the classicizing tendencies just discussed of epic and related genres by bringing its subject, the hero, into "the zone of immediate contact" with open-ended reality and, hence, with laughter. Time becomes relative as the hero's linguistic consciousness becomes multiple. For Bakhtin contemporaneity and laughter are at the center of this process and seem to be almost inseparable. To consider a subject in the context of the unfolding tangible moment is to acknowledge that it has a ridiculous, contingent quality incompatible with the epic aesthetics of completedness and wholeness: "The destruction of epic distance and the transferral of the image of an individual from the distanced plane to the zone of contact with the inconclusive events of the present (and consequently of the future) result in a radical re-structuring of the image of the individual in the novel—and consequently in all literature" (35). This process begins with the carnivalization of the high genres by popular comic traditions that recast myth in comic patterns and replace the distant and heroic with the familiar and mortal. The "first and essential step," he says, "was the comic familiarization of the image of man. Laughter destroyed epic distance; it began to investigate man freely and familiarly, to turn him inside out, expose the disparity between his surface and his center, between his potential and his reality." As a result, "a dynamics of inconsistency and tension between various factors of this image" emerged (35). This novelistic gap between actual and possible selves is expressed in a variety of ways—in a lack of fit between the hero and his fate or situation, in a discrepancy between internal and external identity or between speech and action. "It is precisely the zone of contact with an inconclusive present"—exactly what epic excludes, according to Bakhtin—"that creates the necessity of this incongruity of a man with himself" (37). Hence Bakhtin can conclude that "the novel, from the very beginning, developed as a genre that had at its core a new way of conceptualizing time" (38).

Now if we consider the Greek romances in the light of Bakhtin's criteria, they appear to be an ambiguous compromise between the canonical values of oral epic and those of the novel. Let us take Chariton as an example—the earliest of the extant Greek romances. Insofar as the setting, classical Syracuse, is not mythical, the romance resembles the novel, but insofar as the setting is an idealized, generically classical one without any discernible connection to the anonymous audience's present, it is simply a modernized version of the "absolute past" of epic. Similarly, insofar as we are offered an account authenticated by a scribe who identifies himself—Chariton of Aphrodisias, secretary to Athenagorus—rather than an anonymous tradition, Chariton looks forward to the fully characterized actor-narrators of the Roman novels, but insofar as the story itself follows the compositional patterns of oral epic in both small structures, such as similes and assembly scenes, and in the larger providential design of the plot, we are in a kind of prose epic. In the category of language, Chariton's purity has often been commented on, and this purity, like his concern with decorum, is clearly more akin to epic "homogeneity" than to the dialogue of differing tongues, which Bakhtin associates with the novel and which is clearly central to Petronius's humor.

But the conception of the hero (or "the image of the individual") focuses the generic difference most clearly. The Greek romances revolve around normative examples of the culture: the beautiful and virtuous heroes and heroines who populate this world are as "ready-made" and "externalized" in Bakhtin's sense as are characters in epic—they are frequently compared to Homeric gods—and could scarcely be less similar to Petronius's antiheroes or to Apuleius's randy, curious Lucius, whose salvation precludes the time-honored resolution of romance by substituting vows of chastity for marital vows. Most important, however, is not the social positioning of the characters—significant as this is for genre—but the fact that the distinctly novelistic conception of the hero as subject to a precarious process of change, that is, to time, wedged between past and future, inner and outer, speech and action, is as alien to Greek romance or oral epic as, I would argue, it is central to Petronius and Apuleius. "Heroic romance" from Chariton through Heliodorus to Sidney is a distinct narrative kind defined by the complex conventions of idealization by which fictitious stories are given the aura and value of myth and, hence, of canonical literature. It is primarily this conservative stance toward canonical literary values that distinguishes romance from the novel.[6]

If we accept for the moment Bakhtin's view that oral epic and the novel form the two poles of narrative in antiquity, the classical and the novelistic, how do we move from one to the other in seven or eight hundred years? In his essay "The Problem of Speech Genres" Bakhtin suggests that expansion of the language of secondary, or literary, genres results from "the incorporation of various extraliterary strata of the national language."[7] A change in generic concepts therefore reflects a change in our social orientation to language and, consequently, in our ways of representing the world in language. In "From the Prehistory of Novelistic Discourse" in *The Dialogic Imagination*, Bakhtin argues that the novel differs from other forms precisely in that it is preeminently the form in which language is represented as well as representing. Therefore, when he attempts to explain the evolution of narrative in this same essay, he looks not for particular geniuses who invented new literary languages, nor to social or economic conditions, but for the forms of linguistic experience that enabled the change. He focuses exclusively on two, polyglossia and laughter. By *polyglossia* Bakhtin means the experience of two or more languages in a single cultural context, which would have increased for Greeks with the diaspora following Alexander's conquests and which had characterized

Roman culture from its earliest stages. By *laughter* he means the experience of one's own language from the outside, as, for example, in comic and parodic literature. Thus, both are ways of externalizing language, of experiencing it from the outside as contingent and artificial rather than from the inside as transparent and natural. Where Bakhtin emphasizes polyglossia and laughter we would probably look to the consequences of literacy (as seen in the institutionalization of rhetoric and philosophy in the fourth century B.C.) and the effect this had on the writing and reception of different genres. As it is, we can still say much more precisely what makes Homer's art oral than what makes the ancient novel or romance specifically literary.

Invention or evolution—my two metaphors for describing the process of change in ancient narrative from Homer to Petronius may seem scarcely compatible. Evolution suggests an impersonal process proceeding gradually by natural selection, while invention introduces the idea of conscious, individual creation. But perhaps mixing metaphors from nature and culture is appropriate in describing cultural inventions, because culture does grow or mature and it does so both through unconscious collective action and through unpredictable, individual initiative. The novel, in a sense, grew and was invented by no one anymore than epic was. But just as there appear to be "jumps" and "gaps" in the fossil record of evolutionary change so that species appear fully formed as if they had leapt over the intervening stages of adaptation, so literary innovators like Aeschylus, Theocritus, or Petronius appear to have no real predecessors and yet are inconceivable apart from generations of incremental change in the genres they spliced, recombined, or "carnivalized." The growth of genres seems to resemble the evolutionary model of punctuated change.[8] If Roman narrative was free to develop in more original ways than Greek, it is precisely because it was sufficiently isolated from the constraints of the older, dominant tradition—or "ancestral population." And while I have emphasized the generic differences between Petronius and writers of Greek romance, his accomplishment is of course inseparable from theirs. Their experiments made possible the first response of realism to romance, or, more precisely, the writerly confrontation of conventionally literary genres of speech, popular and classical, inherited from the past with those appropriated from other, extraliterary areas of culture—a definition that Walter Reed has persuasively applied to the Renaissance and modern novel in his *Exemplary History of the Novel*. At least from *Don Quixote* on, he argues, "the novel adopted an antagonistic stance both toward the literary canon and toward its own precursors."[9] This statement is true, I think, if we emend it to read "from Petronius on." What makes the ancient novel different from its modern and early modern counterparts—and therefore seemingly at odds with Reed's model of the genre—is not the lack of a critical stance toward the conventionally literary, but the fact that this stance is refracted through a distinctly aristocratic cultural bias.

In lieu of a conclusion I would like to end with a hypothesis that extends the logic of Bakhtin's reflections into a theory of the dialogic development of ancient narrative. If the ancient novel originates as a comic transformation of Greek romance, then the differences between Greek and Roman traditions of fiction are crucial to understanding either. As a Roman countergenre, the novel represents a critical response to both contemporary (or secondary) epic and heroic romance— the prevailing forms of narrative in the Roman Empire. The novelistic responses to these two forms are closely related, since both romance and secondary epic represent attempts to adapt traditional heroic epic for a bourgeois audience and thus are literate versions of originally oral narrative patterns. The Roman novel, as exemplified by Petronius, is at bottom an omnivorous form of parody that seeks to transform the canonical traditions of idealizing fiction—epic and romance—into a contemporary and, hence, radically mixed form of prose narrative that defines itself through the systematic displacement of the constitutive features of its well-established rivals. Thus the novel first appears as a Roman rewriting of originally Greek traditions and as a writerly response to the modernization of oral narrative that Hellenistic epic and romance attempt. It is not a substitute, derogation, or mere burlesquing of the dominant forms, but a reconceptualization of their principal narrative values beginning with the evaluation of time. Consequently, the very qualities eschewed by epic—the grotesque, realism, and comedy—are foregrounded, and the qualities that epic and its bourgeois descendant, the prose romance, celebrate—decorum heroism, and providence—are inverted in the name of verism.

This hypothesis is thus a reformulation of Bakhtin that would require us to historicize his theory of the novel's origins—based on the contrast between epic and novel, oral and written, popular and high culture—by specifying more precisely the terms of these defining oppositions in the light of the literary practice of Petronius and his Greek predecessors. To approach the development of the novel via the parodic remodeling of symbolic patterns familiar to us, above all, from epic and romance, has the advantage of redirecting our attention to one of the principal thematic preoccupations of the *Satyrica:* the Roman reception of Greek culture, which is subversively explored by Petronius—as the novel's Greek title suggests— as a flexible metaphor for the intellectual and moral metabolism of Roman society collapsing under the weight of an omnivorous empire. The aim of this historicized theory is to place the genesis of the novel as precisely as possible among the competing tendencies of postclassical literary culture and thereby to explain the conditions that made possible the most original works in classical Latin and, hence, why the novel first appears in the Roman Empire rather than in Hellenistic or classical Greece, Renaissance Spain, or eighteenth-century England.[10]

Response and Call: The African American Dialogue with Bakhtin and What It Signifies

Dale E. Peterson

Although it has taken twenty years to achieve, an exotic and somewhat rough-hewn Soviet import has recently approached the height of fashion in the volatile commodities and exchange market that constitutes contemporary critical discourse. Yet, even as Slavic scholars have dared announce the arrival in the West of "the age of Bakhtin," they have, with understandable caution, wondered out loud about the shelf life of this hastily consumed and culturally distant product.[1] Beginning in 1968 with the English translation of *Rabelais and His World*, and accelerating in 1973 with the first American editions of Bakhtin's *Problems of Dostoevsky's Poetics* and V. N. Voloshinov's *Marxism and the Philosophy of Language*, Anglo-American literary criticism began to be infiltrated by a whole new set of terminological oddities borrowed from an embattled circle of unorthodox Soviet semioticians known as the Bakhtin circle.[2] This tendency, enormously aided and abetted by the glossary of terms attached to a widely influential 1981 collection of Bakhtin's essays, *The Dialogic Imagination*, has resulted in a now-familiar critical diction, a Soviet-American creole that is served up in many academic courses and discourses. What accounts, then, for the powerful attraction of a Bakhtinian "dialogic" analysis of cultural signs, despite its off-putting proliferation of polysyllabic neologisms?

The fifty-year delay in the transmission to America of Bakhtin's distinctive linguistic and poetic theories could not have been more timely. The introduction of Bakhtin's particular style of discourse analysis and "sociological poetics" coincided with a massive discontent directed at the failure of old and new modes of literary analysis to acknowledge the expressive power of marginalized and uncanonical forms of articulation. In an American intellectual culture belatedly coming to terms with bracketed and/or hidden signs of cultural pluralism, the critical texts of the Bakhtin circle were able to perform a major intervention. As the central writings became better known, it was increasingly clear that these Russian accounts of effective verbal meaning stood in provocative opposition both to established tradition and to the newest fashions in American literary criticism. To put it directly, the works of Bakhtin and his colleagues, Voloshinov and Medvedev, were explicitly post-Formalist and antistructuralist, and perhaps most interestingly, they were prophetically critical of deconstructionism too. Although the specific arguments advanced in Bakhtin's major books on Rabelais, Dostoevsky, and novelistic discourse have not gone unchallenged in their migration westward, it is the orientation of Bakhtin's own discourse, his radically different point of departure about how words signify in cultural communication, that has most mattered.[3] As I shall argue, Bakhtin's books have come into alliance, for good and profound reasons, with other voices that seek to contest the overly literary notion that textual meaning must either be definitive or infinitely deferred. Or, to reaccent the same point, no matter how folks talk, they be signifyin' all along.

The basic writings of the Bakhtin circle happen to occupy a strategic and distinct position within the contemporary discourse about discourse. They stand in clear opposition to Russian Formalist and American New Critical practices, which attempt to corral effective meaning within a self-sufficient verbal artifact that is, supposedly, a finished work—nothing but the sum of its devices and the unified tension of its managed ambiguities. The Bakhtin circle also rejects the enclosure of the effective meaning of words and texts within the stable binary codes of opposed terms so systematically pursued by linguistic and literary structuralists. Thus, a Bakhtinian analysis of verbal signification insists on freeing cultural signs from that prison-house of language constructed by doctrines that maintain either the autonomy of texts or "the deadlock of dyads."[4] Yet, and this is crucial, despite the Bakhtin circle's partiality for "unfinalized" signification in actual communication, there is not the least trace of sympathy for the radical deconstructionist move toward "the endless play of signifiers."[5] Bakhtin manages to rein in the infinite deferrals of signification by insisting that any utterance, at any given moment of enunciation and/or reception, is projected into a delimited "field of answerability": "Semantic phenomena can exist in a concealed form, potentially, and be revealed only in semantic cultural contexts of subsequent epochs that are favorable for such disclosure."[6] Thus, in the current agitated climate of critical theory, Bakhtin's socially positioned, contextualized understanding of signs and communication takes on a reassuring, rather than an abysmal, open-endedness. Bakhtinian "dialogics" offer a way to open out and ventilate texts in complex social crosscurrents while keeping at bay the heavy weather of a chaotic relativism. But how is this distinctive feat possible, theoretically and practically?

As Bakhtin's translators and explicators have noted, the starting point for his particular analysis of verbal signification is the notion that all speech and writing is "utterance." In Russian, the term (*vyskazyvanie*) is freighted with its own peculiar significance; normally translated as "expression," it literally denotes the active process of speaking out and having one's say, of ex/postulating, to or with an interlocutor. In the beginning, Bakhtin's word is utterance, which is to say that the fundamental verbal sign is already an act of articulation. What is emphatically there is a propulsive energy directed at pronouncing a heard, or overheard, message. In other words, articulation is a primary act of cultural intervention, but it inserts itself into a prevailing discourse; it orients itself toward an anticipated respondent. In Bakhtin, speaking out, or self-expression, is ever mindful of the already spoken and necessarily attentive to the internalized other, the co-respondent. Consequently, we all struggle to in-tone an understanding by others of what we would signify through our words. We do this by reaccenting, as best and as shrewdly as we can, the linguistic rules and cultural codes that inhabit our socialized consciousness. The actual word that gets communicated is for speaker, writer, listener, and reader a contextually embedded, socially constituted, intersubjective event that allows for unfinalized, but not indeterminate, meaning.

From this perspective, which insists on the pragmatic and performative aspect of each word as communiqué, signification is always and necessarily "trans-linguistic." As Voloshinov puts it: "The actual reality of language—speech—is not the abstract system of linguistic forms . . . and not the psychophysiological act of its implementation, but the social event of verbal interaction implemented in an utterance."[7] By the same token, the significance of individual texts is always and necessarily trans-actional. As Bakhtin himself reminds us, any discourse is inherently double-voiced: "Within the arena of almost every utterance an intense interaction and struggle between one's own and another's word is being waged, a process in which they oppose or dialogically interanimate each other. The utterance so conceived is a considerably more complex and dynamic organism than it appears when construed simply as a thing that articulates the intention of the person uttering it."[8] The long and the short of it, and by far the most culturally influential side of it, is that Bakhtinian discourse analysis presumes that utterances come into the world showing and voicing the fact that they are sites of social contestation. Texts display themselves as linguistic arenas in which perceptible cultural conflicts are acting out or acting up. This was a position that accorded well with the growing conviction among a new generation of African American writers and readers that the nation's literary culture had not begun to register what Black expression was signifying.

A major revisionary turn in the perception of the cultural work being performed by African American texts coincided with the gradual transmission of Bakhtinian redefinitions of verbal meaning as culturally situated utterance. Eventually, there arose a genuinely dialogic relation between the two language-oriented modes of cultural interrogation. What emerged first, however, was a richly polyvocal chorus of revisionist readers who were adamant about the need to hear all the voicings simultaneously present in the expressive traditions of African American discourse.[9] A new generation of critics reclaimed and built upon the excluded, rejected, or ignored dimensions of Black American writing. Not by accident, what was retrieved and brought to notice was primarily the "impure" legacy of tricky, artful, evasive, obviously hyphenated "Afro-American" writing. There was a sudden reappraisal of predecessors who had been largely deleted from the canon of Black authorship because their texts were thought to display a "crossing over" from or a "double-crossing" of authentic spokesmanship for the race. Rectifying an earlier neglect or contempt, sophisticated young readers proclaimed the merits of obscure or allegedly obscurantist writers like Jean Toomer, Zora Neale Hurston, and Ralph Ellison and then proceeded to claim a centrality for them as well. University-trained critics sounded the utterances of previously suspect writers and found in them a subtle transcription of the slave culture's crafty oral modes of public expression. The irreverent double-talk that American Blacks had gotten away with in spirituals, blues, and tale-telling was now found to be present in the most markedly "literary" texts within the African American narrative tradition. Once that uncovering discovery was made, it became possible to reevaluate Black texts that engaged in all manner of verbal play and cross-cultural duplicity.

By 1983 two young Black critics had articulated ambitious theories alleging a culturally distinct African American expressive difference; this theorizing emerged from both an intrinsic and an extrinsic critique of the so-called literature of the Black experience. In different but equally effective ways, Henry Louis Gates Jr. and Houston A. Baker Jr. arrived at a primary insistence on the inherent "double-voicedness" of African American writing. Both argued strenuously to restore an ear for the vernacular within the literate texts of American Blackness. Their separate projects each entailed a long overdue foregrounding of the rhetorical and expressive values encoded in African American writing. In a major revision of past critical practices by Blacks and Whites, both called for an end to a tone-deaf and word-blind blanching and blanking out of African American discourse. The traditional reading of Black literature as the plain protest of "humans like us" had reduced a performance of cultural contestation to an "indentured" discourse that seemed to be subjecting itself to an imposed definition of universal sameness. As Gates indignantly announced: "Because of this curious valorization of the social and polemical functions of black literature, the structure of the black text has been *repressed* and treated as if it were *transparent*."[10] Baker put it somewhat differently but no less strongly: "The only means of negotiating a passage beyond this underclass [status] . . . is expressive representation. Artful evasion and illusion are equally traditional black expressive modes in interracial exchange" (*Blues* 195–96). What was being called for was a theory of African American literature that finally allowed for the duplicitous slippage of stable meaning, for the "critique oblique" that prevails in trickster discourses and acts of cultural survivalism.[11]

Had he lived to hear of it, Bakhtin would have delighted in the significant crossover that has now occurred between book-smart definitions of "signification" and street-smart appreciations of "signifyin(g)." Finding useful an elaborate dialogic pun, Gates has devised a mature theory of African American discourse patterns that depends upon rapid, context-specific apprehension of "signifyin(g)" significations. He has in mind a whole range of verbal behaviors, from the behind-the-back double-talk so joyously celebrated in the slave tales of the Signifying Monkey to the complex intertextuality of Ishmael Reed's pastiches of represented Blackness. His core argument is that African American expression has traditionally cultivated a high degree of "metaphoric literacy" because public articulation within earshot of a master discourse requires "monkeyshines" and the "aping" of rhetorical figures. Signifyin(g) is, then, "essentially, a technique of repeating inside quotation marks in order to reverse or undermine pretended meaning, constituting an implicit parody of a subject's complicity"; it is repetition heard as revision in one deft discursive act.[12] By this definition, signifyin(g) is a prime instance of Bakhtin's "internally polemical discourse—the word with a sideward glance at someone else's hostile word."[13]

Though more embedded in a nonlinguistic vocabulary, Baker, too, draws from a theorized vernacular base to argue for a singular process that constitutes "African American expressive culture." In Baker's recent work, cultural specificity is audibly auditory; for him, American Black discourse is figured and refigured in a blues matrix, a performed locomotion of societal cargo that comes to have commodity value in itself: "The blues stanzas . . . roll through an extended meditative repertoire with a steady train-wheels-over-track-junctures guitar back beat. . . . If desire and absence are driving conditions of blues performance, the amelioration of such conditions is implied by the onomatopoeic *training* of blues voice and instrument. Only a *trained* voice can sing the blues" (*Blues* 8). This blues matrix extends northward to literacy in the founding text of Harlem modernism, Alain Locke's *The New Negro*. As Baker hears it, Locke's anthology collects "the fullest extensions of a field of sounding possibilities; it serves as both the speaking manual *and* the singing book of a pioneering civilization freed from the burden of nonsensically and polemically constrained expression."[14] It should be noted, however, that African American discourse may easily become a music unheard unless it is finally and fully appreciated as a mode for *sounding* reality and for *signifyin(g)* resistance to authorized associations.

As both Gates and Baker demonstrate, an ear for Bakhtinian "heteroglossia" comes readily to well-attuned African American literary scholars. In fact, this responsiveness is much in evidence at present, and it has already contributed much to a heightened awareness of textual power in African-American writing. That said, it must also be admitted that there has been a rather selective hearing of Bakhtin's available words, a hearing that has been particularly sensitive to the empowering and emancipatory implications of the Russian's polyphonic discourse analysis, but only gradually and reluctantly attentive to the problematic and double-edged aspects of Bakhtin's theory of the utterance as a site of unavoidable semantic contestation.

Gates, for instance, is fond of citing and re-citing one particular excerpt from Bakhtin's influential essay "Discourse in the Novel." It stands, in fact, as a symptomatic epigraph to Gates's recent discussion in "A Theory of the Tradition." I quote it as given:

> . . . language, for the individual consciousness, lies on the borderline be-tween oneself and the other. The word in language is half someone else's. It becomes "one's own" only when the speaker populates it with his own intention, his own accent, when he appropriates the word, adapting it to his own semantic and expressive intention. Prior to this moment of appro-priation, the word does not exist in a neutral or impersonal language (it is not, after all, out of a dictionary that the speaker gets his words!), but rather it exists in other people's mouths, in other people's contexts, serving other people's intentions: it is from there that one must take the word, and make it one's own.[15]

In this selection, Gates's Bakhtin appears to speak monologically for the successful subversion, through creative "takeover," of the alien implications resident in any discourse. But in the complete passage, Bakhtin goes on to make *his* character-istic emphasis on the resistance of all language to appropriation: "Language is not a neutral medium that passes freely and easily into the private property of the speaker's intentions; it is populated—overpopulated—with the intentions of others. Expropriating it, forcing it to submit to one's own intentions and accents, is a difficult and complicated process" (*Dialogic* 294). To my hearing, some of the finest, and most refined, applications of Bakhtinian analysis in the present-day reconstruction of the African American literary legacy fall short, in their celebratory mood, of listening to the whole story.

With justifiable pride, Henry Louis Gates has claimed that his generation of Black and feminist critics brought Zora Neale Hurston into visibility as a cardinal figure in the African American literary canon. His own powerful argument for Hurston's centrality rests upon a "dialogic" reading of *Their Eyes Were Watching God* that proclaims it to be the first example in the African American tradition of a "speakerly text" (*Signifying* 181). In making this argument, Gates is building the case for a special, innovative form of intertextuality that Hurston's mode of writing realizes. It is a type of intertextuality that Gates rightly associates with Russian Formalist studies of literary ventriloquisms of orality (so-called *skaz*) and with Bakhtin's studies of a hidden dialogicality within modes of narration. It is worth noting that Russian theoretical pre-texts seem to take on a special pertinence in illuminating how certain types of experimental Black prose actually signify.

The crucial point, though, is that Hurston's narrative procedure itself drama-
tizes and enacts the "voicing" of a culturally obscured expressivity. A previously
hidden outspokenness is given its tongue. In Hurston's novel, a Black female
sensibility and sensuality inserts itself forcefully into prior discursive structures
(White and Black, literate and oral) that had little or no room for such expression.
But whose language is it that speaks for Janie Starks's extended backtalk?

Gates correctly emphasizes that the narrative of personal emergence we
overhear is a composite text that blends dialectic speech patterns and formal lyrical
transcriptions of ineffable private experience: "It is a bivocal utterance . . . that
no one could have spoken, yet which we recognize because of its characteristic
'speakerliness,' its paradoxically written manifestation of the aspiration to the oral"
(*Signifying* 208). This mode of double-voiced expression, which Bakhtin understands to be an unstable amalgam of an author's willed monologue and a character's
zone of speech, is inherently problematic. To Bakhtin's perception, such "quasi-
direct discourse" perfectly exemplifies the ongoing struggle of novelistic narrators
to obliterate the linguistic boundaries between authorial and characterized speech
that, nonetheless, remain in hidden dialogue with one another. Gates, however,
chooses to celebrate, in Hurston's name, the achievement of a utopian resolution
of contending languages.

Their Eyes is, for Gates, "a paradigmatic Signifyin(g) text" precisely because
its narrative strategies "resolve that implicit tension between the literal and the
figurative . . . between standard English and black dialect" (*Signifying* 192–93). But
this claim calls a willful halt to dialogic tensions in order to proclaim Hurston's
victorious inscription of a mythical African American speech essence. Ultimately,
Gates sees *Their Eyes* as a canonical text that is engraved in an African American
"third language," in an "oral hieroglyphic" that records the "thought-pictures"
commonly transmitted by Black discourse (215). This is an odd terminus for a
theory of expression that had envisaged a sympathy between the destabilizing
cultural work of "signifyin(g)" and Bakhtin's dialogic model of unfinalized literary
utterance. Sadly, one suspects that Gates has merely re-dressed the discredited
doctrine of American exceptionalism by giving it African American clothing,
cloaking it in Hurston's gorgeous mantle.[16]

Fortunately, Hurston's complex narrative performance begins and ends by
underlining a powerful anxiety about mouth-to-mouth appropriations of life histories. As Janie Starks passes the village "bander log" on which the "porch monkeys"
hold forth with their tall tales, she notes: "Ah see Mouth-Almighty is still sittin' in
de same place. And Ah reckon they got *me* up in they mouth now." This offers a
startling image of folktalk as Moloch, but it also serves as fair and ironic warning
to an act of narration that threatens to consume Janie wholly in its double-voiced
mouth. In the end, Hurston's Janie knows that speaking for others is always a
pretense: "Let 'em consolate theyselves wid talk. . . . It's uh known fact, Phoeby,

you got tuh *go* there tuh *know* there."[17] And Janie's act of speaking for herself, as Barbara Johnson has demonstrated, originates with Hurston's conviction that the impulse to articulate experience arises from not knowing how to mix interior monologue with outside discourses.[18] By this analysis, we can place Hurston's text back in close sympathy with a Bakhtinian understanding of all utterance as the motivated sign of a self-difference struggling to insert itself and to signify within a repertory of given speech genres.

Whereas the notion of African American intertextuality in Gates remains rather self-enclosed and literary, others among the reconstructionist critics have moved more boldly toward the ideological and generic intertextuality envisaged by Bakhtin's dialogic imagination. Houston Baker, for instance, has advanced a sophisticated argument that presents the Trueblood episode from Ralph Ellison's *Invisible Man* as "a metaexpressive commentary on the incumbencies of African American artists" (*Blues* 175). Jargon aside, Baker persuasively situates Ellison's notoriously "race-y" confession of a poor Black man's involuntary incest in an actively dialogic relation with a wide range of signifying systems. Baker is especially keyed to that side of Bakhtin conveyed by Julia Kristeva—the subversive implanting of multiple referents and multiple pitches of address in premeditated acts of "carnivalized" discourse. As a result, Baker sees both the performative value and the ideological tensions within the Black sharecropper's complex act of "bluesy" confession to eager White ears. And Baker further implies that Trueblood's remunerative, bad-ass riff stands in for the yield harvested by that literary "sharecropper," Ellison. Thus what is finally made visible is the problematics of entertainment as the culturally accepted mode of Black expression. Playing up and acting out benightedness is both scam and angst; the exchange between a performance artist and the patronized patron cuts both ways. But having seen all this, Baker too calls a halt to the endless dialogic tension by suggesting that Ellison suggests that "African Americans, in their guise as entertainers, season the possum of black expressive culture to the taste of their Anglo-American audience, maintaining, in the process, their integrity as performers" (194). The integrity of masking is, at best, an unstable concept, one made necessary by an unresolved and inexpressible clash of cultural signals. Ultimately Baker chooses to celebrate Trueblood's bluesy, trickster discourse as a victorious paradigm of "African American expressive culture." But to ears (like Ellison's) accustomed to the defiant yet defensive sounds of self-conscious and class-conscious Russian narrators, what also resonates is that special pathos that informs the protective indirection of all culturally devalued speakers and communities.[19]

In the ongoing African American dialogue with Russian dialogism, the latest development has been to contest the production and enunciation of canon-forming narratives about a singular tradition or language essence. Not surprisingly, the voices of protest have tended to be female.[20] It should also come as no surprise that the correction of these "master narratives" has taken place with some strategic assistance from the Bakhtin circle. The current controversy raises a challenge to the notion of cultural paradigms by demonstrating how alternative discourses are themselves shaped by and immersed in shifting social contexts. Black texts, like other doubly addressed utterances, are culturally produced and contextually interpreted within specific sets of social dynamics. The reconstructionist project itself, as Hazel Carby has argued, is embedded in sociolinguistic variables: "The struggle within and over language reveals the nature of the structure of social relations and the hierarchy of power, not the nature of one particular group. The sign, then, is an arena of struggle and a construct between socially organized persons in the process of their interaction. . . . we must be historically specific and aware of the differently oriented social interests within one and the same sign community."[21] This is dialogism extended into critical discourse itself, and the argument, as Carby generously acknowledges, derives from Voloshinov's pioneering work in contextual linguistics.

As Bakhtin argued in *Problems of Dostoevsky's Poetics*, "every literary discourse more or less sharply senses its own listener, reader, critic, and reflects in itself their anticipated objections, evalutions, points of view. In addition, literary discourse senses alongside itself another literary discourse, another style." This may seem to some like a very Russian generalization, since it is in Dostoevsky's embattled and contending polyphonies that "almost no word is without its intense sideward glance at someone else's word."[22] Yet Toni Morrison has recently spoken of African American literariness in terms that evoke a similar restless reconstitution of identity: "Now that the Afro-American artistic presence has been 'discovered' actually to exist . . . [w]e are not, in fact, 'other.' We are choices. And to read imaginative literature by and about us is to choose to examine centers of the self and to have the opportunity to compare these centers with the 'raceless' one with which we are, all of us, most familiar."[23] It does seem that a never-complete ex/postulation of difference has particular significance for both the Russian and African American cultural imaginations.

There is obviously a particular pointedness, a special ground of receptivity, when Bakhtin's theory of the utterance gets carried over into the African American literary critical community. Consider yet one more formulation of the Bakhtinian position on "speech-acts": "Our speech, that is, all our utterances (including creative works) are filled with others' words, with varying degrees of otherness or of 'our-own-ness,' with varying degrees of familiarity and of alienation. These words of others bring with them their own expression, their own intonational value, which is assimilated, reworked, and reaccented by us."[24] Given this understanding, the very language by which "we" would articulate our being is experienced as an occupied zone. While this depiction may seem theoretically acute or even generally valid, it certainly applies, practically speaking, to the situation of literary discourse in the Russian and the African American language communities. Literature itself, in cultural-historical terms, was introduced as a European institution that was both alien and central as an exclusionary norm of articulate identity.[25] Under these circumstances, Russian and African American literary texts were, from their inception, bound to be performative and contestatory speech acts. It is no accident that Russian and African American literary texts tend toward formal anomaly and "hidden polemic." In both communities, literate texts became theaters of enactment for self-conscious and "double-voiced" utterances pitched against a presumed illiteracy. It has taken a while, but Bakhtin's philosophy of articulation as a contextually formed struggle to disrupt or modify cultural conventions has fallen on sympathetic ears. At present, the African American reconstructionist critics are culturally situated to give Bakhtin an especially full hearing and creative response. They understand, as Russians do, that in cultural communities presumed to be inarticulate, literature necessarily takes the shape of Utterance Writ Large. But no one is excluded from understanding the dilemma this dialogue speaks to. Ralph Waldo Emerson, too, had intimations that self-expression must always antagonize on, kicking against the rubrics of inherited speech: "It is very unhappy, but too late to be helped, the discovery we have made that we exist. That discovery is called the Fall of Man. Ever afterwards we suspect our instruments."[26]

Moral Perception and the Chronotope: The Case of Henry James

Lisa Eckstrom

Toward the end of "Forms of Time and of the Chronotope in the Novel: Notes toward a Historical Poetics" Bakhtin describes the chronotope of the threshold, a chronotope "highly charged with emotion and value." It is "the chronotope of *crisis* and *break* in a life. The word 'threshold' itself already has a metaphorical meaning in everyday usage . . . and is connected with the breaking point of a life, the moment of crisis, the decision that changes a life (or the indecisiveness that fails to change a life, the fear to step over the threshold)."[1] Bakhtin's example of a writer whose work is suffused with this chronotope is Dostoevsky; but the reader of Henry James will recognize here what is also a central Jamesian concern. Throughout James's work, the crucial moments, the scenes of recognition and crisis, the episodes of poignant drama, are all figured on the threshold or figured by related chronotopes: "those of the staircase, the front hall and corridor, as well as the chronotopes of the street and square that extend those spaces into the open air."[2] Moreover, a significant change in James's worldview can be traced by charting the modification of his treatment of this chronotope from novel to novel. Here I focus on two exemplary texts: *The Portrait of a Lady* (1881) and *The Golden Bowl* (1906).[3]

For the early James, threshold moments are moments of morally charged insight: the truth is glimpsed, if not fully appreciated; veils are lifted, and the character becomes, increasingly, the ideal Jamesian agent, the sort of person on whom nothing is lost, "finely aware and richly responsible." Revelation in the earlier novels conforms to what we expect from an "epiphanic" moment. For the later James, by contrast, knowledge and insight are no longer unmitigated goods. The threshold scene figures a refusal to come to know what is half suspected. The ideal is no longer one of perfect and intuitive comprehension, but rather the subtler (and less clearly "ideal") ideal of strategic self-deception in the interests of maintaining a domestic modus vivendi: a stable way of getting along together given our imperfections and the complications of our circumstances.

James's most perceptive philosophical critic, Martha Nussbaum, has, I believe, missed this development. Her work presents a brilliant articulation and defense of the moral content of James's earlier work.[4] Central to this reading is the identification of the Jamesian ideal of perspicacity and perceptual sensitivity to the nuances of one's immediate situation with the Aristotelian conception of the virtuous agent as someone who in some sense *sees* the particular ethical requirements a situation presents.[5] For Nussbaum, in other words, virtue consists in a perceptual capacity—to be a good human being is to be the sort of person who takes in a scene and sees what is to be done without mechanical appeal to general principles served up by pure practical reason or some other authority—and she takes this to be James's view as well. The novels are novels of moral education. A sensitive but imperfectly schooled ingenue acquires the ability to pierce through veils and lift curtains, and so to see what is to be done. In my view this represents a double misreading. Nussbaum is in part right. Isabel Archer in *The Portrait of a Lady* begins to acquire such perception, and her doing so is a part of growing up and becoming a morally capable adult. But the capacity Isabel so painstakingly develops is one that the worst characters in the novel already enjoy. Gilbert Osmond and Serena Merle are paradigms of the sort of person on whom nothing is lost. But if this is so, then being this sort of person cannot be a sufficient condition for virtue. James seems to insist that something else is needed—something that sets off Ralph Touchett from Gilbert Osmond and Isabel Archer from Serena Merle. The inadequacy of Nussbaum's view is then only compounded when we notice the reconsideration of this ideal of perspicacity in *The Golden Bowl*. Here the activity that passes for virtue—the activity that Nussbaum herself treats as exemplary on James's behalf and her own—consists in a turning away from what is to be seen, in not facing facts. If the early James is not quite Aristotle, the later James is not even close. And all of this emerges with real clarity when the chronotope of the threshold becomes the object of our considered attention in the two novels.

Finely Aware and Richly Responsible: Nussbaum's Reading of James

In her call for moral philosophy to acknowledge that some forms of literature (specifically long and complex novels) indeed constitute forms of moral philos- ophy, Martha Nussbaum insists, in effect, that moral knowledge consists in the ability to see the most complex knot of chronotopes, the image, without reducing it: "Moral knowledge, James suggests, is not simply intellectual grasp of propositions; it is not even simply intellectual grasp of particular facts; it is perception. It is seeing a complex, concrete reality in a highly lucid and richly responsive way; it is taking what is there, with imagination and feeling" (*LK* 152). Novels are important for moral philosophy in part because the image as it figures in the literary work serves as the embodiment of an unrecuperable, nonsystematic *concreteness*. Our encounter as readers with the literary image is an analogue for the moral subject's encounter with the moral situation. But Nussbaum goes further, arguing that it is more than an analogy: "the work of the moral imagination is in some manner like the work of the creative imagination, especially that of the novelist. . . . this conception of moral attention and moral vision finds in novels its most appropriate articulation. . . . according to this conception, the novel is itself a moral achievement" (*LK* 148). In reading the novel, moral attention and moral vision will not try to ignore specificity and unrepeatability but, rather, will try to make those very qualities the focus. Attention to particulars is everything. Moreover, some novels—complex, psychologically intricate ones—make it palpable to us that this sort of fine attention is demanded; that to be anything but thoroughly vigilant is to miss what *matters*. Since for Nussbaum this capacity to attend to details with feeling is identical with the capacity for moral judgment, the encounter with the novel both exercises the moral faculty and calls our reflective attention to the nature of its operations. Because this is the task of moral philosophy as well, the novel is not just the matter for philosophical reflection but a work of philosophy itself.

In "James's *The Golden Bowl*: Literature as Moral Philosophy" Nussbaum provides an eloquent and extraordinarily Jamesian-sounding account of what moral philosophy ought to be. She argues in particular that *The Golden Bowl* is a work of moral philosophy in whose "sustained exploration of particular lives" (*LK* 139) readers find the opportunity to acquaint themselves with multitudes of repeated and shifting chronotopes (although she does not use Bakhtin's term).

Nussbaum begins with a response to an anticipated objection: "First to prevent confusion, we must have some rough story about what moral philosophy and the job of moral philosophy are—for on some accounts of these things, particularly the Kantian account, this text obviously falls entirely outside of moral philosophy in virtue of the empirical and contingent nature of its content" (*LK* 138–39). For Kant, the principles of morality are categorical imperatives binding on all rational creatures independent of their historical situation, emotional or personal attachments, and contingent desires or inclinations.[6] Against this, Nussbaum insists that principles play only a peripheral role in real moral judgment and hence that a list or catalog of them is at best only the raw material for an adequate philosophical account. The central moral judgments are the deliverances of trained perception. By their nature they resist cataloging, so a work of moral philosophy cannot be anything like a comprehensive account of the moral verities. Rather, it must contain reflection on particular illustrations of the operation of this perceptual faculty. But of course, in order for these illustrations to be illuminating and so to deserve the name of philosophy, they must capture at least some of the concreteness and specificity of the real phenomenon. And more than this, in order for them to be at least potentially *edifying*, the representations of these exercises of perception must somehow engage the reader's own moral sense, applied in imagination now to the complex circumstances of the judgment in question. The Jamesian novel of moral consciousness is just what is called for.

Here Bakhtin's distinction between abstract cognition and living artistic perception (a perception that incorporates all that Kant would dismiss in matters of moral judgment) finds application in a field outside the artistic. In *Toward a Philosophy of the Act* (1919–21)—written well before his discussion of the chronotope (1937–38)—Bakhtin's central concern is just this: he wants to ground Kant's categorical imperative in the particulars and concreteness of an individual life. He wants what most philosophers deem impossible: to detranscendentalize Kant while preserving ethical judgment from relativism. The central problem is how to save judgment from abstraction: "When I contemplate a picture showing the destruction and completely justified disgrace of a person I love, then this picture will be quite different from the one I see when the person destroyed is of no interest to me. . . . And this will occur not because I shall be trying to justify him contrary to sense and justice. . . . This will not be a biased, subjective distortion of seeing"[7] Bakhtin's later work on chronotopes may be seen as one of his solutions: chronotopes such as those of the threshold and the encounter provide a narrative ground for the representability of moral judgment. Nussbaum's solution holds much in common with Bakhtin's.

Nussbaum's positive account of the aim of moral philosophy is this: "The aim of the study will be to produce an intelligent ordering of the 'appearances'—the experiences and saying of human agents and choosers. It cannot, then, in any way be cut off from the study of the empirical and social conditions of human life" (*LK* 139). This conception of the aim of moral philosophy is, of course, opposed to one traditional conception according to which the behavior and speech of actual people in concrete situations is at most a partial starting point for the development of moral theory, and no part of the end point of moral philosophy. On Nussbaum's view, the appearances here are "the experiences and sayings of human agents and choosers," and our access to these appearances is through experience and education. Kant would call such a study not moral philosophy at all, but "practical anthropology"[8] since it takes in—as James's Madame Merle says in *Portrait of a Lady*—"one's house, one's furniture, one's garments, the books one reads, [and] the company one keeps" as necessary observations for moral theory. The upshot of the inquiry, moreover, is not a system of rules for conduct, but at best an account in rough outline of the good life for man. As a guide to practice this outline is useless. It's too sketchy and rough. But the end of moral philosophy is practice. So the discursive text that the philosopher produces is only part of moral philosophy. To act well in any particular case requires in addition the capacity for judging what precisely constitutes the exercise of virtue in one's concrete circumstances. This capacity cannot be represented as a mastery of a system of rules, and it cannot be learned by reading a book. It is a habit inculcated by practice. At best the philosopher can illustrate and assist its exercise.

Nussbaum's central example of moral judgment as refined perception is a scene between Maggie and her father late in *The Golden Bowl* (bk. 5, chap. 3). For Nussbaum, Adam's offer to return to America and Maggie's acceptance of it are morally exemplary acts. "He must let her go, loving her, so that she can live with her husband as a real wife; loving him, she must discover a way to let him go as a 'great and deep and high' man and not a failure, his dignity intact" (*LK* 149). What is especially important, however, is not the general plan of mutual "sacrifice" but rather the peculiarly elliptical way in which the plan is hatched. "The general sacrificial idea . . . is in itself no solution. For it to become a solution it has to be offered in the right way at the right time in the right tone, in such a way that she can take it; offered without pressing any of the hidden springs of guilt and loyalty in her . . . offered so that he gives her up with greatness, with beauty, in a way that she can love and find wonderful" (*LK* 150). This is the ideal of Aristotelian virtue as manifest in the capacity to act not according to general moral rules but rather according to the ineffable and highly specific perceptually given details of one's circumstance. Adam and Maggie are heroes, here, because each manages, by steering the conversation just around the real subject, to prevent the other from feeling the guilt and ambivalence that this necessary choice might have inspired if otherwise considered. "[Maggie's] vigilance, her silent attention, the intensity of her regard, are put before us as moral acts. . . . She measures her moral adequacy by the fullness and richness of her imaginings . . . And her imagination . . . achieves its moral goal in the finding of the right way of seeing. Like an artist whose labor produces, at last, a wonderful achieved form, she finds . . . a thought of her father 'that placed him in her eyes as no precious work of art probably had ever been placed in his own'" (*LK* 152). For Nussbaum this scene on the bench is the culmination of Maggie's moral development. Finally Maggie is capable of real goodness. "By finding a way to perceive him, to imagine him not as father and law and world, but as a finite human being whose dignity is in and not opposed to his finitude, Maggie achieves an adult love for him and a basis of equality" (*LK* 153). This goodness is not just the Kantian ideal of irreproachable conduct, but the Aristotelian idea of eudaimonia, or "human flourishing."[9]

Nussbaum's effort to read Maggie as an Aristotelian moral exemplar generates what seems to me (ultimately) a powerful misreading of the novel. It is powerful because she is on to something: James's focus is once again on highly perceptive characters, worried in some way or other, perplexed by their own objectification. Where Nussbaum's reading goes astray, or does not go far enough, is in the reading of the novel's solution—the separation of the couples—as an unambiguous success. Maggie saves her marriage. She is the first Jamesian heroine to fight back, not to acquiesce in the manipulations of others. But Maggie's plan *not* to be used becomes darkly confused with an interest in her betrayer's pain.

To put the moral "success" in context, recall Maggie's thoughts of Charlotte just after this moment of allegedly exemplary moral communion. Maggie imagines her old friend as a black spot against a field of light, "removed, transported, doomed." According to Nussbaum, that Maggie has this thought is evidence that she has achieved the moral maturity that consists in being able to bear in mind the values that weigh against one's choice in any tragic circumstance where some good must inevitably be sacrificed. "Choose as well as you can for overt action, but at every moment remember the more comprehensive duties of the imagination and emotions. If love of your husband requires hurting and lying to Charlotte, then do these cruel things, making the better choice. But never cease, all the while, to be richly conscious of Charlotte's pain, and to bear, in imagination and feeling, the full burden of your guilt as the cause of that pain" (LK 135). Nussbaum's Maggie is a new Antigone: torn between two genuine obligations, she performs one, and her virtue consists in bearing the weight of the other in mind all the while.

But Maggie's consciousness of Charlotte's pain bears a darker and ultimately more tragic reading as well. Maggie's rich consciousness is adept at so arranging appearances that she, Maggie, is never implicated in Charlotte's pain although she is acutely conscious of it. She does not feel under any obligation to Charlotte. In fact, some critics who have emphasized this aspect of Maggie's character have come to the opposite conclusion. Sallie Sears in The Negative Imagination asserts that Maggie's idea that she can fight Charlotte without sacrificing her own "moral poise" is "a diabolic combination, for really sustained, it is probably the nearest thing to psychic invulnerability that can be achieved, and under its guise any action, however destructive, may be justified."[10] While Sears's reading is compelling, I cannot completely agree. James does not mean for Maggie to be diabolical; there is a real pathos surrounding Maggie even at her most disagreeable.

Maggie's lack of guilt, her ability to keep her "moral poise," depends upon her own self-understanding. At her worst, she never sees herself as harming anyone. Instead, she sees herself as saving everyone at her own expense. And strangely, it is in just this sacrifice (which "saves" the Prince) that she sacrifices her future happiness—but not in the way that she supposes at the time. The strange machinations of her conscience become clear when we examine James's use of the threshold as a narrative ground for revelation in The Golden Bowl. Indeed, James's use of the threshold is so unusual in The Golden Bowl that it helps to bear in mind earlier Jamesian revelation scenes.

The Normal Case: The Portrait of a Lady

The development and dramatic use of the threshold in The Portrait of a Lady is relatively straightforward. The chronotope of this opening, the relation between time and space, is almost the direct inverse of the chronotope of the threshold. We might call it the chronotope of the summer lawn. Time has slowed down to the point of suspension. The affect associated with the chronotope (an essential ingredient, as Bakhtin notes) is pervasive goodwill among friends. Spatially, James goes out of his way to mark the lack of a threshold between the house and the lawn: "The wide carpet of turf that covered the level hill-top seemed but the extension of a luxurious interior." The sloping lawn, with its cushions, rich colored rugs, books, and papers, becomes an indefinitely extending space of domestic repose.

James balances this antithreshold in *The Portrait of a Lady*'s beginning with a dramatic instance of the threshold at the end of the novel. The chronotope there, reflecting the general crisis of Isabel's life, and in particular the crisis of what to do with Caspar Goodwood's proposal, is reflected in the changed relation between the house and the same summer lawn: "There were lights in the window of the house; they shone far across the lawn. In an extraordinarily short time—for the distance was considerable—she had moved through the darkness (for she saw nothing) and reached the door. Here only she paused. She looked all about her; she listened a little; then she put her hand on the latch" (chap. 55). The lawn itself becomes the threshold between the bench and the door of the house, the threshold proper. Time speeds up—large distances are crossed instantly and in darkness—and then stops as she pauses at the door. At the door, Isabel comes to see something new. She understands that "she had not known where to turn; but she knew now. There was a very straight path." On the face of it, this is the chronotope of the threshold just as Bakhtin describes it: an epiphany at a spatial border, a flash of insight. And this is the last the reader "sees" of Isabel. Her return to Rome and presumably to Osmond is reported by Henrietta Stackpole to a mystified Caspar Goodwood and thereby to a mystified reader as well. Gilbert Osmond, her malevolent husband, is clearly not the right path. And yet James leaves her there, on the threshold of the door, her hand on its latch, leaving open the possibility of a sequel or an epilogue that was contemplated but never written.[11]

Contrast this ambiguous epiphany on the threshold—ambiguous in the sense that what is "revealed" is not clearly true—with the two central moments of recognition earlier on. These are both explicitly figured in strikingly similar terms as incidents near—but not quite on—the threshold. In chapter 40, Isabel's hitherto inarticulate apprehension about the circumstances of her marriage is focused for an instant in an image glimpsed through a doorway: "What struck Isabel first was that he [Gilbert Osmond] was sitting while Madame Merle stood; there was an anomaly in this that arrested her. . . . the thing made an image, lasting only a moment, like a sudden flicker of light. Their relative position, their absorbed mutual gaze, struck her as something detected. But it was all over by the time she had fairly seen it." James has reduced the more standard "flash" of light that accompanies enlightenment to a "flicker." In a flash of insight something comes to be known; in a flicker what is glimpsed is the possibility that something exists to be known, without an articulate conception of what it is. As she stands just beyond the threshold here, Isabel does not hazard an interpretation of what she has seen. Isabel keeps it as "something detected," much as Maggie in *The Golden Bowl* will later keep an insight "held in her breast, till she got well away." This is not an epiphany, a becoming apparent of something hidden. The sense of something hidden strikes Isabel in an instant—"it was all over by the time she had fairly seen it"—but the knowledge that flows from this glimmer does not arrive on the threshold, but only later and in a very different chronotope.

Isabel's long meditation before the fire in chapter 42 allows the instantaneous nature of that flicker of insight to mature. The chronotope of the vigil gives James a chance to draw out all the consequences of this vision, which the instantaneous nature of threshold-time does not. What emerges after hours of wide-ranging reflection on the circumstances of her life and of her marriage is the sense that Isabel has "thrown away her life" and also a practical resolution not to abet Serena Merle's plans for Pansy. These insights are hard won and anything but instantaneous. And strikingly, even after they are in place and the vigil is finished, the original image remains fundamentally uninterpreted. "When the clock struck four she got up. . . . But even then she stopped again . . . and stood there gazing at a remembered vision—that of her husband and Madame Merle, grouped unconsciously and familiarly."

The interpretation of the image depends on a second revelation: In chapter 51, in the second revelation scene, the Countess Gemini pauses just beyond the threshold of Isabel's room "noiselessly, unperceived." She explains to Isabel that her first sister-in-law had no children, that Serena Merle is the mother of Osmond's child. This is not a straightforward epiphany. This time Isabel does come to know a fact, with full and articulate consciousness. But she does not come to know it by "seeing" it. She comes to know it by being told. The *reception* of this testimony does, however, involve the operation of Isabel's dawning perceptual sensitivity. What Isabel sees here is not the fact of her husband's deception; it is rather the fact that the Countess Gemini, a famous liar, is in this instance telling the truth. Isabel's response takes the Countess off guard: "She [the Countess] had expected to kindle a conflagration, and as yet she had barely extracted a spark." James saves the fireworks for Caspar Goodwood's kiss like "a flash of lightning."

Goodwood's kiss followed by Isabel's rush to the door is as close as we come to a genuine threshold epiphany in *The Portrait of a Lady*. Something becomes clear in an instant, and the decision it forces changes a life. And yet even here the type is realized only obliquely. Isabel's resolution to return to Rome is inscrutable. It is simply not so clear that what she has "realized" in this moment of "insight" is really right.

The More Complicated Use of
the Threshold in *The Golden Bowl*

The novel opens with the Prince meandering through London streets thinking vaguely and fitfully about the change his life is about to undergo. His solicitor has just come to an agreement with his prospective father-in-law's lawyers. So now it is settled: he will be married in a few days. This decisive step has left him restless. And so for the rest of this long summer afternoon, he walks through the city. His natural first thought is to gravitate toward the great public spaces that signify the grandeur of the modern imperium: London Bridge, Hyde Park Corner. But for no reason he cares to fathom, he finds himself instead in Bond Street. And as he thinks, he window-shops.

James transforms this mundane activity into a sort of parable that the Prince takes in but does not understand. The parable of this new sort of threshold sets the tone for the novel. Standing before the plate glass windows of Bond Street, the Prince—a metaphorical *morceau de musée* according to his fiancée's remembered description—sees the real thing in the display cases of antiquaries and jumble shops. Having been bought by Adam Verver that afternoon, the Prince is now of a kind with the objects "massive and lumpish, in silver and gold," that were "as tumbled together as if, in the insolence of the Empire, they had been the loot of far-off victories." He is, as he remembers his fiancée telling him, "one of the things that can only be got over here. You're a rarity, an object of beauty, an object of price." He thinks of himself as a rare coin "of a purity of gold no longer used, stamped with glorious arms, mediæval, wonderful." What is striking and a bit confusing is that despite the centrality of this metaphor in the Prince's stream of thoughts about himself, he never once notices the harmony between this figure and the real "treasures" that stare him in the face. He has no "consistency of attention." It is obvious enough to us that the Prince finds himself in Bond Street in part because this is where these symbols of himself are collected. But this impinges on his consciousness only as the registering of a vague agitation.

The chronotope here is a version of the chronotope of the threshold, of course. But it is very different from any Bakhtin discusses. Time here is not the frozen crucial instant, as it is in the paradigm scenes of threshold recognition. Instead time is experienced as running out. The Prince has an appointment for dinner. It is some hours away, so he has time to spend, but not all the time in the world. And this figures the more significant impending deadline. He will be married, not now, but soon and at a definite date. The space is not a single threshold but an indefinitely extended row, and the movement is not across the threshold but laterally from one threshold to the next. The emotional value that suffuses this space-time is not focused intensity, but rather a vague uneasiness that never manages to settle down upon a single object.

The shop window as threshold differs from the doorway in other crucial respects. Signally, the opening is not passable and perfectly transparent, but covered by glass. Think too of the image the Prince confronts in this glass. It is a palimpsest: the items behind the glass are overlain in his visual field by his own reflected visage. And of course this is not just an accidental double exposure. The objects of the Prince's visual attention—objects he can only see by looking past his own reflection—are concrete metaphors for himself. Given the figurative content of the Prince's thought, this double image holds out the possibility for genuine threshold recognition, an instantaneous focusing of the so far diffuse anxiety that animates him. But this is just what does not happen. The correspondence between what he sees across the threshold and what he thinks escapes him, and he learns nothing.

The impassability of the shop window threshold matters as well. The plate glass prevents direct contact with the objects it protects: here figures the Prince himself. And as if to reinforce this, when the Prince remembers that he is about to become "futile," he "screens out" this memory, "much as, just in front of him . . . the iron shutter of a shop, closing early to the stale summer day, rattled down at the turn of some crank. There was machinery again, just as the plate glass, all about him, was money, was power, the power of the rich peoples. Well, he was *of* them now, of the rich peoples; he was on their side—if it wasn't rather the pleasanter way of putting it that they were on his." Being on the same side of the plate glass is an illusion. The difference between doorways and plate glass windows is that doorways are thresholds through which we pass all the time without incident. One does not become a different sort of thing for being on the other side of a doorway. But the items on the other side of a shop window—the merchandise—are very different from the shoppers who view them. The passage from one side to the other is not an ordinary event. To contemplate moving across is to contemplate a horrible ontological transformation. The iron shutters here figure the Prince's turning away from this prospect before fully facing it. And this is a general feature of threshold moments in *The Golden Bowl*, as Ruth Yeazell's brilliant analysis of language in late James points out.[12]

Later, when Maggie buys the golden bowl and understands that the Prince and Charlotte knew each other intimately before her marriage, she places the bowl on the mantel so that it can be seen by the Prince as soon as he crosses the threshold of the room. "'I've stood it out for my husband to see; put it where it would meet him almost immediately if he should come into the room. I've wanted it to meet him,' she went on, 'and I've wanted him to meet *it*, and to be myself present at the meeting.'" But—and this is characteristic of *The Golden Bowl*—although the Prince has been in the habit of coming into the particular room quite often, "he hasn't showed to-day." Heightened sensation in this novel warns the characters when they are about to be confronted with a threshold moment. "It's quite as if he had an instinct—something that has warned him off or made him uneasy. He doesn't understand, naturally, what has happened, but guesses, with his beautiful cleverness, that something has, and isn't in a hurry to be confronted with it. So in his vague fear he keeps off" (bk. 4, chap. 9). The second half of Bakhtin's description of the threshold chronotope—as figuring the indecisiveness that fails to change a life, the fear to step over the threshold—dominates this novel. Perception here becomes a way to avoid perception. And nowhere is this theme of the sensitive capacity to know when not to know more central than in the passage Martha Nussbaum discusses as the focal point for her reading of the novel and of James's moral philosophy.

Epiphanic Terror

Maggie and Adam have "sloped" off together, desperate all of a sudden to be alone together, "father and daughter" again. The ostensible topic of Maggie and her father's conversation is the recent arrival of Mrs. Rance to the estate, which brings them back to the days when Adam Verver was a pursued bachelor and marrying Charlotte seemed to simplify everything. But the language throughout is abstract and pregnant with the appearance of double meaning.

> It was . . . as if . . . in their acceptance of the unsaid, or at least their reference to it, [they had] practically given up pretending—it was as if they were "in" for it, for something they had been ineffably avoiding, but the dread of which was itself in manner a seduction, just as any confession of dread was by so much an allusion. . . .
> "Oh, I'm not talking about my husband!"
> "Then whom *are* you talking about?"
> . . . She wondered if he weren't expecting her to name his wife then . . . she produced something that she felt to be much better. "I'm talking about *you*." (bk. 5, chap. 3)

Their exchanges are almost completely opaque, even to each other. While intimates speak elliptically and in a sort of private shorthand, so that conversations overheard in the park will always be hard to interpret, here Adam and Maggie manage to communicate in this way only because of an intense and motivated concentration on the conversation. This "mutual vigilance" is required of them if they are to keep themselves from inadvertently bringing the real subject out into the open: "This was the moment in the whole process . . . in which it decidedly most hung by a hair." Their figurative threshold is covered by a transparent tissue: "Their thin wall might be pierced by the lightest wrong touch. It shook between them, this transparency, with their very breath; it was an exquisite tissue, but stretched on a frame, and would give way the next instant if either so much as breathed too hard. She held her breath."

Maggie apologizes to her father for having had to spend so much time with her husband—or, in her more melodramatic idiom, for having had to "sacrifice" her father. Maggie is speaking in the past tense in order to alert her father to what will have to happen in the future. The reader knows, as do Adam and Maggie, that in fact neither has given up or sacrificed the other in any way. The real prospect of such sacrifice arises only now, in the aftermath of the adultery. Maggie continues in the past tense, "You don't claim, I suppose, that my natural course, once you had set up for yourself [i.e., married Charlotte], would have been to ship you back to American City?" Adam replies:

> "Why you make me quite want to ship back myself. You make me quite feel as if American City could be the best place for us."
> It made her all too finely vibrate. "For 'us'—?"
> "For me and Charlotte . . . "

So Adam Verver offers the solution, without of course saying so explicitly. To keep Charlotte and the Prince apart, and so from destroying their marriages, Adam will take Charlotte back to American City. And without saying that she sees that this is what he has done, Maggie sees how perfect it is: "*There* was his idea. . . . It was a blur of light in the midst of which she saw Charlotte like some object marked by contrast in blackness, saw her waver in the field of vision, saw her removed, transported, doomed. . . . It was as if she had held a blank letter to the fire and the writing had come out still larger than she had hoped." Charlotte's secret doom, written here first in invisible ink, increasingly fascinates Maggie.

While Nussbaum and others cite Maggie's ability to imaginatively experience Charlotte's suffering as evidence of Maggie's goodness, I am not so sure. Immediately after Maggie and her father determine that Adam will take Charlotte to America, the exquisite decision Nussbaum explicates, images of Charlotte flood Maggie's consciousness. Maggie does not think of her father at all. Instead she imagines scene after scene in which "poor Charlotte" slowly and painfully comes to realize that she has lost. Maggie imagines what it is to be Charlotte, "to feel her own heart in her throat, " and "to [look] with Charlotte's grave eyes" (bk. 5, chap. 4). She breathes Charlotte's "cold air" and turns with her "in growing compassion, this way and that, hovered behind her while she felt her ask herself where then she should rest." Maggie's "fancy" is "let loose," and she is fascinated with Charlotte's agony: "Marvelous the manner in which, under such imaginations, Maggie thus circled and lingered—quite as if she were, materially, following her unseen, counting every step she helplessly wasted, noting every hindrance that brought her to a pause." Charlotte has become Maggie's prey. "There were hours of intensity for a week or two when it was as if she had guardedly tracked her step-mother . . . from room to room, and from window to window." Nussbaum's reading cited earlier—"never cease . . . to be richly conscious of Charlotte's pain, and to bear, in imagination and feeling, the full burden of your guilt as the cause of that pain" (*LK* 135)—does not register the sense James conveys that Maggie is richly conscious of Charlotte's pain but does not feel especially guilty.

Maggie's imagination creates an elaborate simile for the new position of her stepmother: "the likeness" of Charlotte and Adam's connection "wouldn't have been wrongly figured" as one in which her father was holding a rope that ended in a "silken halter" around Charlotte's neck: "He didn't twitch it, yet it was there; he didn't drag her, but she came." Adam's smile is like the "soft shake" of that "twisted silken rope." Maggie demurs from any conscious sadistic pleasure in her rival's fall, but her imagination develops the simile further (and continues to return occasionally to the simile until the novel's close). Her translation of the smile "held in her breast, till she got well away, came out only, as if it might have been overheard, when some door was closed behind her. 'Yes, you see—I lead her now by the neck, I lead her to her doom, and she doesn't so much as know what it is, though she has a fear in her heart which, if you had the chance to apply your ear there, that I, as a husband, have, you would hear thump and thump and thump.'" Maggie's interpretation of her father's glance is first of all "held in her breast"— which is to say not that she keeps it to herself by refusing to say it aloud, but rather that she keeps it out of *mind* for a moment: she represses it by pushing it beyond the threshold and closing the door. Moreover, when it does finally emerge in consciousness, it emerges as "something overheard." She is alienated from the image, as if it were not quite her own thought. This is not an instance of a fine and fully reflective discernment of the facts, as would befit Nussbaum's Jamesian exemplar. Here the silken thread that binds Charlotte to Adam entangles all the characters. It prevents all, and most especially Maggie, from being self-objective. It points to the huge difference between Maggie and Charlotte: Maggie is not being led, even if she can imagine the scene. Maggie and Adam have the power to pull the narrative thread—to lead Charlotte to America—while Charlotte loses all.

James raises the question of whether or not Maggie ought to feel remorseful as early as book 4, when she begins her first manipulations of Charlotte and the Prince. Fanny Assingham calls her "terrible," but Maggie dissents:

"No, I'm not terrible . . . but surprisingly mild . . . "

Mrs. Assingham . . . bridled. "Is that what you call it when you make them, for terror as you say, do what you like?"

"Ah, there wouldn't be any terror for them if they had nothing to hide."

(bk. 4, chap. 6)

In a late conversation with Fanny Assingham, Maggie continues to hold her earlier views, but she is more defensive: "'They're the ones who are saved,' she went on. 'We're the ones who are lost. . . . Lost to each other—father and I. . . . Oh yes . . . lost to each other much more than Amerigo and Charlotte are; since for them it's just, it's right, it's deserved, while for us it's only sad and strange and not caused by our fault'" (bk. 6, chap. 1). While separation for Charlotte and the Prince might be just, right, and deserved, it gains Maggie and her father little. But we see in these two similar conversations with Fanny Assingham that Maggie has moved from blaming Charlotte's terror on Charlotte ("There wouldn't be any terror for them if they had nothing to hide") to seeing herself as sacrificing her own happiness for that of Charlotte and the Prince ("They're the ones who are saved. . . . We're the ones who are lost"). And this change comes about as a result of a threshold experience, an epiphany, which ought to be central to the book. That is, it ought—by convention—to bring about a change. It ought to be the sort of thing that in Bakhtin's words is a "breaking point of a life, [a] moment of crisis, [a] decision that changes a life (or the indecisiveness that fails to change a life, the fear to step over the threshold)." Instead it is neither. Having passed over the threshold, Maggie retreats and comes up with a new translation of herself as powerless.

The Epiphany

Maggie pauses, importantly, on the threshold of a gallery. James rigorously adheres to all the dramatic conventions that announce that a revelation is about to take place, conventions that play so large a part in Bakhtin's description of the threshold: Not only is Maggie poised on a literal threshold, but her father is as well. Charlotte is midway between them, speaking in a "high voice" whose "quaver was doubtless for conscious ears only, but there was verily thirty seconds during which it sounded, for our young woman, like the shriek of a soul in pain. Kept up a minute longer it would break and collapse—so that Maggie felt herself . . . turn . . . to her father. 'Can't she be stopped? Hasn't she done it *enough?*'" (bk. 5, chap. 4). Here the threshold seems to have "worked": Adam Verver is delicate enough to receive his daughter's mute communication and, blushing, turn away. Upon hearing Charlotte's voice, Maggie's fictions cease, and Charlotte is no longer a suffering stage heroine in whose body Maggie thrills to one agony after another. In meeting her father's gaze, Maggie seems to see, for a moment, the futility of the punishment. Self-examination should follow if James holds to the general conventions, and self-renunciation should follow if he holds to Jamesian conventions in the novel.

Maggie seems to be at a turning point, but nothing happens. Later, when Fanny Assingham speculates aloud about what Charlotte's life in America will be like, Maggie disowns her knowledge:

"I know nothing. If I did—!"

"Well, if you did?" Fanny asked as she faltered.

She had had enough, however. "I should die," she said as she turned away.

Maggie must redeem herself in some way. She can't feel guilty because she hasn't done anything wrong. But she no longer sees herself as "mild" and has had an intimation that both she and her father are capable of being "terrible." Having seen Charlotte, in the highly perceptive way Nussbaum describes, and in the sort of spatiotemporal relation Bakhtin describes as framing the realization that changes a life, the reader expects Maggie to call off the separation, to realize its pointlessness. But in this last novel, James portrays the fragility of moral cognition. The revelation is undermined by stronger psychological forces at work. Maggie is agitated. If she were to know Charlotte's fate, she would "die." Surely this should excuse her from the burdens of such knowledge. But Maggie goes further: she exonerates herself. And this is the direct outcome of the threshold scene.

The Exoneration

Maggie's justification scene begins when she joins Charlotte outside on a bench. Note how Maggie begins to supplant Charlotte in her role as a suffering and helpless stage heroine, a role she herself created for Charlotte: "Our young woman was to have passed, in all her adventure, no stranger moments; for she not only now saw her companion fairly agree to take her then for the poor little person she was finding it so easy to appear, but fell, in a secret responsive ecstasy, to wondering if there weren't some supreme abjection with which she might be inspired" (bk. 5, chap. 5). Maggie manipulates Charlotte into assuming the pose of a powerful and triumphant second wife. When Charlotte does so, Maggie assumes the air of the defeated stepdaughter. But Maggie's response does not stop there: she responds with raptures described in metaphors usually reserved for sexual ecstasy: "Maggie took it and for a moment kept it; held it, with closed eyes, as if it had been some captured fluttering bird pressed by both hands to her breast." Here the reader is confused. The "secret responsive ecstasy" and the "supreme abjection" of the scene escape Maggie's understanding of it.

Maggie does not understand the connection between (1) her earlier fascination with Charlotte's plight and the palpable ecstasy with which it inspired her, (2) her vision from the threshold of the gallery, and (3) her new ecstatic *abjection*. From the threshold, for a brief moment, Maggie does not imagine herself commingled with Charlotte's sensations. Instead she is startled by the shriek of a soul in pain—a soul different from hers, but a soul with as much right to happiness as her own. Maggie does not understand that her earlier visions of Charlotte were fueled by impulses darker than empathy. Nor does she understand that this new desire to see herself as more abject than Charlotte, as more in need of pity than Charlotte ("She too might have been for the hour some far-off harassed heroine"), is in any way connected to the threshold scene. James leaves such connections to the reader, experimenting, as he explains in the preface, with a new sort of point of view.

By now it is clear that James has abandoned the more straightforward use of epiphanic knowledge that predominates in *The Portrait of a Lady*. James in *The Golden Bowl* has taken the dramatic convention of having an actor or a character stand on the threshold and confront "reality" and be forever changed—the dramatic situation so admired and reproduced in the novel—with a much more complicated psychological model of revelation that acknowledges the role repression plays in our lives. As Charlotte claims in book 3, chapter 9, "Ah for things I mayn't want to know I promise you shall find me stupid."

Stasis

By *The Golden Bowl's* end, the Prince and Charlotte have become the Ververs' acquisitions once again. Maggie's conception of Charlotte is of a woman held behind a pane of glass "frantically tapping from within by way of supreme entreaty" (bk. 6, chap. 1). Maggie again thinks of Charlotte's being led to America by means of a silken tether around her neck. And by book 6, chapter 3, the Prince and Charlotte have become, in Maggie's consciousness, "high expressions" of "human furniture." The moment shares much in common with the earlier moment Nussbaum explicates. James, however, draws the reader's attention to what is disconcerting in the image: "The fusion of their presence [Charlotte and Amerigo's] with the decorative elements, their contribution to the triumph of the selection, was complete and admirable; though to a lingering view, a view more penetrating than the occasion really demanded, they also might have figured as concrete attestations of a rare power of purchase" (bk. 6, chap. 3). Charlotte and the Prince are now under their purchasers' control. Maggie perceives Charlotte and the Prince's stillness as a "submission to the general duty of magnificence; sitting as still to be thus appraised." They are unable to cry out or object. New thresholds are in place and honored. Maggie is sure that her father would not press on his threshold "by the tip of a toe." The odd foursome is united in its careful observation of individual boundaries: "they remained in fine, the four of them, in the upper air, united through the firmest abstention from pressure. There was visibly no point at which . . . either Amerigo or Charlotte had pressed." We wait for something to break the spell, but nothing ever happens. Time is "stale." It is "the end of a dull day" in September. The atmosphere is dominated by the "strange finality of relation" between the four characters.

The photograph James chose for this volume of the New York edition is of a solitary carriage leaving a desolate Portland Place, the very name of which recalls *portal*. The photograph echoes the novel's strange finality. There is no turning back. This might not seem strange; it is a familiar enough convention: Huck Finn heads West. But that is not what is happening here. What is strange in *The Golden Bowl* is the sense that nothing will ever change again for the four principal characters. Their fate has been sealed as if it had been placed under glass.

Charlotte will be the beautiful wife of the rich American museum founder. She will pay official visits and will always behave as impeccably as she does on her final visit with the Prince. The possibilities of divorce or even of her husband's death seem nonexistent. Adam will be the rich but (if we are to understand Charlotte's explanation of why they will have no children) impotent American with a magnificent spouse his daughter's age. The Prince, like Charlotte, will behave well and will try to please his wife—even when he is not certain how—as happens in the final scene. But he, like Charlotte, has no illusions: he is no longer ruler, prince, but ruled.

The sobering atmosphere of the final pages suggests that Maggie has not met her match in the Prince. She has struggled to win a pleasant enough man who does not understand her. She has avoided the crises that mark the threshold for Bakhtin, "the falls, resurrections, renewals, epiphanies, decisions that determine the life of a man." Instead she has preserved her dignity (cf. *LK* 153).

The question that lingers after one has finished the novel is not what will happen next. The plot is finished. The heroine is not left *en l'air* as Isabel Archer was in *The Portrait of a Lady*. Instead, one asks a strange question for a novel: Is this a success? That is, is this arrangement between the couples a success? Are we meant to think of it as one? In Nussbaum's reading, Maggie's ability to appreciate Charlotte and the Prince aesthetically testifies to Maggie's moral maturity, her success: "At the novel's end, [Maggie's] ability to view the other people as . . . a . . . living breathing painting expresses her commitment to several features of James's moral ideal . . . : a respect for the irreducibly particular character of a concrete moral context and the agents who are its components; a determination to scrutinize all aspects of this particular with intensely focused perception; a determination to care for it as a whole" (*LK* 162). But what James would have us question with the photograph of the carriage leaving Portland Place is whether "the vulgar heat of Maggie's wrong" might not have led to a world much more conducive to human flourishing (*eudaimonia*). Maggie's "success" is puzzling. The language throughout the last book suggests that Maggie has "won," but her triumph is tempered for the reader by a sense that she has lost what she has desperately tried to win, namely her husband, and paid dearly for her triumph with the loss of her father, figured in the photograph of his carriage leaving Portland Place.

For Nussbaum, Maggie's moral development is complete, in the sense that she now possesses the faculties of perception and reflection necessary for the good life for human beings, *eudaimonia*. Whatever frustration, regret, and unhappiness she will feel is a consequence of tragic circumstances, not of any inner lack. But our consideration of Bakhtin's chronotope of the threshold must lead us to doubt this irenic picture. Maggie's central feature is the capacity to avoid self-knowledge and the lucid responsibility it brings with it. Maggie's picture of the Prince and Charlotte as possessions is not an expression of a calm and objective response to their sufferings, but rather a convenient illusion, an illusion designed to exculpate Maggie and her father in Maggie's eyes. But this illusion simultaneously sabotages the possibility of mature and mutual love between Maggie and the husband she has "saved." This is the Jamesian tragedy. On Nussbaum's reading, Maggie is now finally prepared to be a wife, a real woman.[13] But Maggie (still innocent, at least in her own eyes) has so painted the Prince in her delusory picture that he is now, for her, not the sort of man to whom one can be married. He is an object, not a subject. This guarantees something short of human flourishing, and the fact that Maggie cannot bring to consciousness the structured self-deception that makes happiness impossible for her guarantees its permanence.

Part 2
Bakhtin and Social Theory

Literature as Social Knowledge: Mikhail Bakhtin and the Reemergence of the Human Sciences

Stanley Aronowitz

In recent years, literary methods have been widely used to reread some of the texts of social sciences, particularly ethnography. James Clifford and George Marcus's collection, *Writing Culture* showed us that "evidence" can be taken as discourse—specifically, that the ethnographer engages in rhetoric and other weapons of persuasion—metaphor, metonomy, tropes, and so on—that render power to discourse.[1] Moreover, as the recent debate over ethnography has shown, the researcher is bound, ethically, to take responsibility for the choice of subjects as well as their method of inquiry. The notion that anthropology, for example, is assigned by a neutral division of intellectual labor to study the subaltern in "third world" settings is today completely shattered. The investigator is obliged to set out her or his social and political presuppositions, including what may be described as the "intention" of the investigation. In sum, knowledge for knowledge's sake is under severe attack.

The problem of taking literary and other artistic works as reliable sources of social knowledge presents somewhat greater difficulties. In the first place, artists, critics, and philosophers have since the eighteenth century insisted upon the "autonomy" of art, especially from the economic and political matrix we call society.[2] Others have modified this judgment by admitting that art is intertwined with moral and ethical precepts of a given culture, in which case the relation of art to philosophy and other forms of systematic knowledge is a reasonable inference. At the same time, the art world—artists, critics, theorists, patrons—tends to acknowledge the internal relations of art to everyday life or, in another register, to what Bakhtin often refers to as culture.[3] Literature may be self-referential insofar as its formal attributes, such as narrative and linguistic traditions, play their significant part in artistic production, and aesthetics insists that the creative act is autobiographical, that is, objectifies what George Bataille has called inner experience.[4] Yet as we know, the common root of both self and other precludes a purely subjective origin.[5] We are ineluctably bound to our social relations; culture may be taken both as the civilizing process—where the assimilation of art and its traditions is understood as one of the crucial elements of self-creation—and, in the anthropological sense, as the practices (and, as Bakhtin argues, utterances) that constitute everyday life.[6]

The second difficulty is the conventional separation of science, including the sciences of society, from art. According to the so-called two cultures thesis, the methods and the apprehended knowledge derived from these spheres of human existence are both logically and existentially separate.[7] While literature provides insight into the subjective or psychological aspects of being, its ability to offer reliable systematic, conceptual, and generalizable knowledge as compared with, for example, history or sociology is, quite limited.

Until the discovery of the work of Mikhail Bakhtin by European and American theorists and critics, the debate concerning the possibility that literature might be a source of social knowledge was determined by the tenets of realist epistemology, according to which the literary text corresponds to an objective reality and, in fact, is determined by it, albeit not in a one-to-one copy. Even in the more sophisticated versions of this position, such as that of Georg Lukács, the problem of the epistemological status of representation is never avoided. Within this framework one needs no theory of language, only a theory of narrative. Recall that in Lukács's second excursions into literary criticism and theory (chiefly in the 1930s), he argues that narratives are constituted formally by social types derived as an abstraction from social life and are, consequently, independent of the text or literary traditions. The "great" novelists in his canon—among them Balzac, Scott, and Thomas Mann—draw their sources from these typifications of bourgeois society; the contradictions of everyday existence refer to real, historical contradictions, and in the best novels, narratives lose their self-referential character. Thus, despite the enormously complex categorical and interpretive apparatus invoked in Lukács's later work (e.g., *The Historical Novel, Realism in Our Time, Studies in European Realism*), significant literature holds up a mirror to sociohistorical time. Lukács draws his canon of European literature from those works that conform to the requirement that the economic and social character of a period is expressed in and through concrete characters and situations.

Of course, in this paradigm of literature as social knowledge, literary forms themselves are taken as mediations of an external reality that is quite independent of them. In our time of keen interest in the formal methods of criticism, Lukács's work has become a monument to an important but apparently surpassed discourse, precisely because of its realist historical epistemology. Consequently, for much of the interwar period, when literature and art were not understood in their formal-aesthetic dimensions to the exclusion of any possible social referent (a move conditioned by Marxism's intellectual hegemony over much of the literary intel-ligentsia during the 1930s), the social investigation of literature was subordinated by conceptions according to which literature may be taken as a kind of language game that obeys certain rules, some of which owe their effectiveness to literary conventions. In semiotic criticism, the text is a signifying practice whose meaning can only be derived from how it functions with a specific context. In turn, *context* connotes not chiefly a sociohistorical "reality" but a system of codes.

For example, Roland Barthes's *S/Z*—which may be taken as anti-Lukács—purports to show that the literary text of Balzac is actually fractured by a gaggle of codes, the interplay of which constitutes the narrative. Barthes transforms the social code from a master discourse into one of six relatively autonomous systems, the juxtapositions and combinations of which constitute the text. As with other works of structuralist criticism, diachronicity is subordinate to synchronicity, but equally important, the social loses its privileged place in reflection upon literary production. Barthes's methodological move consists not in obliterating the social referent, a position easily dismissed by the perspective of critical realism. Rather, the social code is relativized; its effectiveness becomes indeterminate in advance and must be evaluated anew in every concrete situation.

At first glance, the recent interest in Bakhtin may be considered paradoxical, since he appears to privilege *parole* over *langue*, time (history) over space, and, perhaps more puzzling, his work may be interpreted as profoundly ensconced in a subtle but unmistakable realist epistemology that, despite its differences from Lukácian Marxist criticism, shares a sociohistorical referent.[8] Indeed, the similarities between the two are by no means frivolous. Yet, as I argue, by exploring Bakhtin's category of chronotope and, perhaps more urgently, his use of the musical figure of polyphony, we have here neither conventional materialist discourse abetted by dialectical logic nor a precursor to post-structuralism. For the chronotope, along with Bakhtin's other key categories—heteroglossia, dialogic narrative, and polyphony—may be seen as a critique of historicism from the perspective of a new conception of historicity.

Bakhtin offers a theory of language that privileges agency over structure while working with, but not within, linguistic boundaries.[9] Most important of all, from the perspective of social and cultural theory, his perspective addresses, within a critique of literary texts, the complex relationships between humans and nature and social relations, without, however, succumbing to correspondence theory. In fact, Bakhtin offers an incipient theory of the relation of nature to human interaction that falls neither into biological nor social reductionism. It remains virtually singular in the past century of literary scholarship, during which the culturalist position of the *Geisteswissenshaften* (spiritual or human sciences) has dominated cultural studies.

Perhaps his stature as a social historian is unknown to literary scholarship. But Bakhtin's wide influence on European social history is largely due to the pertinence of his "method," not uncontested, to historical sociology of the medieval and early Renaissance period. For what Bakhtin achieved, long before the richly detailed historical and sociological studies by George Rude, Eric Hobsbawm, and E. P.

Thompson, to name only some of the best known, of what is variously termed the Crowd, "the people," or simply popular culture, was to provide a series of rigorously constituted categories of description. Yet some admiring historians have persisted in privileging social scientific methods that purport to achieve direct knowledge of the past.

Here is Carlo Ginzburg: "The stereotyped and saccharine image of popular culture that results from this research is very different from what is outlined by Mikhail Bakhtin in a lively and fundamental book on the relations between Rabelais and the popular culture of his day. Here it is suggested that Gargantua or Pantagruel books that perhaps no peasant ever read, teach us more about peasant culture than the Almanach des Bergers, which must have circulated widely in the French countryside. The center of the culture portrayed by Bakhtin is the carnival, myth and ritual in which converge the celebration of fertility and abundance, the jesting inversion of all values and established orders, the cosmic sense of the destructive and regenerative passage of time."[10] According to Bakhtin, this vision of the world, which had evolved through popular culture over the course of centuries, was in marked contrast to the dogmatism and conservatism of the culture of the dominant classes, especially in the Middle Ages. By keeping this disparity in mind, the work of Rabelais becomes comprehensible, its comic quality linked directly to the carnival themes of popular culture: cultural dichotomy, but also circular reciprocal influence between the cultures of subordination and the ruling classes that was especially intense in the first half of the sixteenh century. "These are hypotheses to a certain extent and not all of them equally well documented. But the principal failing in Bakhtin's fine book is probably something else. The protagonists of popular culture whom he has tried to describe, the peasants and the artisans speak almost exclusively through the words of Rabelais."[11]

But what is the epistemological status of Ginzburg's own text? Can the "reports" of the captors of his own protagonists, the miller Menocchio, be called more "reliable" than Bakhtin's protagonists of popular culture read from Rabelais's Gargantua? Says Ginzburg, "The very wealth of research possibilities indicated by Bakhtin makes us wish for a direct study of lower class society free of intermediaries. But for reasons already mentioned, it is extremely difficult in this area of scholarship to find a direct rather than an indirect method of approach."[12]

Ginzburg believes that we can avoid the "indirect approach," yet he is properly concerned that this claim exposes him to the charge of positivism: "But the fear of falling into a notorious, naive positivism combined with the exasperated awareness of the ideological distortion that may lurk behind the most normal and seemingly innocent process of perception prompts many historians today to disregard popular culture together with the sources that provide a more or less distorted picture of it."[13] Ginzburg implies that something other than "distortion" can be derived from a direct method of research, that historical research can reliably get back to the "things themselves," that history can be recovered in some extratextual manner. So, like other social historians such as the Annales school (Bloch, Braudel, Fevre, Le Roy Ladurie), he scans official records in an effort to capture the moral economy of the period, the rhythms of everyday life, and the elusive but discernible agency of the people. Yet his method is inevitably indirect. The people rarely if ever "speak for themselves." They cannot represent themselves either because they cannot read or write or because they are denied access to preserved documents. They must be represented through the reports of official bodies, which, until fairly recently, monopolized the means of communication and whose texts are always edited. Social history is, regrettably, an indirect history subject to the exclusions and inclusions of interested informants. The texts of social history, however valuable, are warranted inferences whose epistemological status may be compared in their documentary status with that of the novel. Events are inevitably and doubly fictionalized: by the institutional authority of the Church and its courts and by the professional authority of the historian. While it is admirable that some, notably the various schools of social history, choose to construct the agency of the people, the methodological ensnarements are frequently severe.

Bakhtin seems to anticipate these criticisms. In his essay on "the text" he claims that, "the text (written and oral) is the primary given of all these distinct disciplines and of all thought in the human sciences and philosophy in general (including theological and philosophical thought at its sources). The text is the unmediated reality . . . the only one from which these disciplines and this thought can emerge. Where there is no text there is no object of study and no object of thought either."[14]

Even the social historian (and of this genre Carlo Ginzburg is an unsurpassed practitioner) relies on texts—letters and diaries—and in order to get at everyday life, especially of the nonliterate classes, the historian or ethnographer is obliged to construct a narrative out of the raw materials provided by public records—court transcripts, tax rolls—among which Braudel and other members of the Annales school found lists of agricultural products and their money or barter values—property deeds, and so forth. And others, such as Le Roy Ladurie and Le Goff, worked in the genre of historical scholarship that relied, in part, on civil and ecclesiastical courts. If Bakhtin is right that, whatever its form, "the implied text (if the word is understood in its broadest sense is any coherent complex of signs)"—then even the study of art deals with texts.[15] For Bakhtin "our discipline" is not literary criticism or social history, but the "human sciences," which for him are distinguished by the centrality of interpretation in them, in contrast to the natural sciences' penchant for direct modes of authentication.

However, if it can be shown that the natural sciences themselves are theory-laden and, therefore, that their evidence is heavily mediated by interpretation, then we may refer to the positivist doctrine of authentication through experiment, rational calculation, or whatever, but the actual as opposed to the imputed differences between the two broad disciplines begins to break down. Bakhtin:

> We will give the name *chronotope* (literally, "time space") to the intrinsic connectedness of temporal and spatial relationships that are artistically expressed in literature. This term [space-time] is employed in mathematics, and was introduced as part of Einstein's Theory of Relativity. The special meaning it has in relativity theory is not important for our purposes; we are borrowing it for literary criticism almost as a metaphor (almost but not entirely). What counts for us is that it expresses the inseparability of space and time (time as the fourth dimension of space). We understand the chronotope as a formally constitutive category of literature; we will not deal with the chronotope in other areas of culture."[16]

For Bakhtin, in literature the primary category of the chronotope is *time*. And, as his essay shows, time constructs narratives by its intersection with social and symbolic space. Moreover, in the sections on Rabelais in the chronotope essay, Bakhtin shows that the history of the novel itself may be configured in relation to chronotopic categories, as multitudes of spatiality whose cores are forms of temporality. Bakhtin abstracts from the texts of Rabelais, for example, no less than seven forms of what he calls "productive and generative time" in the preclass agricultural stage of human societies (the folkloric time), all of which are marked in various ways as "unified" and "unmediated" totalities in which means of production, ritual, and everyday life are not yet differentiated into the private and public spheres. Rabelais's Gargantua comes at the end of this era: its series are primarily spatial, since, as Bakhtin says, "The folkloric basis of (even) the entire grotesque images is patently obvious."[17]

Laughter and grotesquerie mark these series of eating, copulation, death, and so forth that are, despite their phantasmagoric imagery, still ensconced in the worldview according to which we are part of natural history. Thus, in contrast to the sublimated form of sexuality—love—that transmogrifies the Romantic novel in the eighteenth century, Rabelais invokes the popular conception according to which sex is a natural practice unmediated by extrinsic influences such as religious morality. All of this is concentrated in the spatiotemporal specificity of the carnival.

In contrast, modernity is marked by the separation of public from private, that is, the separation of means of production, ritual, and everyday life, each of which becomes the site of the well-known fragmentation of the social world in which the commodity form, in all of its permutations, gradually displaces (but does not destroy) popular culture.[18] With the rise of the individual, the social chronotope is replaced by the individual chronotope. We must now speak of the multitude, not

so much of series, but of voices, the combinatory effects of which are polyphonic, a term that signifies the dissonant harmonies of individual voices.
Bakhtin:

> When the immanent unity of time disintegrated, when individual life-sequences were separated out, lives in which the gross realities of communal life had become merely petty private matters; when collective labor and the struggle with nature had ceased to be the only arena for man's encounter with nature and the world—then nature itself ceased to be a living participant in the events of life. Then nature became, by and large, a "setting for action," its backdrop; it was turned into landscape, it was fragmented into metaphors and comparisons serving to sublimate individual and private affairs and adventures not connected in any real or intrinsic way with nature itself.
>
> But in the treasure-house of language and in certain kinds of folklore this immanent unity of time is preserved, insofar as language and folklore continue to insist on a relation to the world and its phenomena based on collective labor. It is in these that the real basis of the ancient matrix is preserved, the authentic logic of a primitive enchaining of images and motives.[19]

In these lines we can hear echoes of the neo-Marxist critique of modernity associated with Lukács and the Frankfurt school but with a significant and, perhaps, a decisive difference: Bakhtin insists on the primacy of the popular, which itself is associated with the unity of humans and nature mediated through labor. His vision—against all privileging of high culture—is the idea that what appears as trivial to culture in what Norbert Elias calls the "civilizing process" may be taken as the authentic when seen from the perspective of its historicity.[20] For a unique conception of historicity underlies Bakhtin's chronotope, within which all categories of social space-time are employed. Since in the final accounting, language is subject to temporally induced transformations but also stands outside, one may infer its relative transhistoricity as well. Otherwise, how could language "preserve" the "immanent" unity of time? But folklore enjoys the same status. Contrary to the myths of modernity, Bakhtin shows that, although fundamentally marked by the totality (in which subject and object are unified by the body), folkloric time is anything but static. Unlike the later incarnation, history is not coded as a series of external events to which private life is consigned to "petty affairs," but it consists in the chronotope of the carnival, which is part of everyday existence. Although Bakhtin's object of knowledge is literary, the sources of literature are plainly "extraliterary," insofar as language in its informal mode, folklore (popular culture), is part of the oral tradition, texts that are transformed into the verbal mode by writing.

Surely the idea that literary texts may be taken as reliable objects of social knowledge is precisely what Bakhtin has in mind in his *Rabelais* or *Dostoevsky*. The distinction between the social sciences, including history and the so-called humanities is refuted in Bakhtin's invocation of "human sciences," a term he employs to signify what he calls "the unity of culture" in describing his own discourse.[21] Of course, the appropriation of his categories by the disciplines and subdisciplines in the United States without showing the implications of the large claim represented by the chronotope for constituting categories of experience, literary or otherwise, is entirely conventional, just as Bakhtin's own disclaimer for the universality of the chronotope in relation to the natural sciences may be comprehended within the framework of Marxist-Leninist scientism, to which he was subject, at least bureaucratically. However, if we recall the ambiguity of his own statement, he proposes to employ space-time as a fourth dimension of space in literature, but not really metaphorically. For his meticulous typology of the various series that constitute the temporal-spatial contexts for the medieval and Renaissance novel and the modern novel illustrate the claims of contemporary philosophers of science, that all empirical science is theory-laden. The "chronotope" as a physical category mediates observation, measurement, and their results. Bakhtin uses space-time in a fairly rigorous way, from which he derives his own categories of narrative.

Moreover, in the work of Vernadsky, Oparin, and other biologist contemporaries from whom Bakhtin drew as much as from Einstein's relativity theory, the chronotope, one of the main ideas that appears in the *Rabelais*, became a crucial element in the study of the evolution of the biosphere and problems such as the origin of life.[22] In the mid-1920s Soviet biologists and biochemists, together with some German and British colleagues, developed a theory of biochemical evolution that abandoned the older view that posited the appearance of life in images of linear temporality. They held that green plants fed by radiation made the earliest appearance, followed by other organisms. These scientists, led by Vernadsky and Oparin, advanced the hypothesis of heterotrophic sources of life, the simultaneous appearance of life-forms, and the close relation and ultimate interdependence of organisms and their organic and inorganic environments, which interact interdependently. That is, once having emerged, life-forms enrich or impoverish the environment. And Vernadsky employs the category of chronotope to describe and explain the series of events that constitute evolution. It is a Darwinian hypothesis but also one in which synchronic relations of a horizontal kind remain pertinent.

So although Bakhtin identifies with the view according to which literary studies are part of the human sciences, he departs from one of its major tenets: the logical and existential divide between natural and human sciences corresponding to a parallel gulf between nature and history. The concept of the "unity" of culture refers to art, everyday life, and postmodern scientific culture. But unity does not assume identity. To space-time he inserts polyphony, that is, the multiplicity of voices that are definitively *not* dialectical, if by this term we connote internal contradictions that are resolved through the subordination of one of the terms by the other and its incorporation into a "higher" unity.

Thus Bakhtin's philosophical position resembles more that of Nietszche than of Hegel. While the rhetoric of the eternal return is absent from his discourse, there is also an emphatic, albeit implied, argument for the continuity of formal categories in the wake of historically determined transformations of speech genres. Yet the chronotope, the heterogeneity of voices, signals the importance of the utterance as a dynamic category through which time may be apprehended. The importance of utterance in Bakhtin's later thought can be understood in several dimensions: its role in literary production, its centrality to what we mean when we speak of "style." But Bakhtin's ambition is, finally, to read history through discourse, especially through a close reading of the transformations of utterances. In his essay on Bildungsroman, Bakhtin comments on Goethe's description of geographic terrain in his *Italian Journey*:

> The living, dynamic marker provided by flowing rivers and streams also gives a graphic idea of the country's water basins, its topography, its natural boundaries and natural connections, its land and water routes and transshipment points, its fertile and arid areas and so on. This is not an abstract geological and geographical landscape. For Goethe, it reveals potential for historical life. This is an arena of historical events, a firmly delineated boundary of that spatial riverbed along which the current of historical time flows. Historically active man is placed in this living, graphic, visual system of mountains, waterways, boundaries and routes. . . . One sees the essential and necessary character of man's historical activity.[23]

Bakhtin draws on the travel genre as he draws on novels to demonstrate that embedded in the writer's craft of invoking nature is human activity, that writing is a kind of speech whose status is fundamentally historical even when its ostensible referent is the natural world.

Bakhtin commends his work to our attention now because, underneath the current fashion of European-inspired formalisms, other currents are struggling for a place in the critical sun: the new literary history, much of which is not new; a strong claim inspired by the later works of Roland Barthes for relieving criticism of its obligation to produce science in favor of a return to the text of fiction, to discover its pleasures. In some ways, interest in Bakhtin is unlikely in either literary criticism or linguistics because, until now, his social perspective on literature was out of fashion. Since the 1960s, American critics have been smitten by formalisms of various sorts: structuralism and semiotics, deconstruction. A considerable coterie also hangs on to the New Criticism. Even Marxism, which is historical, whatever else it might be, is forced to adapt to the French turn or face marginality in current debates. Bakhtin and his circle were the collective precursor of anti-Formalist criticism; the *Freudianism* book is a pitiless critique of the fundamental psychoanalytic ideas from the point of view of a social linguistics. Their theory of language, which forms the basis of all the work of what became know as the Bakhtin circle, is fully developed in *Marxism and the Philosophy of Language*, like the Freud book, ostensibly written by V. N. Voloshinov.

In the language work, Voloshinov's fire is directed against Saussure's *Course in General Linguistics*, which took Soviet linguistics of the 1920s by storm and provided a broad basis for a new literary formalism, against which the Bakhtin circle argued throughout the decade. *Marxism* is perhaps the most persuasive statement in our century of a conception of language alternative to that of Saussurean structuralism, for which the structure of language really inheres in the biophysiological makeup of humans and, like the gene, is relatively independent of its social and historical environment. Long before Saussure's French legatees discovered the pragmatic rule that signification was situated, not chiefly in structure but in the uses of language, Bakhtin insisted that even if the capacity for language is given, its structure as well as its meaning derives from its uses (and its consequences) within a definite social context. Words and sentences do not refer principally to their structure but to the dialogues in which they are employed.

Speech, or, as Bakhtin calls it, utterance, is intimately linked to the space-time (chronotope) that constitutes the speech act as well as narrative. In fact, the utterances in literature, as much as daily communication, are the crucial sources of knowledge about modernist daily life. We learn about what people are saying, but even more important, inner and outer dialogues (conversations between people and the self and its own other) tell us by the mode of expression who these people are.[24] And as we have seen, descriptions of the external world are signifiers of conditions of historically situated time, signs of the self-production of humans.

So, although taken up in the United States mostly by literary critics because most of the translated work under his own name concerns methods of literary theory or studies of such novelists as Dostoevsky and Rabelais, Bakhtin may be considered better as a close student of culture, both in the anthropological and artistic sense. His wide use of historical, sociological, and aesthetic categories defies the neat cubbies of academic disciplines, although this has not prevented scholars from recoding his work in their specialized debates.

Like Walter Benjamin, whose writings animated the literary critical scene in the late 1960s and 1970s, Bakhtin is rapidly becoming the subject of a new cottage industry.[25] Among others, of course, the Slavists have appropriated him. In the context of the anti-Stalinist revival of the post-Brezhnev era, he is portrayed as a "religious man" persecuted by the Soviets for his faith. Consequently, his writing, ostensibly about Rabelais and Dostoevsky as well as about language, psychoanalysis, and literary forms, are sometimes taken as codes of an antiauthoritarian political intervention precisely during the Stalinist era.[26] On the other side, the Marxists gravitate to Bakhtin after long years in the modernist wilderness, where their insistence on socially rooted interpretations of literature were considered by the critical avant-garde to be quaint, when not dangerous in light of Zhdanovian repression of artistic dissent until the partial thaw of the late 1950s.

More than Benjamin, who, despite his Communist fellow traveling, was among the first of the truly modernist critics, Bakhtin rails against modernism in art and criticism on both technical and ideological grounds. His attack against Formalism, the revolution's most daring and internationally appreciated aesthetic experiment, not only puts him, at least in the immediate postrevolutionary decade, outside the cultural mainstream in his own country, but also places him out of step with modern art of the first half of the twentieth century. If he remained relatively obscure after the 1920s until his belated and conjunctural discovery in the highly charged political context of the waning years of the Khrushchev era, modernists could argue "with good reason," for even when Bakhtin reads Dostoevsky, he looks for different things. What he wants to discover in the novels are the voices of those excluded from written history; he wants to dredge up the details of everyday life, not until very recently a legitimate object of the historian's eye.

But Bakhtin is not just another critic for whom the popular voice constitutes the basis of the aesthetic and social value of a literary work. Although there is a great deal of evidence that he is not only a literary critic, historian, or aesthetician but a social theorist and a social linguist for whom literature functions as social knowledge, his great attraction for us, despite his denunciation of formalisms of all sorts, is his penchant for category-making, which corresponds, ironically, to our (if not Bakhtin's own) will to scientificity.[27] Bakhtin's category-making is an elective affinity that places him, loosely, in the Kantian mode of cultural criticism that was extremely powerful in the years just before and immediately after the Russian Revolution. At the same time, his great admiration for Goethe belies any facile attempt to place him in either the religious or the Kantian camp: "All we have said reveals the exceedingly chronotopic nature of Goethe's mode of visualization and thought in all areas and spheres of his multifaceted activity. He saw everything sub specie aeternitatis [from the point of view of eternity] as his teacher Spinoza did but in time, and in the power of time. Everything— from an abstract idea to a piece of rock on the bank of a stream—bears the stamp of time, and is saturated with time and assumes its form and meaning in time." To Goethe's world of "emergence" Bakhtin counterposes the "mechanical materialism of Holwachs and others. . . . These same two aspects clearly separate Goethe from subsequent romantic historicity as well."[28] Unlike the old literary essayists whose discursive meditations grabbed the reader by their sheer force of style, and who performed criticism by making the assumption that the work of art violated or was sympathetic to our collective sensibilities, Bakhtin gets us to think in his categories. If you already know that Dostoevsky is the modernist whose major achievement was to capture interior dialogue, as our first great modern psychological writer, then Bakhtin shows that this is merely an instance of a far greater contribution, his polyphony, the multitude of voices that inhabit his texts. He is the master narrator of the vicissitudes of modernity, where the petty affairs of private life become identical to the excluded history of the space-time that his characters inhabit.[29]

Bakhtin contrasts the monologue, in which the authorial voice dominates the text, to dialogue, where characters speak for themselves, voices that Dostoevsky articulates against his own political will, speaking values and ways of life that are in profound disagreement with his own precepts. For Bakhtin, Dostoevsky's greatness consists in his loyalty to truth, even if this truth of diversity, of plurality, opposes his own exquisitely hierarchical religious worldview. Like his critics and biographers, Dostoevsky may have believed he was a chronicler of the existential choices to which humans were ineluctibly wedded, but Bakhtin persuades us that his work provides, first of all, a window to the Russian middle class, which forms the context of nearly all his most important novels and stories. Not that Bakhtin's Dostoevsky is a sociological naturalist who, like Emile Zola, contents himself with recording the world as a botanist classifies the forest flora. The novels and stories do not describe a social environment "objectively."

Bakhtin writes: "Not a single element of the work is structured from the point of view of a nonparticipating 'third person.'" In the novel itself they "are not represented in any way." Dostoevsky has created a "plurality of equally authoritative ideological positions and an extreme heterogeneity of material," the achievement Bakhtin calls polyphony.[30] The musical metaphor could be transposed to a political metaphor, since Bakhtin's study was published when Stalin's dominance in Soviet life was just taking hold. And 1929 was the year of Bakhtin's arrest for his religious activities, an event that led to his exile from the Soviet metropole to the provinces, where he was to spend most of the rest of his life except for the last decade, after being "discovered" by a post-Stalinist student generation. He returned to Moscow in the late 1960s, when the Soviet Union was still in the first period of post-Stalin reform. In fact, this obscure provincial teacher of linguistics and literature was rediscovered in the context of the debate, initiated by Khrushchev, about the monologism of the previous era. For a new intellectual generation Bakhtin became a democratic prophet, but also a great Marxist critic. Certainly it is this "Marxism" that many current claimants to the Bakhtinian legacy would deny, substituting instead an aestheticist interpretation on this work, which may be perhaps the least literary of all twentieth-century schools of thought for which textual criticism is the crucial method.

The first chapter of *Problems of Dostoevsky's Poetics* lays out Bakhtin's standpoint: Dostoevsky has invented the polyphonic novel out of his own ambiguous and ultimately contradictory personality and ideological position. Although the work is rooted in its own time, the validity of the achievement does not die when the conditions under which it was produced have been surpassed. Like only Dante and, perhaps, Dickens before him, Dostoevsky has the gift of presenting many voices simultaneously and with equal amplitude. The dialogic imagination reaches its highest point here, precisely because Dostoevsky cannot resolve the conflicts that constitute his life and art. Nor can Bakhtin. For he was a religious individual, profoundly at odds with postrevolutionary Russia. At the same time he is influenced by Marxism's *intention* to deliver literature from its formal bonds, especially in his attempt to develop a truly social theory of literature in which not only whole discourses and even sentences embody the dialogic principle, but even the word itself becomes an instance of discursive activity—a sign of the "subject." A member of the so-called Bakhtin circle, Medvedev, writes a harsh critique of Russian Formalism, and another, Voloshinov, produces a theory of language as a system of signs whose meanings depend upon their use within the context of communication. The social semiotics suggested in this work is compelling to members of French post-structuralist circles, particularly Julia Kristeva, who finds in Bakhtin a precursor to her own work, which, however formalistic, nevertheless adopts the idea that language means as language acts.[31]

We resonate to Bakhtin, particularly his conception of the plurality of voices and the intimate link of language to action, in part because his position bears some affinities to pragmatism, which I understand here as democratic philosophy, according to which a discourse may be evaluated chiefly, not in relation to a transcendent "truth," but through its practical consequences. He offers criticism a way to explore the relationship between text and context that is resolutely antireductionist but insists that social life is embedded in the narrative in a way not available to more abstracted disciplines such as sociology, economics, and even historiography.

For what is found here is the experience of the ordinary, retold and recast in the novelistic text, which, since the seventeenth century, has taken the quotidian as its discursive object. For Bakhtin there are no resolutions of the contradictory, "heteroglossic" nature of human interactions in categories of class, history, or other formalisms that inevitably transcode experience into information. This is not to deny that Bakhtin is acutely aware of the class dimension to the novels of the bourgeois era. What he refuses is precisely the tendency of social criticism toward class reductionism, to encode all experience and its aspects in a version of social relations that derives from a priori, eternal essences such as those he perceives in Spinoza.

This is Bakhtin's strong program for a criticism that seeks to recover experience, wiped out by the processes of abstraction—both social and scientific—

among other monologisms. Bakhtin demands that we reconstruct history through explorations of literature, because in his view "life below the waist" is erased from our collective memory by official historians, those employed by the victors to tell the past in images of the present. This perspective is perhaps made clearest in his dissertation, *Rabelais and His World*, published belatedly after Bakhtin's rehabilitation in 1963. Bakhtin argues that the two major Rabelais novels, *Gargantua* and *Pantagruel*—judged by leading historians and critics to be "merely" comic masterpieces—are profound constructions of the popular critique of aristocratic society and culture, monuments to the power of laughter as political and social criticism. Moreover, the novels are veritable snapshots of the social worlds of the transition between peasant and bourgeois societies, portraits hidden in the histories in which peasant culture remains invisible.

Bakhtin's *Rabelais* book has become a major influence on recent social history of the sixteenth century, as we have seen in the work of Carlo Ginzburg. Rabelais's peasants work hard all year, too hard, under the stern authority of the Church and the aristocracy and their retainers, the local officials. The carnival is that time when the peasants are free to break the rules, rules imposed from on high, and appropriate by inversion the sacred practices of high culture by means of parody and ridicule. The carnival is a *ritualized transgression*, the place to display gross violations of conventional sexual morality, to engage in a temporary raucous public celebration of the body, a sphere strictly interdicted by established authorities. Bakhtin shows that the wild peasant dances, the laughter, and other outrages creep into high culture just as popular culture absorbs, albeit in comic form, the art of the masters. Even the Church is infected with popular art, so that although possibly not a single peasant could or did read *Gargantua*, Rabelais's novels represent the intervention of the popular into literature, an art of the ruling classes by definition.

Ginzburg, still tied to the positivist premises of historiography, does not grasp the full power of Bakhtin's approach. It is not that Bakhtin has somehow avoided dredging up direct evidence to demonstrate resistance through popular culture and other means; he is making two different points. The first is that high culture does not stand as the polar opposite of the popular. The split between intellectual and manual labor is a wall created by ideology but does not, in fact, describe the real relationship between the two. And he is, tacitly, making a crucial historiographic point. He challenges the positivist assumptions of social historians who, since Thompson's magisterial *Making of the English Working Class* and Trompé's *Les mineurs de Carmaux*, have revolutionized the writing of working-class history through their archaeological investigations of everyday life. Bakhtin invokes the social world through literature because, among other things, he holds that the novel is the premier form through which the popular is defined by an oral tradition not available to historiography except through *indirect* accounts. Moreover, he shows that much of high culture is constituted, in part, by its appropriation of the popular and that since it is an oral tradition, it can speak only indirectly through its incorporation by high cultural works. The people of Rabelais's time cannot speak for themselves directly; in order to enter "history" they require intermediaries.

Our knowledge of their hidden history—even information culled from records, of ecclesiastical courts in Ginzburg's justly famous studies or manorial rolls where clerks recorded commodity exchanges between lord, serf, and merchants and accumulated debits and credits—is always filtered information, since our informants are servants of the mighty. Of course, Rabelais's account differs only in degree; his eyes and ears are unique only because the novel is a form that depicts everyday life and is not restricted by the function within which peasants appear—as defendants, debtors, or whatever additional subordinate positions they occupy. The historian is not likely to discover the grotesque—as, representations of aristocratic culture or the orgies of pleasure—in the trial of a heretic or a report of a highwayman apprehended by the county police (the sources from which many social histories of the last centuries of the old regimes are gleaned). Nor can the lower classes emerge as real subjects, no matter how much we learn about them by dredging official records, without the historian's narrative constructions. The formal context of a tribunal tells one thing, a novel another.

Consistent with his work on the early modern novel, Bakhtin investigates later novels to reveal the underside of the space-time of the characters they represent. Unlike criticism derived from structural linguistics, which recognizes that signification derives from its use but disdains its historicity, Bakhtin holds language as a historical category; utterance is the clue to the "socioideological" situation of characters: "The novel is an expression of a Galilean perception of language, one that denies the absolutism of a single and unitary language—that is, that refuses to acknowledge its own language as the sole verbal and semantic center of the ideological world. It is a perception that has been made conscious of the vast plentitude of national and more to the point social languages . . . all of which are equally relative, reified and limited, as they are merely the languages of social groups, professions and other cross-sections of everyday life."[32] According to Bakhtin, the modern novel is marked by "linguistic homelessness of literary consciousness," by which he means that authorial individuality, prized by some critics as the mark of great writing, is "decentered" by what might be described as the experience of modernity itself. The fragmentation of the social world, the relativity, and relationality, of the worldviews of any of its actors, is the real subject of the novel. Against poetry that preserves the myth of language—that the singular voice may be contained in the form itself—the "truth" of the novel is its "vast plentitude" of voices. The best works of fiction dissolve the singular voice of the author. The characters take over, as in Pirandello's play, where the authorial voice is sought but has, regrettably, disappeared.

This theory of literature and its companion theory of language are analogous to the propositions of relativity and quantum physics, both of which put the observer in the observational field and therefore can make no statements about nature that are independent of the framework of investigation. Poetry may be described as the Newtonian period in art: its ideological assumption is the separation of the inner and outer life; its language is characteristically the monologue. This was precisely the reason that the New Criticism privileged poetry over fiction. Stories and novels have a quality of anonymity, especially if they fulfill Bakhtin's critical criteria, while poetry is still the work of the ego whose sole possession, a mythic yet individual language, aspires to transcend the muck of everyday existence to achieve higher truth. Of course, much of twentieth-century poetry has violated these rules by its aspiration to descend "below the waist." One hears the otherwise muffled voices of the populace in the epic of William Carlos Williams or in the declamations of Mayakovsky. These are not the world-weary consciousnesses of a Pound or Eliot who speak for the unified voice of their generation, however distinctively. What many critics find wanting in Williams is precisely the degree to which his utterance approaches the vernacular, and they complain that there are too many separate voices in his long poem, *Paterson*, that the transcendental monologic subject, the unique personal voice that has become the subject of modern poetry, disappears. Besides the cardinal sin of merging aesthetics and politics, Mayakovsky feels too "prosy": he has taken everyday speech as the vehicle of his poetry.

Still, despite the blurring of the lines between prose and poetry in a growing genre of poetic works that explicitly renounce the evaluative criteria enunciated by high cultural critics for this form, Bakhtin prefers prose, because "in the poetic image narrowly conceived (in the image-as-trope) all activity—the dynamics of the image-as-word—is completely exhausted by the play between the word and the object. . . . The word forgets that its object has its own history of contradictory acts of verbal recognition, as well as that heteroglossia that is always present in such acts of recognition.[33] The word cannot stand alone apart from its object, but the object does not exist solely for the wordsmith; Bakhtin insists that language refers to something outside the speaker's sensibility. Or to be more precise, the poetic trope cannot be the product of pure consciousness or stylistic convention but points to an inexhaustible variety of expressions whose reference is the space-time of the world. For Bakhtin, rather than stretching the multiplicity of its uses and its references, poetry closes down the word.

My point in this essay is emphatically distanced from an attempt to appropriate Bakhtin for the social sciences but is to show, instead, how Bakhtin shows the way, through his paradigm shift from the standpoint of the disciplines to that of the human sciences—an antidisciplinary intervention into the construction of knowledge—to transform the disciplinary basis of historical, literary, and social knowledge, all of which are separated in contemporary culture by parameters that are institutionally and ideologically derived. Bakhtin's is the way of the transgressor, for the disciplines have fiercely defended their respective domains and, with few exceptions, have clung to that portion of their canons that justify their separate existences.

Needless to say, this work points to the emergence of the intervention that has appeared under the rubric of "cultural studies." This intellectual movement has been marked by three distinct features, all of which have been elaborated by Bakhtin. We have already seen the interplay of the "low" culture of Rabalais's peasants with high Church culture. There is *mutual* appropriation of each by the other, although the forms of utterance are dissimilar: peasant appropriation is accompanied by mockery and laughter; the Church incorporates peasant culture within its own rituals, but without calling attention to it. The second feature is culture studies' alternative to the monologism of the dominant culture's canonical works of literature and art, proposing instead that the human sciences recognize the diversity of voices— not only with respect to the emerging discourses of women, people of color, lesbians and gays, and workers—but also the criteria for privileging utterance. This request articulates with Bakhtin's emphasis on genre which provides space for "emotion, evaluation and expression" that are foreign to the mainstream.[34] Finally, as I have argued, Bakhtin introduces the concept that literature may be an authentic, perhaps *the* privileged site of social knowledge, precisely because of its polyphonic character, as opposed to the monologisms of the philosophy of language and historical writing that remain unaware of their passive character.

I suspect that it is Bakhtin's challenge to the claims of science, with its positivist methodologies of discovery, particularly its artificial separation of fact and fiction, of theory and observation on the one hand and "expressive" forms on the other, that is the most enduring contribution of this amazingly prescient thinker. If we are on the verge of a paradigm shift in the constitution of social knowledge in which the categories developed by literary theory, especially of discourse, utterance, and polyphony, are no longer conceived as an internal, aesthetically saturated discourse, and where the distinction between nature and culture is once more blurred, then it is in Bakhtin's work that we will find a beacon for the new.

The Postmodern Crisis: Discourse, Parody, Memory

Vincent Crapanzano

The process of making equal is the same as the process of incorporation of appropriated material in the amoeba.

—Nietzsche, *The Will to Power*

In writing about the baroque *Trauerspiel*, the mourning play, the play of melancholy, Walter Benjamin notes that the allegorical physiognomy of history conjoined with nature—"The word 'history' stands written on the countenance of nature in the characters of transience"—is present in reality in the form of the ruin. "In the ruin history has physically merged into the setting."[1] Today, in an age that has been declared postmodern, indeed, by some, in Spain for example, as neobaroque, the ruin has been replaced by the quotation, the trace, really a pseudo-trace, a detritus, a re-ferent, a carrying back to/from a past, that is so completely decontextualized, so open to recontextualization, that it, the quotation, the trace, becomes at once an emblem of a past evacuated of history (history understood as a somehow meaningful account of the past) and a signal of the artifice of any such account, any history. Ironically, demonically if you will, the denial of the possibility of a "real" mimetic account, of any master narrative, proclaimed by the relentless signals of artifice does in fact announce an overarching narrative of—a consuming obsession with—artifice. As baroque mourning, constituted on the experience of transience, of death and the corpse, gives way—I need not pass, I suppose, through the defiles of neoclassicism and romanticism—to today's (ideologically bruited) *jouissances*, constituted on the experience of change, of difference, *différance*, of rupture, the bit, the flickering image, the digital sound, no doubt masking a postcoital emptiness, nostalgia, and the longing for repetition and reunion, so allegory, whose artifice, at least during the baroque, was mournfully relished, surrenders to artifice, whose allegorical possibility is playfully denied. There is in all play a danger that the truth alluded to (from the Latin *ludere*, "to play") will break through and arrest the play.

    I will be concerned with putative discursive changes associated with post-modernism and with their relationship to memory understood as a structural precipitate of any dialogic engagement in which a change of perspective or the illusion of a change of perspective occurs. This "new" discourse, at least in cross-cultural settings, is structured, I will argue, like parody. Parody, Linda Hutcheon writes, "is a perfect postmodern form, in some senses, for it paradoxically both incorporates and challenges that which it parodies."[2] It stresses difference and through the inscription of that difference in a literary or artistic tradition masters it. Its assumption is imperial.

Many definitions of *postmodern* have been advanced, and for the most part, as even the most superficial reading reveals, they are vague, overgeneralizing, and contradictory.[3] Some stress epistemological skepticism, hyperreflexivity, and the artifice of all accounts, including those that articulate a perduring self. Others emphasize play, language games, the "logical operations of cultural terms" within a structure that seems independent of its medium of expression, indeed of reality itself. And still others point out the arbitrariness, the conventionality, of those temporal connections that give us the illusion of history and continuity and take ironic delight in a sort of promiscuous quotationalism that subverts history, continuity, and memory.[4] "Pouvons-nous aujourd'hui continuer à organiser la foule des événéments qui nous viennent du monde, humain ou nonhumain," Jean-François Lyotard asks, "en les plaçant sous l'Idée d'une histoire universelle de l'humanité?"[5]

Postmodern commentary, that is, commentary on postmodernism by contemporary postmodernist critics, stresses the reflexivity. Commentary and its subject, criticism and its subject, metalanguage and primary language, are entangled and declared inseparable. There can, as such, be no external vantage point for commentary, criticism, indeed reading and perception. We are caught within the play of arbitrary signs that are loosened from their referents and no longer systematically constrained by grammars of style, say, or narrative. (The postmodernist debt to Saussure, as understood by the deconstructionists, is enormous.) Not only is the arbitrariness of the sign in any act of signification paradigmatically proclaimed, but so is the arbitrariness of its syntagmatic, its syntactic, placement. There is—there can be—no longer a "natural" or "naturalized" sequence. The concatenation of signs becomes an ironic montage, ultimately a self-subverting comment. In architecture, where a postmodern ideology has flourished, the juxtaposition of disparate styles is no longer justified on transcending aesthetic or decorative principles (as were the juxtapositions of Egyptian, Greek, Roman, and Oriental motifs on Empire furniture). When Philip Johnson couples immense vaults, reminiscent at once of Sabastiano Serlio and a stage setting for grand opera, with a Chippendale scroll that reminds one of the secretary back home, he is making a statement about the artifice of his project, about its place in the "history" of architecture, about history itself, and about the conventionality of aesthetic theory. So at least it can be read—and is read by the postmodernist reader.[6]

As Fredric Jameson has observed, postmodernism seems always to be understood as some sort of "radical break" with *another* moment of socioeconomic organization and cultural and aesthetic orientation.[7] It is defined against that which it is not, against conditions that no longer prevail or are somehow irrelevant. For Marxists like Jameson, it is rooted in a "consumer society" that differs structurally from other moments of capitalism.[8] I stress "another moment"—"other moments"— for postmodernist theorists seem to be particularly concerned with the relationship between postmodernism and modernism. Although some see postmodernism as simply following modernism, others, who are anxious not to succumb to "the illusions of history," attempt to describe the relationship between modernism, or romanticism for that matter, and postmodernism in some more complex, often dialectical way. The Italian philosopher Gianni Vatimo likens the *post* of postmodernism to Heidegger's *Verwindung* and *Überwindung*. According to Vatimo, *Verwindung* is analogous to *Überwindung*—to overcoming—and yet different from it. Unlike *Überwindung*, *Verwindung* has no relationship to *Aufhebung*. It is the leaving-something-behind of a past that has nothing to tell us.[9] Postmodernism is then both part of, an extension, a sublation, of modernism and, despite the modernist traces (the detritus) it exploits, wholly different from it.

This concern with the *post* of postmodernism, with the relationship between one period and another, however arch it may seem to us, reflects a far-reaching discontent with—an epistemological anguish over—the conventions of historical, indeed, at times it seems, of any kind of understanding. Sequencing, the causal assumptions that underlie that sequencing, continuity, the experience that fosters that sense of continuity, selecting and framing of events, the theoretical understanding that sanctions that selection and framing of events, the adoption of an appropriate vantage point, the authority that authorizes that vantage point, are all questioned. The skepticism appears here to be as thorough but by no means as terse as Hume's. It is clotted theoretically; it lacks Hume's ultimate confidence. It does take a certain delight—some critics would say nihilistic delight—in the impossibility of any universal understanding, any incontestable truth, any indefeasible argument, any ultimate authority. God is surely dead in the postmodernist world. There is, as Lyotard remarks, no faith in metanarratives that legitimate science and other totalizing (emancipatory) visions of the world.[10] Included among these are the Marxist and the psychoanalytic, which in their causal overdetermination, in their totalizing assumption, resemble the magical systems Levi-Strauss describes. I would also include the quasi-articulate, commonsensical stories we tell ourselves about everyday life that assume meaning, totality, progress, and emancipation. These metanarratives are as subject to deconstruction as their narratives of reference.

When I write that God is dead in the postmodernist world, I am at once playing with a popular postmodernist conceit—Nietzsche is of course a postmodernist hero—and making a very serious point about the world the postmodernist postulates. I am referring to the authoritative function—elsewhere I have called it the Third—that mediates any interlocution.[11] In any dialogue, conversation, or exchange there is always an appeal to a complex, stabilizing authority that authorizes a particular linguistic code, a grammar, a set of communicative conventions, allocations of power among the interlocutors, criteria of intra-, inter-, and extratextual relevance, and appropriate interpretive strategies. This function is, in technical terms, metapragmatic, for it determines the way the communication indexes itself, its personnel, its context, and its possible interpretations. It is symbolized, I believe, abstractly by such notions as the law, grammar, or tradition, more concretely by totems and fetishes. It may be embodied by father, king, or priest—more rarely by female figures—by spirits and deities, and even by a third person (the audience) in any dyadic exchange. It may be appealed to directly or indirectly in any of its symbolic guises. In ordinary exchanges, it is usually taken for granted or easily negotiated. In some extraordinary exchanges—cross-cultural exchanges before they are routinized, for example, or exchanges during periods of crisis or, less well understood, creative fervor—there is no mutually acknowledged Third to whom rhetorical appeal can be made. When the Third is simply an empty function, there can be no communication.

The postcolonial world has been called postmodern: an off-centering juxta-position of contradictory styles that are not supported by any single, seemingly unified vision—or narrative—of the world. Observers stress surface, the spectacle, the multimedia nature of social life, its polyphony, its heteroglossia, the rapidity of change, the uncritical adoption of modern technology (from the pocket calculator to the submachine gun), the absence of historical awareness, the lack of compelling criteria for contextualization, interpretation, and understanding, the "protean" nature (to use an anachronistic term) of postmodern man, his lack of depth, his uncritical narcissism, his interminable quest for gratification. The description appears to be altogether too specular, too literary, like something out of Salman Rushdie, having more to do with the New York art scene, the Milan world of fashion, or the Paris bar in Berlin than with the pathetic conditions of a Bangkok slum where a man may wear a women's lib T-shirt, enslave his wife, spend his evenings in a brothel listening to Michael Jackson on a cassette recorder made in Japan, and hope his daughter will win a Miss Thailand contest so that he can open a little restaurant for workers in the center of the city and have his teeth capped in gold.

The post of postcolonialism is not subject to the same play, not yet at least, of the post of postmodernism. The past of postcolonialism is not yet a repertory of self-referential citations. For the postcolonialist the past evokes the imposition of a history, no doubt in alien form, that has been used, paradoxically, in the failed struggle to overcome that history, that imposition. It calls attention to the absence of voice—and what is worse, the absence of a responsive interlocutor. However real their source, phantasms, like ghosts, can never respond, not truly, for they can never add anything to what is already known. The past of postcolonialism is the past of the Aufhebung. It cannot be overcome. It cannot be controlled by citation. It cannot yet be reduced to trash, the trace, the *pseudo-trace. It is too painful. Like the shoddy borrowings of that other culture, those cultures of reference, the polyester shirts, the tinny transistors, the expired penicillin, and the Mercedes Benz, it calls attention to difference—difference framed in equality—and the locus of power that perpetuates that artifice of equality.*

There is of course considerable truth in the postmodern vision of the world despite its overgeneralizations, its literariness, and its loose associations. It challenges us. It can be neither simply accepted nor simply rejected. This results less perhaps from what it says than from how it says it, and this we find particularly disturbing. Postmodern discourse, at least the discourse that comments on it, not only entangles primary-level discourse with secondary- or metalevel discourse, but it confounds description with prescription. Insofar as it is descriptive of a state of affairs, we are free to accept or reject it according to its accuracy, its truth value, but insofar as it prescribes (programmatically in the works and writings of architects like Paolo Portoghesi or in the commentaries of Hutcheon and others) a particular orientation toward reality, including perhaps the rejection of those metanarratives that justify our criteria of accuracy and truth, we can neither accept nor reject it according to accuracy and truth.[12] We can take a moral, or even a political, stance toward its prescription, but again, insofar as the prescriptive is confounded with the descriptive, we can neither accept nor reject fully the prescription. We are confronted, or more accurately, incorporated, into a totalizing hermeneutic—a sort of epistemogical antinomianism—that rejects totalization, questions the authority of any hermeneutic, and refuses any transcendental position.

Now, let me do precisely what the postmodernist rejects. Let me take, arbitrarily, an *external* vantage point. They do, despite themselves. Let me suggest that what the postmodernist describes/prescribes is the result of a change in the manifest articulation of power relations—the result of a failure of hegemony—that creates the illusion at least of an anything-goes egalitarianism at the discursive level. (I stress "the discursive level" since I am not arguing that there is in fact today a "real" egalitarianism or a "real" hegemonic failure. It may well be—the Marxist would certainly argue the point—that discursive egalitarianism, hegemonic failure, and all this self-reflective talk about postmodernism are in fact contemporary mystifications, a bit decadent no doubt, of real class relations.) There is, in the terms I used earlier, no stabilizing Third in any dialogic engagement to which a final appeal may be made. It is not that the Third qua function is rejected, but it is depleted—not completely, however—of its pragmatic force. Its symbols become rhetorical, but not fully. Depleted, symbolically reduced, the Third is still "required" for any successful communication. This is one of the sources of the tension we find in the commentaries on, if not the discourse of, postmodernism itself: the strained conflation of the prescriptive and the descriptive. Herein lies a danger: assertions of sheer power, uncritical declarations of a correct version, if you will, of reality, fevered affirmations of maimed symbols. These are of course the characteristics of that other discourse, that other movement, that seems to accompany the postmodern: fundamentalism. I do not refer here only to religious fundamentalism but also to ideological and scientific fundamentalism.

The evacuation of the Third and its symbolism, the breakdown of authoritative conventions of communication, and the consequences of this evacuation, this breakdown, if it does in fact occur, have yet to be examined on the ground. Postmodernists, even in their descriptive mode, are given to largely unsubstantiated generalizations. From careful, clever readings of literature and the arts, they generalize to a "reality" and read that constituted reality as though it were empirically real or simply another "text." It seems likely that it is in declaredly egalitarian cross-cultural contexts, particularly those that are not yet routinized or have resisted routinization, in which the discursive conditions that are reflected in the postmodern outlook are most salient. As any good anthropologist knows, the communicative conventions of all the participants in a sensitive, cross-cultural encounter are always put into question, and the progression of such encounters is largely determined by the response to this questioning. The threat may be denied. Established conventions may be reaffirmed and enforced. New conventions may be negotiated. The communication may be ended. In most such encounters all of these responses occur over time.

By "an egalitarian dialogue," I refer to an exchange between participants who presume with whatever illusion or pretend that they are equals and have equal rights in the exchange. This dialogic egalitarianism may in fact be purely ideological, a mystification of "real" differences in power, and these real differences may— certainly do—affect the plays of power that occur within the egalitarian-framed dialogue. The framing—the convention, the pretense—of the dialogue is not of course without its effect. Itself no doubt determined by power relations exterior to it, the framing constrains the way these external power relations are given or denied expression. There is a double indexing that occurs within any exchange: an intra- and extradialogic indexing of the participants, for example, as equal within the dialogue but as unequal outside the dialogue, in real life, as we say. The difference may be masked metapragmatically by the dialogue's pretense. Court speech, diplomatic exchanges, conventional hypocrisy, and, of particular interest to us, those cross-cultural exchanges "between equals" in this postcolonial era that just a few years ago, during colonialism, were manifestly hierarchical are especially revealing of this double indexicality, but it occurs, I would argue, in all exchanges.

Despite their pretense, the declaredly egalitarian, yet to he routinized, cross-cultural dialogues are never in fact between equals, for the absence of a fully governing convention, of a mutually acceptable Third, fosters hierarchy—a (silent) assertion of authority over, an "understanding" of the position of the interlocutor (or its opposite). There is little to mediate—to attenuate—the challenge that each participant, coming, as it were, from somewhere else, poses to the other. Whatever the reasons for the exchange and its continuation, whatever the source of its egalitarian pretense, the challenge of a different orientation, of a different cognitive outlook, and a different set of values that has to be reckoned with among equals, threatens the respective orientation, the stability, the outlook and values, of each participant. We are, in extreme cases, at the limit of relativist artifice and can well understand the appeal of one fundamentalism or another.

There are many different responses each of the participants can have to this challenge. One is to deny the challenge and play the game. A second is to seduce the other into one's own orientation. A third is to succumb to the other's orientation. A fourth is to negotiate a shared orientation. A fifth is to suspend the game. With the exception of the fifth, all of these have to be accomplished within the egalitarian pretense. No doubt all of these (again excepting the fifth) occur within any of these special exchanges. The danger of my formulatlon is that it presupposes a degree of lucidity and control that, I believe, is precluded by participation within any dialogue. Our language is intentionalistic and tends to weigh any description or analysis of interlocutory space, of the *Zwischenraum* or the *Zwischenzeit* of dialogue, by comparison with the actors and their intentions.

Here, recognizing the dangers of intentionality, I should like, nevertheless, to discuss two types of response to the other that occur in all dialogues, but particularly in the cross-cultural ones I have been describing. I refer to what Mikhail Bakhtin calls *stylization* and *parody*.[13] I will focus on parody. Both stylization and parody can be related to the challenge posed by the other and can reveal the witting and, more often, I suspect, unwitting assertions or denials of power that occur in such exchanges. In postmodern discourse, there are times when it is impossible for the external observer—the audience, including perhaps the interlocutors' self-reflection—to determine the hierarchical relations that lie behind these two stylistic responses. We end up with something like what the literary critic Gary Saul Morson calls metaparody and, I would add, metastylization.[14]

For Bakhtin, parody and stylization are double-voiced words, that is, words that are to be interpreted as the expression of two speakers. The words of one speaker are appropriated by a second speaker as the words of the first speaker but used for the second speaker's own purposes "by inserting a new semantic intention into a discourse which already has, and which retains, an intention of its own."[15] In other words, they are recontextualized, or, in Hutcheon's terms, "transcontextualized"—revised, replayed, inverted.[16] Such double-voiced words are—and here I quote Morson—"best described not simply as the interaction of two speech acts, but as *an interaction designed to be heard and interpreted by a third person* (or a second 'second person'), whose own process of active reception is anticipated and directed."[17] For Bakhtin the difference between stylization and parody lies in the relationship between the two utterances. In parody the relationship is antithetical; in stylization it is corroborative. Both are evaluative; both objectify, more so perhaps in parody than in stylization, the stylized or parodied discourse; both attribute symbolic value to that discourse. Stylization can be read as either an indication of submission to the discourse, the position, the authority, of the other or as a sign of mutuality. Parody is essentially hierarchical. It dominates its target. Unlike imitation, quotation, or allusion, it requires critical, ironic distance.[18] Though it is incorporative, it calls attention to difference. (*Parody* is derived from the Greek *parodia*, a countersong but also a song beside, a neighboring song.[19] It need not be comic. According to Morson, it must evoke or indicate another utterance, it must be antithetical in some respect to that utterance, and it must have a clearly higher semantic authority than that utterance.[20] Where the semantic authority cannot be determined, we have metaparody. Where we cannot determine the relationship between stylized discourse and its reference, we have metastylization. This indeterminacy occurs, I suggest, when there are no shared conventions of interpretation and evaluation.

These criteria of parody also apply to egalitarian, cross-cultural discourses. Insofar as the response is meant to engage with the other's "in some meaningful way," it has to evoke or indicate that response. The speaker has to use the other's language (as he understands it) in order to engage with him for whatever ends. But insofar as the speaker does not share the other's orientation and may well resist that orientation, his response is antithetical to the other's. It may in fact be marked as such, or it may only be "understood" as such (though I suspect that careful stylistic analysis will reveal some sort of antithetical marking where the response is only *understood* by the speaker as being antithetical). Insofar as the speaker accommodates to the other's language for his own purposes, his response has "higher semantic value" for him and may well be marked as such—that is, within the parameters set by the egalitarian pretense. In other words, at least at the level of understanding, the target is recontextualized and in its new context (ironically) evaluated.

More specifically, the other is recontextualized, most often, I suspect, stereo-typically, and his words are treated as symptoms of that stereotyped contextu-alization. We understand and evaluate his words because we know "where he is coming from." This process leads to a practical engagement with, or manipulation of, the other, justified often enough on crude utilitarian grounds, and precludes a real engagement with the other's point of view. In blatantly nonegalitarian cross-cuitural exchanges—during the colonial period, for example—the hierarchically inferior other's response presented, so to speak, only an administrative challenge. He was expected to respond, often did respond, was certainly taken to respond, by accepting, as best he could, the outlook, the language, of the speaker; that is, he was to respond—to learn to respond—corroboratively. That his response might well have been parodic was ignored. (Here I should note that the response of South

African Blacks to South African Whites is often understood by Blacks parodically and only occasionally so by Whites. They say the Blacks are being cheeky. Indeed, the Blacks have a tradition of parodying Whites, onstage even, as in the play *Wozu Albert.*) Where the commitment to the egalitarian pretense is, for whatever reasons, very strong, it may well be that no participant to the exchange can admit that his recontextualizing response to the other has higher semantic authority. It is this metaparodic situation that resembles the discourse the postmodernist postulates. It is, I believe, potentially a highly creative moment, one whose essential relativism forces us to recognize and reconsider the moral basis of our cognitive outlook that is so masked by taken-for-granted communicative conventions. It is an equally dangerous moment, for it can always stimulate backlash.

Here is an example of the type of exchange I have been talking about abstractly. It is rather more complicated, certainly not as pristine, as I should like. It occurred more than a year ago at an academic conference attended by American, Indian, and Chinese scholars. The Chinese, most from Beijing, had been active in Tienanmen Square and were in exile in the United States. One of them had just finished telling us about a greater individuation of the self in recent Chinese literature. After a somewhat disorderly discussion of her presentation, including frequent reference to the Chinese government's brutal reaction to the student protest, one of the Indian participants, a poet, spoke.

> Let me try to approach many of the things we have said this morning from a completely different angle. As you spoke, I have been thinking of the problem of violence and nonviolence in India. In many ways India faces, has faced, the same problems as China . . . and one of the things that we know in Indian literature and politics is the problem of—let me characterize it as Orientalism. Let me also say outright that it seems to me the way you presented the whole problem [of violence] seems to give in to the Orientalist paradigm set up for China by the West. This is constantly surprising to me coming from the Indian context. In a sense the self is one of the major themes of the Orientalist discourse about the Orient. Why pick up on this? Why concentrate on individualism? . . . In the Indian case, much the same thing happened, but it happened in the nineteenth century in alarming ways. Once India opened up, it picks up prepackaged ideas from the West, jumps on the bandwagon, and repeats, as it were, the history of the West . . . and loses its own cultural identity.

The Chinese reaction to his observations was immediate, violent, emotional. (Most of the Chinese participants were not familiar with the debates on Orientalism that Edward Said's work has inspired. Most of them did not have the command of English that the Indian poet did.) The American participants listened for an unusually long time before entering the discussion. The first respondent was one of the principal leaders at Tienanmen Square. He spoke angrily.

I don't think you will reform China according to Western patterns. . . . At the same time, I think no people can go their way only according to their own way, their own culture. Chinese can only develop in a Chinese way. But what we are trying to do, what we hope to do, is to introduce some concepts, some institutions [from the West] that will be useful to us—not all concepts and institutions.

The Indian poet interrupted with "a quick footnote"—one of his favorite expressions—about how in India being modern meant being Western, being traditional meant being tribal. He was in turn interrupted by a second Chinese participant who just managed to utter, "on the surface you are right, but actually you are not," before he was interrupted by a third, highly articulate Chinese man—I'll call him Wenzhong—who reiterated the leader's comment while emulating (parodying), so it seemed to me, the style of the Indian poet. (He spoke slowly, ponderously, using "we" as the Indian had and turns of phrase like "up-to-the-minute" and "wholesale borrowing" reminiscent of the Indian's "bandwagon" and "prepackaged.") His discourse was, so to speak, triple-voiced! It was very controlling.

When we introduced these up-to-the-minute concepts, we were quite aware of the danger of wholesale borrowing, blindly borrowing, copying, from Western models. We discussed their limitation. We were always aware of their [being] obstacles to Chinese culture. We see them on only a utilitarian basis or a basis of expediency. No, we study them, we scrutinize them for an essence that can hold out something for us, be healthily absorbed into the Chinese way, and play some positive role.

The Indian poet—he was now standing up—was irritated. A second Indian participant also stood up and tried to mediate, by paraphrasing with some critical distance his countryman's position. He concluded by contextualizing it, stereotypically, as an Indian propensity toward the mimetic—"the quoting of passage after passage of a Western text, encapsulating it."

I cannot pursue the discussion in detail. The Indian poet asked the Chinese if there was a Chinese equivalent to the Indian mimetic tradition. No one answered. A fourth Chinese participant from Taiwan, an outsider among the Beijing intellectuals, argued that one could not speak of a single Chinese response and said that he saw his own participation in Tienanman Square as a painful way of discovering his own selfhood. No one followed up on his observation. Wenzhong spoke again, offering the possibility of resolution by invoking the different historical traditions of China and India and their different relations with the West, but before anyone had time to respond to him, an American participant, the first to speak, seemingly oblivious to what was happening, offered a manifestly Orientalist view of how the Chinese often mistook the Western ideas they borrowed. He was ignored. The discussion turned to history and repetition, with references to Kierkegaard, without anyone noticing that "history" and "repetition," as understood by Kierkegaard at least, were distinctly Western. At one point I intervened, noting that "Orientalism" was a Western category. Several Chinese agreed; several ignored my intervention; the Indian poet simply asked, "So what?" There was no final resolution, though an American political scientist, a Frankfurt school Marxist, tried to mediate by invoking the inevitable progression of social change. He said talk about Orientalism was a red herring. What was important was the discontinuity that was occuring or would occur in India and China as it had occurred in the West with the development of modern capitalism (or some other economic arrangement), that this discontinuity, this break with tradition, would be painful.

After the meeting, there was a lot of talk about what had happened, and although I was not privy to most of it, what I did hear and overhear from Chinese, Indian, and American participants was an attempt to reframe the argument according to different historical traditions and responses to the West. History, evacuated of content, served rhetorically to preserve the "egalitarian tone" of the meeting. No one wanted to talk, for example, about notions of cultural confidence and cultural superiority or about feelings of losing one's cultural identity by being identified with another culture. No one took an ironic stance, noting that despite all the critical talk about, and the resistance to, "prepackaged," "up-to-the-minute" Western ideas, the discussion was in fact couched in distinctly Western terms.

The violence of the encounter stemmed, I believe, from the Indian poet's failure to preserve its egalitarian tone and thereby exposing its pretense. He had revealed the "superiority" of his own parodic response and broken the metaparodic illusion of egalitarianism. He had also revealed his own vulnerability, for though he made use of Western categories in a structurally parodic fashion, he did not have, so it seems to me, a critically ironic distance from them. The Chinese response, at first angrily confrontational, was in its own way parodylike, insofar as it evoked and was antithetical to the Indian's comment and assumed a higher semantic authority. There was, however, no compelling authority—not even Orientalism, certainly not the Westerners present—that could be appealed to to mediate, to reconstitute the egalitarian pretense. So serious was the betrayal that ironic understanding of the metaparodic situation was precluded, even in the retrospective accounts. No one wanted to analyze, at least semipublicly, the dynamics of the encounter. Only one alternative was left if the meeting was not to break off completely and if any claim to egalitarianism was to be preserved: namely, the appeal to a symbol, *history*, that was so empty as to pose no threat to any position. "Orientalism played itself out differently in India and China," one of the Chinese participants observed toward the end of the discussion and was seconded by the Indian poet and the Americans. History here becomes one of the maimed symbols of that metapragmatic function that I have referred to as the Third.

That history was the chosen symbol for preserving the egalitarian pretense of the meeting is significant. It is history—memory, I would prefer—that has been radically altered by the changes in discourse that the postmodernists have postulated. History, that is, *narratio rerum gestorum* and not *res gestae*, whatever that may be, is a positioned narrative that affirms among other things its position—hence its importance in nationalism, territorialism, and group and individual identity. History or memory or some objectification—some emblem or monument that stands for it—can serve as an authoritative reference point, whose artifice has been traditionally denied, in dialogues within one culture or across cultures when one of the cultures is manifestly dominant. Where there is a failure in hegemony, history can no longer serve as such a reference point, for each of the parties to an encounter has his own "legitimate" position, his own history, his own memory. The artifice of historical assumption—the incorporation of multiple positions into a single, consuming narrative—is revealed. The strain—to share or not to share, to be incorporated into or to remain independent of any historical tradition—is enormous. (Hutcheon stresses the ex-centricity of the postmodern outlook and the play between incorporation and differentiation in parody.) When universalist narratives, like the Marxist, lose their legitimacy as metanarratives, then history becomes an evacuated symbol of only rhetorical or pragmatic interest. Or again, there is always the possibility of some nationalistic, religious, racial, or ethnic appropriation—or invention—of a historical narrative whose encompassing authority is affirmed through ritual, through the sacralization of chosen, iconic events. We are of course familiar with these in the fascist states of the 1930s and 1940s, in White South Africa, and in many contemporary fundamentalisms.[21]

As a speculative coda, I should like to consider the relationship between new discursive—parodic and metaparodic—forms (or, perhaps more accurately, the privileging of existent forms) and memory, understood as a precipitate of these forms. (Hans-Georg Gadamer, writing in a different vein, asks us "to rescue the phenomenon of memory from being regarded as a psychological faculty and to see it as an essential element in the finite historical being of man." "Memory must be formed," he writes, "for memory is not memory for anything and everything."[22]) I suggest that insofar as memory is articulated in conventional forms, it, at least its expression, is constrained by these forms, and that when there is a change in a conventional discursive form, there will be a corresponding change in memory or its expression. In other words, memory is determined by the metapragmatic function, the Third, that determines how various communicative *Einstellungen*, or functions, including, notably, the intra- and intertextual, are indexed.

Traditional, empirical approaches to dialogue have assumed the continuous identity of the participants and have regarded dialogue as simply an alternation of speakers and hearers.[23] They have ignored what the Viennese poet Hugo von Hofmannsthal called the *allomatish*, the allomatic, the "mutual change," the *gegenseitige Verwandlung*, that occurs between two or more persons who are engaged in some way, say dialogically, with each other.[24] They have assumed, in other words, that Speaker A before hearing Speaker B's response is the same as Speaker A after hearing Speaker B's response, and no doubt this assumption can safely be made for most conventional conversations—for what Heidegger calls *Gerede*, or idle talk. But there are of course occasions, often dramatic ones, like conversion, a sudden insight, an epiphanous experience, a new way of seeing things, triggered by Speaker B's words, that radically change Speaker A's perspective, his understanding, his sense of self, his identity even. The dialogic situation becomes far more complicated. Speaker A (and in another way Speaker B) have now to reckon with Speaker A's previous dialogic incarnation, all that that incarnation symbolizes, and the challenge to (the artifice of) personal continuity it poses. (It may indeed become a symbol of the Third.) We ought perhaps to regard any conversation as an exchange not between Speaker A and Speaker B but between Speaker A prime, double prime, and so on, and Speaker B prime, double prime, and so on. It is the gap between the dialogic incarnations of each speaker that affords the space of memory—and forgetting. We must remember Nietzsche's observation: "Forgetting is no mere *vis inertiae*. . . . it is rather an active and in the strictest sense positive faculty of repression [*positives Hemmungsvermoegen*]." Forgetting as well as memory is implicated in the perduring self.

Hofmannsthal was writing about the allomatic, or, more correctly, trying to capture it, in *Andreas*—a novel he was never able to complete—and in *Die Frau ohne Schatten*, which took several forms, during a period of great discursive turmoil and invention. At this time another Viennese was developing a new discursive genre of revolutionary import, the psychoanalytic, and was also elaborating the most systematic theory of memory and forgetting we have ever had. Freud's theories of screen memories, of distortion, condensation, displacement, repression, foreclusion, and sublimation, which were largely discovered from within this new speech genre, can all be seen as ways in which an individual negotiates the gap between his present self and his previous ones. Freud provided a compelling metanarrative for preserving the sense of continuity, which, paradoxically, was subverted, altered certainly, by the discursive form he invented.

We should ask what is happening today to memory, and by extension to history, if there is in fact a radical change in discursive forms and practices of the sort I have been describing and the postmodernist postulating. We do not live easily with our ghosts, with the traces of the past. We talk about a loss of history among young people, for example, as though it can be regained. We try desperately to preserve—and pass on—the memory of events, so often traumatic events, that we once found significant and perhaps still do, in another way, we know grudgingly, as they enter our personal and our collective rhetoric. We document them, we commemorate them, we memorialize them, to the point even of sacrificing ourselves to them. And particularly where we have no narratives that support our memory, we are left with only the truth of its evacuation, its rhetorical reduction, and the certainty of the artifice of our documentation, commemoration, and memorialization. We understand despite ourselves the enchantment of retrogressive movements, like the fundamentalism, the racism, and the nationalism to which I have referred obliquely, and we know the risks of such enchantment. We have to recognize the inescapable dangers—and the extraordinary creativity—of those discursive changes that trouble our complacency, and we have to resist the facility, the cant, with which they can be described and ultimately reduced.

Those who argue that postmodernism does not reject history and those who argue that it does miss the point. *History* is no constant. It is a discursive practice, subject to change, that presupposes a particular temporal organization and bears a particular symbolic (existential) weight. It changes as discursive practices change. If there is any truth in Lyotard's contention, for example, that the citations of past architectural forms in postmodern architecture are like diurnal residues in the dream, then it follows that the "history" that arises from such citations has a radically different temporal organization than that of our traditional narrative histories.[25] It is autonomous, closed in on itself, frozen. The unconscious, the dream, knows no time, Freud tells us. We are not particularly comfortable with this history. Nor are we comfortable with the Roshomon effect of the dialogically open, self-questioning, multiperspectival histories that are appearing today.[26] We may delight in the artistry of their montage, but underlying this delight is, I believe, anxious nostalgia for the modernist preoccupation with the wounded tales of emancipation. Benjamin observed that it was "common practice in the literature of the baroque to pile up fragments ceaselessly, without any strict idea of a goal, and, in the unremitting expectation of a miracle, to take the repetition of stereotypes for a process of intensification."[27] Benjamin's words can also be applied to the postmodern, that is, if one erases but does not expunge "the unremitting expectation of a miracle." Would this erased miracle be the return of the Third—*our* Western hegemony—and the capacity to escape metaparodic indeterminacy by knowing whose parody is empowered? To repeat? The parody and metaparody I have described are serious.

The Emergence of
Language from Dialogue

John Dore

Bakhtin has inspired researchers in several traditions to reconsider some of their most entrenched beliefs. His work has had an especially strong impact on those who approach language from a structuralist perspective. After having been trained in the tradition of structuralism, I have been persuaded by Bakhtin to reexamine some fundamental assumptions about the origins of language in the mind of the child. Rather than assuming that the greater part of language is explainable via a small set of mental structures, I now view language as emerging from a primarily social context. The psychologist Lev Vygotsky proposed this view long ago, but Bakhtin's concepts of genre, voicedness, dialogue, and discourse expand upon this view considerably. This essay argues for a reversal of one of the most basic beliefs about child language: Rather than simply claiming that "children acquire language," I argue that it is equally true that "language acquires children."

The history of child-language studies can be seen as a struggle toward clarity about two major issues. The first concerns the conceptualization of language itself: Which terms best describe the phenomenon of language?—or in other words, Whose theory will hold sway? The second issue is, given some set of theoretical terms, how do we know what a child's language abilities are at any given moment of development? This concerns the methods we rely upon to reveal exactly what is changing in the speech produced by a child at the time we are analyzing. In this essay I will examine the pre-sleep monologues of a prolific little girl. Not all linguists agree that language must be described in light of its social conditions, and those of us who believe this vary in how much we are committed to the social determination of the child's language development.

Here I propose an account of how language emerges out of a social matrix. Regarding the corpus of a child's monologues and dialogues with her parents, my central claim is that her monologues "reenvoice" the features of dialogue that she experiences. This notion of reenvoicement is taken from a theory of the social dimensions of language, called dialogism, articulated in the works of Bakhtin.[1] Reenvoicement is a concept that replaces the reliance upon imitation on the one hand, and upon "sentence creativity" on the other, for describing language development.[2] Here I make the claim that reenvoicement takes place via the unit of analysis called the genre.[3] Thus, developments in this child's monologues are described here as changes in the features of genre they manifest. One implication of this analysis is that the language spoken by those close to the child influences language development at least as *much* as the child's genetic endowment does. Language is *between* speakers.

A general concern of this essay is to show how language functions and how it is structured in a recurring scene from one family's daily life. I begin by discussing some perspectives as background to the kind of theory that informs the data analyses. (The theoretical perspective proposed here derives primarily from insights proposed by Bateson, Vygotsky, and especially Bakhtin.) Then I describe the scene of putting the child to sleep from an ethnographic viewpoint. In large part the scene is a social struggle between the parents, who require that their child sleep alone, and the child, who resists this.

The data to be analyzed here are the speech productions of a little girl, Emily. They are in the form of conversations between Emily and her parents before she goes to sleep, and her talk to herself after her parents leave the room. The conversation is referred to as dialogue and the crib talk to herself as monologue. After proposing the units of analysis, I describe the features of the adults' talk in the dialogues. These features are primarily from the father's conversations with Emily, and they do not change much throughout the corpus. Then I analyze a pivotal example of narrative from one of Emily's monologues, using the same units, and compare it with the features in the dialogue preceding it. This comparison shows the influence of dialogue on Emily's monologues at this transitional period of her development. I then analyze three months of her earlier and her later monologues to specify what changes in the course of her development.

Background: Mind as Social System

Gregory Bateson conceived of "mind" as a cybernetic system of "messages" defined as transforms of differences traveling in circuits around the system. He described mental systems in general as having several properties: they process information by trial and error; they operate via feedback loops and mechanisms of comparison that allow for adaptive change; they are hierarchically organized in levels of learning and signaling; and they are self-corrective. But the "total self-corrective unit which processes information, or thinks and acts . . . is a system whose boundaries do not at all coincide with the boundaries either of the body or what is popularly called the 'self.'"[4] Rather, mind is immanent in the larger system of man plus environment, and "large parts of the thinking network are located outside the body" (320).

To illustrate a total "thinking" system, Bateson used the example of a blind man tapping his way along a street with a stick. He argued that the "stick is a pathway along which transforms of difference are being transmitted." If we are to explain the blind man's behavior, the total system of man, stick, and street must be involved. And "the way to delineate the system is to draw the limiting line in such a way that you do not cut any of these pathways in ways which leave things inexplicable" (459). Regarding the status of the "self" in such systems, Bateson made two points of crucial importance for this essay: First, that a "human being in relation with another has very limited control over what happens. . . . He is part of a two-person unit, and the control which any part can have over any whole is strictly limited" (267). And second, at the higher levels of learning to act in relation to the context of contexts, the "concept of the 'self' will no longer function as a nodal argument in the punctuation of experience" (304).

Depending on whether they are inside or outside of the body, the pathways along which "messages" travel differ, but not absolutely so. There is a certain amount of compartmentalization segmenting the system. But there is also a "'semiperme-able' linkage between consciousness and the remainder of the total mind. A certain limited amount of information about what's happening in this larger part of mind seems to be relayed to what we may call the screen of consciousness" (432). What gets into consciousness is highly selected. Bateson thought that there was little known about the rules and preferences of selection by consciousness, but that the limitations of language must play a role (444). Using the analogy of the map to its territory, he claimed that the "process of representation will filter it [the territory] out so that the mental world is only maps of maps of maps" (454). But he felt it was dangerous to attempt "to separate intellect from emotion" or "to separate the external mind from the internal" (464).

Bateson's notion of mind is useful in describing language, especially as language is involved in "thinking" and as it develops in the child's mind. Bateson himself spoke of language occasionally, usually as a symbol system (along with art, ritual, myth, and others) for organizing cultural experience. Although he offered no structural account of language itself, he stressed the need to describe "meaning" within a hierarchy of contexts: "The word only exists as such—only has 'meaning'—in the larger context of the utterance, which again has meaning only in a relationship. . . . without context there is no communication" (402). As discussed below, this view fits nicely with Vygotsky's theory of how language develops in the child's mind, and with Bakhtin's notions about how language functions. But here it is most useful to speculate about how some of Bateson's notions might apply to the language of our corpus. The following discussion is not a set of claims about the Emily data so much as a larger-scale theoretical framework through which the claims I will make below can be understood.

Emily and her parents form a kind of cybernetic system of feedback loops. They form a sort of "collective mind," a "mind" that strictly circumscribes whatever is "in" Emily's mind. "Messages" circulate among them in the form of words, tones, and narrative story lines. These forms are transformed as they move among the members of the system. From this perspective Emily's monologues can be viewed as trial-and-error productions, hierarchically organized in certain linguistic units, operating as self-corrective feedback mechanisms, and adapting to related models of language forms used by her parents in the wider system of language they all share. Emily is only one part of the three-person language system of her family. Any control she may be able to exercise over her monologues is strictly constrained by the properties of the larger family system. Her consciousness is, I suggest, quite permeable to the expressed features of this system. Her monologues will inevitably be "maps" of her parents' larger "maps."

Now let us extend this discussion to include the work of a thinker who focused on child development. Lev Vygotsky proposed a theory describing how any higher intellectual function, such as language, could appear in the child's mind. He offered the example of how an infant's grasping for an object becomes the communicative act of pointing. At first the infant struggles alone to reach an object by grasping toward it. When a parent observes this, she interprets the gesture as indicating something. She assumes that the infant is pointing to a particular object and that he wants to receive it. "Consequently," Vygotsky argued, "the primary meaning of that unsuccessful grasping movement is established by others. Only later, when the child can link his unsuccessful grasping movement to the objective situation as a whole, does he begin to understand this movement as pointing."[5] For Vygotsky the meaning of any language unit can emerge in the child's mind only by means of such social collaboration in objective situations.

Vygotsky theorized that "the process of internalization consists of a series of transformations." First, "an operation that initially represents an external activity is reconstructed and begins to occur internally" (56–57). Second, "an interpersonal process is transformed into an intrapersonal one." And third, this transformation is "the result of a long series of developmental events." That is, intellectual functions that take place at first between individuals are transferred to inner processes and "are incorporated into a new system with its own laws" (57). A recent retranslation of Vygotsky clarifies his position and provides an important vantage point for viewing the Emily data: "Speech for oneself has its source in a differentiation of an initially social speech function. . . . The central tendency of the child's development is . . . a gradual individualization that emerges on the foundation of the child's internal socialization."[6]

Elsewhere I have argued that this model of development accounts for the emergence of word meaning in the child's mind based on the process of dialogue with parents.[7] Although the present case concerns larger units of language, I suggest that Vygotsky's theory applies, to a point, here as well. The "initial external activities" that serve as models for Emily's monologic narratives are her parents' narratives in their dialogues with her. Emily tries to "reconstruct" these internally, transforming what was an external process of narrative in dialogue into an internal process of monologue. But in order for her to establish "a new system" of her own narrative structures cognitively, she must undergo "a long series of developmental events," namely, successive attempts at reformulating monologic narratives. The challenge here is to show the "gradual individualization" of her narratives—to show how her monologues are reflections on dialogues, sometimes reproducing dialogic segments almost exactly, while at other times refracting (or otherwise assimilating) them through her own newly emerging internal system.

Speech Genres: The Organization of Discourse Meanings and Functions

Speech has most often been analyzed structurally, with reference to language as an abstract system, most notably as a grammar. But speech, of course, serves numerous functions, and a grammar is not a theory of these functions. The structural properties of sentences tell us little about how utterances express intentions, acts, and social conventions, much less about how they express emotions, motives, attitudes, and social stances. Yet since speech works simultaneously as both structural knowledge and social function, we need a unit of analysis that captures both structure and function simultaneously. Vygotsky proposed that the minimal unit of the analysis of thought and language that met this criterion was "word meaning," since it reflected both the conceptual and the linguistic aspects of words.[8] Beyond the word level, previous analyses have usually kept structural and functional analyses separate: for example, an utterance might be seen as having a sentence containing a proposition on the one hand, while expressing a speech act (attitude or intention) on the other.[9]

For describing the Emily corpus we need a larger unit, one that provides for the analysis of narrative sequences in monologues and dialogues. A unit that captures the overall functioning of narrative and conversational sequences is the "genre." Some ethnographers have identified different types of genres. Dell Hymes, for example, described the "complex genre of a church service" as comprising "elementary genres" such as sermons, hymns, litanies, psalms, and so on.[10] Erving Goffman apparently had a similar notion in mind when he spoke of "frames" of talk, where some "key" will shift the frame, affecting the way in which some strip of talk is done.[11] And a genre in this sense functions as one of the kinds of context that Bateson had in mind when he argued that an utterance can have meaning only in its relationship to a larger communicative context (402).

But the most extensive treatment of the genres of everyday speech is to be found in the work of Bakhtin. According to him, "speech genres" are "relatively stable types" of organization for the "thematic content, style and compositional

structure" of utterances as expressions.[12] A set of speaker assumptions and expec-
tations, of emotions and attitudes, are expressed, primarily through intonation, by
the genre in which one speaks. A speech genre is the central functional mode for
the analysis of sequences of speech. In scope a genre may range from a single retort
in conversation to the tone of an entire formal speech. But in the data analyzed
here the same speech genre will cover several successive sequences of utterances.
In the literature on child language the phenomenon that comes closest, at least
to the stylistic aspect of a genre, is "baby talk," that is, the register of talk in
which adults simplify, repeat, differentially intone (with higher pitch, elongation,
emphatic stress, and so on), and otherwise tailor their speech to young children.
But baby talk has not been proposed as a unit that organizes the style, content,
and structure of adult speech to children. Moreover, in our corpus the adults mix
baby-talk features with those of a more adultlike talk. So a certain interweaving of
genres occurs.

A genre in Bakhtin's sense is a functional format for organizing content, style,
and structure simultaneously. It is a routine means, sometimes even a ritual way,
of accomplishing a verbal interaction. The dialogues of our corpus manifest a
strictly circumscribed set of styles, contents, and structures; the forms of this talk
are determined by the kind of social scene they are motivated to achieve. The
actual scenario of putting Emily to bed is enacted through several genres. These
are complex genres, which are made up of several kinds of elementary ones. These
genres are not strictly ritualized, but they are fairly routine. And genre, I propose,
is what most deeply organizes Emily's speech.

This notion of genre must be distinguished from the social orders of the scene
and the scenario on the one hand, and from the internal states of individuals on
the other. When a scenario is actualized in a scene, the actualization is typically
performed in varying mixes and levels of genres. An individual may bring any
number of conscious intentions and strategies to a scene, and probably brings
many unconscious motives and needs as well. For example, in the dialogues to be
analyzed it seems to me uncontroversial to say that Emily's father is motivated to
get his child to go to sleep, and that he often uses the strategy of promising her
rewards if she does so. Similarly, Emily is presumably motivated (though perhaps
less consciously) to keep her father in the room, possibly for fear of being alone;
and she accomplishes this by continually questioning him, eliciting repetitions,
crying, pleading, and otherwise delaying him.

These internal phenomena are not the object of study when we analyze the
genres of speech. Nor does the specification of genre appeal to any pragmatic
explanation of the participants' purposes for interacting. A genre is (before it
can be internalized) a social performance, requiring recognition, uptake, and
collaboration in order to be sustained. It is thus explicitly displayed by interacting
members, even when the "speaker" is writing to an "audience." Genres orchestrate

the themes, styles, and discourse structures and functions of a scenario. And in the case of a child's emerging monologues with herself, various pieces of content, structure, and style are what gradually evolve into the organized format of a recognizable genre.

The notion of genre proposed here is the functional counterpart to grammar. While sentence structures are organized grammatically, discourse functions are organized generically. However, a grammar operates with a fixed set of syntactic rules, a systematic set of semantic meanings, and a narrow array of phonological realizations. Genre, in contrast, organizes dynamically shifting sets of fluctuating meanings, of situated messages, and of varying discourse functions.

Genre can be viewed as analogous to Wittgenstein's notion of "family resemblances."[13] When we look for the common meaning among the uses of the same word form, as with the word *game*, for example, we do not find an exclusive set of conceptual criteria or semantic features shared by each use of the word. Rather we find something like "fuzzy family resemblances," enabling us more or less to recognize a meaningful use of the word when it is extended to refer to a new object. Similarly, the set of thematic, stylistic, and structural features that constitute a genre often vary widely from one occasion to the next. For instance, while content and structure may vary, a speaker may persist in the style of the same genre nevertheless.

This is so because there seem to exist wide arrays of options available to be actualized in the three components of genre. Within each component of theme, structure, and style there are elementary genres that together constitute the larger and more complex genres. Moreover, unlike the rather limited variations of grammatical speech, genres are less fixed formats for organizing the situated functions and momentary meanings in a conversation. Also, in everyday speech grammatical expressions are rarely too complex to be decoded, and speakers of the same dialect rarely have difficulty in understanding one another grammatically. But multiple genres are typically woven together in ordinary conversation, and the quality of experience needed to recognize the more subtle features of genre shifts differs from one person to another. Because of all this complexity, it takes years for a child to acquire consistent control over genre formats. In fact, it is not likely that such complex formats could be acquired at all without enormous amounts of specific socialization in the ways that speech can be used. This subtlety of genre formation is quite challenging, not only to the child learning language but also to the analyst trying to describe it.

The Family Scene and Its Emotional Significance

In order to appreciate fully the relations between dialogue and monologue in these data, we must understand the nature of the scene in which this talk occurs. The central fact is that Emily is being put into her crib for a nap or a night's sleep. It is a necessary scene of family life. The activity to be accomplished is that Emily lies down to sleep and her parents leave the room. We must appreciate that this entire activity could be accomplished silently: placing her in the crib and exiting through the door could do it. And this scene must indeed be done this way in other cultures, in other families, and perhaps at times in this family. However, the encouragement of talk is a primary ethnographic fact in this family's life.

We can ask, then, what these dialogues accomplish. And the prima facie answer is that the dialogues negotiate the conditions for going to sleep. The central fact for Emily is that she must sleep alone; and the father, whose "job" this is, must leave the room. Many other conditions are also negotiated. Among the required conditions are that the door be closed and the light put out, that Emily stay in her crib, and that she not cry. There are optional conditions as well: she may lie down at one end of the crib or the other, may have a blanket on, may have "friends" (toys) with her, and may request other conditions, such as having the shades shut.

All of the above facts are explicitly discussed by family members, but much else also goes on. The parents answer Emily's questions; they perform naming routines (of her "friends," of objects in the room, of their colors, and so on); they make lists (of who is sleeping, of who is "big" versus who is a "baby," of who is coming to visit, of where they will be going when she awakes, of what they will buy, and so on); they engage in baby talk, apparently for solidarity and emotional alignment; they describe events, sing songs, explain rules, and so on. Moreover, the parents sometimes cajole, indulge, and placate Emily. They make promises of "fun" to come after she sleeps; they try to convince her of the rationale for sleeping. Emily often cries in anticipation of the parent's departure, and she persists in asking questions, naming things, requesting repetitions, and, in general, resisting being left alone to sleep.

Obviously a good deal more is being done in the dialogues than the verbal pleasantries of taking leave of one another. The emotional significance of being left alone to sleep is great for Emily, as is evidenced by her frequent crying, delaying the talk, lingering on topics, refusing conditions of sleep, changing her mind, and much else. The practical necessity of getting his daughter to sleep is uppermost in her father's mind; this is evidenced by his persistence at the task, his occasional exasperation, and his frequent ignoring of what Emily says.

But there is a tacit contract, as it were, that the negotiation of the scene will be done civilly, even affectionately. The parents want it to be pleasant; for Emily it is often threatening. And herein lies the struggle at the heart of the discourse: how to accomplish the practical task at hand and at the same time preserve positive relations. In this respect the scene is like many other social encounters. But the emotional significance for Emily here is enormous. It is not only that she may feel abandoned by her parents each time she must sleep; at a critical, transitional point in the collection of our data a baby boy is born into the family. The mother is nursing him, which is apparently why the father is handling Emily at sleep time. All of this contributes to the considerable emotional impetus motivating Emily's talk, in both the dialogues and the monologues. Descriptively then, if metaphorically, the music of the father's rational rhythms (alternating with the sweet sounds of baby talk) clashes with Emily's plaintive cries and pleas, even screams, in their dialogues as well as in her monologues. I suspect that the emotionally charged style of her monologues is due to these conflicts, which may accelerate her growth.

Throughout these data, a certain scenario is played out in the dialogues before Emily goes to sleep. That scenario may be schematized as follows:

1. *Negotiatory*	*Obligatory*	*Promissory*
2. (First/now)	(When/if)	(Then/after)
3. We talk about X	You/Em sleep	We go/do Y
	I/Dad leave	They come/go Y

The first line labels phases of the drama that is often played out in the Father-Emily dialogues. The three phases are optional talk about an array of routine topics, an obligatory component about sleeping conditions and the father's departure, and a promise of things to come. The X on line three represents several kinds of talk routines (naming colors, labeling toys, answering questions, and so on). The negotiation of the conditions for sleep (blanket, toys, and so on) is virtually obligatory. And the Y at the end stands for such promises as going shopping, visiting playmates, making breakfast, and several others.

I call this the sleep-bargaining scenario, and it is often actualized by a complex weave of genres. At this level of generality the pre-sleep talk genres might be comparable to "meal talk" genres, or "shopping talk" genres, and so on, where different rules and means for talking apply. That is, each complex genre can combine different structures and styles. The pre-sleep talk, for example, contains elaborate narrative, descriptive, explanatory, and promissory structures. These can be delivered in varying styles of singing, baby talk or a more businesslike adult talk, or even a mixed style of "adult-baby cajoling talk." As a further subdivision within this intermediate level, there occur even more basic elements of genre, such as naming, questioning, answering, and listing routines. Thus a shifting set of features of theme, style, and structure constitutes each genre.

Genre Descriptions of Our Data

When Emily was 23½ months old a remarkable shift took place in the coherence of her monologues. Before that time, though she produced many word forms in several of her monologues, the words that appeared in coherent sequences of narrative were far fewer than occurred later. A coherent narrative sequence is defined as any stretch of words that contains two or more clauses related semantically. These could range from "when Emmy wakes up, Carl come" at 22½ months to "Oh mother, no hat, mother. I am not wearing a hat. I got fancy clothes, see, mother" at 25½ months.

Figure 1 displays the first three months of this data analysis, at half-month intervals, in terms of the percentage of words that occurred within coherent sequences in Emily's monologues. That is, the total number of words produced in each monologue was divided by the number of words that occurred within coherent sequences. So, for example, of 147 words produced at 22 months, 18 days, only 48 occurred in the 5 coherent sequences in that monologue, yielding a .33 ratio of words in coherent sequences. Compare this with the 157 words produced at 25 months, 20 days, of which 114 occurred in 12 coherent narrative sequences, yielding a ratio of about .73.

The dialogue and monologue of 23 months, 15 days, at exactly the time when the shift in Emily's coherence took place, are especially revealing. This point in her development shows the closest connections between the dialogue she hears and the monologues she produces. Before this time she can barely reenvoice in her monologues what she hears in dialogue. After this time she becomes more and more able to reenvoice the features of dialogue in her own monologues. A thorough analysis of the features of genre in the data for 23 months, 15 days (called the Childworld episode) will show how closely monologue can reenvoice dialogue. After this is clearly shown, I will look at Emily's early and later monologues to see how reenvoicement develops.

Following Bakhtin, we can describe the features of genre of the father's speech in the Childworld dialogue in content, style, and structure. Now, for the sake of coherent analysis, I propose that for these data the three components of genre are construed as follows. Content concerns the primary "propositional themes"; in this case the father's first long narrative is about "buying," and the second is about "crying." These predicates of "buy" and "cry" organize the content of his utterances about what is to be bought and who does the crying. The two major themes of his talk, then, might be concisely stated as follows: "We buy X on Saturday at Childworld"; and "Little kids cry, but big kids don't." Example 1 in the appendix to this essay codes the dialogue.

For these data two styles of talk are systematically identifiable: baby talk and (for lack of a better contrasting term) adult talk. These styles are manifested primarily through prosody, but at times the lexicon and syntax also mark a style shift. For example, looking at the father's first Childworld narrative, we see these features of baby talk (called the BT style): he whispers, "We're gonna go"; repeats "we're gonna" four times; uses a slow rhythm of speech, with unusually long pauses between and within phrases; sustains a cadence with emphatic stress on

Figure 1. Percentage of words appearing in coherent sequences, Emily's monologues, 22 months, 17 days–25 months, 17 days.

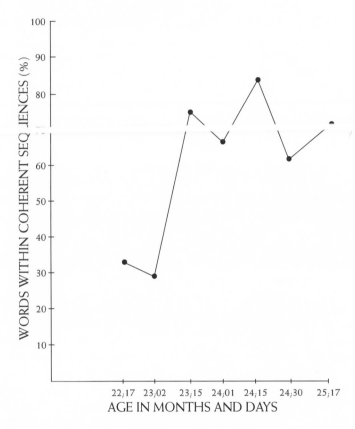

words like "diapers" and "Stephen"; elongates the ("wavy") intonation of words like "house" at the ends of clauses, and so on. However, there is a shift away from this slower, simpler, cadenced BT style toward a more rapid and complex adult talk (AT style) when he introduces the word "intercom," follows it with the "so" clause, and then gives the "upstairs-downstairs" explanation. The successive repetitions of the "buy at Childworld" theme have closely analogous patterns of BT rhythms punctuated by occasional AT features. In a still more subtle mix, in the third round of the Childworld narrative, the father uses an extremely wavy intonation on the "inter" syllable of "intercom," as if to make it more accessible to Emily through the BT style.

The third component of genre, what Bakhtin called compositional structure, is close to what is referred to today as discourse structure. There are two sorts of discourse structures. Narrative structures are those relations that connect the parts of long speech monologues or of written prose, ranging from connections such as causal, temporal, and locative among clauses in sentences, up to the plots and story lines that organize paragraphs and larger units. And the second sort of discourse structure is the exchange structure found in conversation: for example, question-answer, summons-response, statement-acknowledgment, command-compliance, and the other "adjacency pairs" that organize conversation.[14]

In the first part of the Childworld episode Emily's father structures his discourse in the following way:

Question	You know what we're gonna do this weekend?
State	We're gonna go . . . to Childworld . . . and we're gonna buy . . .
List	diapers for Stephen, and . . . Emily . . . an intercom system
Explain	. . . so that we can hear Stephen . . . downstairs
Evaluate	. . . it's neat. You're gonna like it.

So in three repetitions of this Childworld narrative we see the "buy" theme take various objects ("diapers," "intercom"), various temporal phrases ("this weekend," "on Saturday"), and various explanations of how the intercom system will work. Stylistically, these narratives are delivered primarily in the BT register, punctuated briefly by the AT style around the "intercom" object. And structurally the five discourse categories described above are repeated, but Emily supplies the initial request or question in the last two rounds.

This kind of organizational format, integrating theme, style, and structure, is a clear and fairly simple example of a speech genre. It can be labeled a "promissory genre" because of the simple thematic content, the predominance of baby talk, and the structural boundaries of promising to take Emily to an interesting place she will like, if she goes to sleep.

Example 1 in the appendix is a transcript of the entire Childworld dialogue, coded for style and structure. The themes are clear from the text itself. The father initiates the two major themes of buying and crying. Emily collaborates in these themes with requests, questions, repetitions, and extensions. She also repeats a "sleep" theme five times, and she mentions blankets and alligators. Stylistically, only the father's speech is coded: each time his tonal features shift between baby talk and adult talk, this is coded. For example, he begins with BT features in his repetition and agreement with Emily about sleep, using a high-pitched, slow, singsong intonation while elongating the first and last syllables of "Y-e-s you a-r-e"; then he shifts to the more tense, clipped, and rapid tones of AT in explaining the intercom system. The exchange and narrative structures in the speech of both

Emily and her father are coded. They begin with the standard exchange of the "state-agree" type, and then the father goes on to produce a "state-list-explain" narrative sequence.

The dialogue of this pre-sleep scenario exemplifies a weave of genres on the father's part, and Emily's minimal participation in these genres. Both of his extended "buy" and "cry" narratives begin when Emily is crying: his talk is at least partly motivated to stop her from crying. The genre function of the "buy" narrative is to promise Emily the reward of shopping at Childworld if she stops crying and goes to sleep (or, more precisely, if she allows him to leave the room without crying and talks to herself before sleeping). So I call this a promissory genre of speech since it is organized to prevent her from crying by supplying the entertaining information in the promise of shopping.

The second set of narratives, the "big kids don't cry" sequences, also begins as Emily is crying. But these do not entertain or make promises. Rather, they are in a more explanatory genre, containing as they do so many categorizations, contrasts, arguments, and explanations. Whereas the "explain" structure in the "buy" narratives is a secondary addendum to the "buy" theme, the "explain" structures at the end of the "command-state-list-contrast-explain" sequences of the "cry" theme are primary. Not only are the discourse content and structure of the "cry" narratives more complex, but stylistically there are more AT and more rapid alternations of BT and AT in them. Thus, while some of the same features appear in both sets of the father's narratives, the first "buy" theme is articulated in a promissory genre and the "cry" theme in an explanatory genre. The overlap of features weaves the two genres together.

Example 2 in the appendix is a transcript of Emily's monologue after the Childworld dialogue. It is not coded for style and structure, because although Emily's narratives do contain many of the empirical features of her father's genres, they are not yet stabilized in conventional genre formats. The purpose here is to compare the features of the Childworld dialogue and monologue in order to specify how Emily's monologue reenvoices features of the dialogue. An obvious early reenvoicement occurs when Emily reproduces her father's line, "We're gonna buy some *diapers* for *Stephen*, and some *diapers* for *Emily*, and we're gonna buy an *intercom* system," as her own "buy *diapers* for *Stephen* and Emmy and buy *sokething*." This is neither an imitation nor a creation of her own, but intermediate between the two. Emily reenvoices the theme of buying diapers, the structural feature of listing names, and the stylistic feature of emphatic stress on names of people and objects. She substitutes "sokething" for the complex word *intercom* and introduces all this with an apparently indirect quotation, "Daddy said."

Moreover, a subtler version of reenvoicement can be seen if we compare Emily's opening lines, "I member the . . . e- *D-a-d*dy said," with the father's "member what we said about big kids" in the dialogue. This example illustrates a different degree of reenvoicement, involving the blend of features in monologue from different genres in dialogue.

More globally, notice that this monologue reproduces first, in 1a and 1b, the minor theme of "sleep," which was one of Emily's own contributions to the dialogue. Then she reenvoices the father's "buy" theme (in 2), followed by a fragment (3) and her own "broken seat" narrative (4). And the monologue ends with her version of the father's "cry" theme (5 and 7), with a slight interruption by another fragment (6).

Stylistically Emily not only reenvoices the frequent emphatic stress on the same nouns stressed by her father, but she also adopts the cadence of most of his phrasing; for example, the rhythm of 2d ("buy *dia*pers for Emmy and *dia*pers for the baby") is virtually identical to the father's version, despite minor differences in content. Furthermore, Emily reenvoices close analogues of her father's exaggerated, elongated, and "rippled" intonation patterns. However, she often produces these patterns with words of her own. For instance, the father says "Y-e-s you a-r-e!" and "*house*" and "N-o-o-o" with quite dramatic melodies. Emily reproduces similar melodies in her monologue on "T-*a*-*n*ta's" (4a and d), "*any*body" (2g), and "*bl*-*a*-*n*kets" (1a), respectively.

In general Emily preserves her father's two major themes while varying the content within them; for example, she inserts word forms like "sokething" in 2b, "chocalik" in 2e, and "croutes" in 2i into phrase structures provided by her father. She places the "Saturday" and "Childworld" phrases later in the narrative, she drops complicated explanations, and she inserts her own "broken seat" theme.

Beyond the obvious borrowings of style and theme from dialogue in this monologue, there are numerous reenvoiced discourse structures, as well as a few structures that Emily introduces herself. Among the latter is her opening complaint in 1a: "I can't sleep with the *bl*-*a*-*n*kets." (Her father had put a blanket on her, and in the past this complaint had often brought him back into the room.) It appears at this point that Emily addresses this monologue to her father, but her "*D*-*a*-*d*dy said" mitigates this probability. Semantic anomalies such as this occur repeatedly in Emily's monologues up to this date. See, for example, "I went to sleep" in 1b. These anomalies, along with syntactic and narrative fragmentations in the monologues, make it diffficult to track her speech for discourse structures. In fact, overall, the utterances in her monologues fluctuate between reenvoicements of parental genres, attempts at her own themes, and fragmentations of both of these.

The reenvoiced structures in the monologue's segment 2 are evident: the lists of people, the repetition of "plug in," the paraphrase of "say ahhh" for the father's "we'll hear [Stephen] cry," the reduced statement "on Saturday go Childworld," the repeating of the predicate "buy" with lists of items, and the recycling of the whole narrative theme. Similarly, in segments 5 and 7 we see reenvoiced lists of the names of "big kids" (5a), statements (5b, 7c), contrasts (7a, 7f, and so on). Moreover, line 5a represents in microcosm the essence of the reenvoicement phenomenon. Emily begins with an apparently interrogative structure (the auxiliary verb *do*) as if to ask a question, then lists kids' names, but ends with the statement form "don't cry." Notice how this one utterance reproduces in fragmented miniature the father's dialogic sequence of structures: question-list-state. Yet in 7a she reproduces an almost flawless version of the father's argument—the contrast of "big" and "little kids" ("babies") and the explanation of who cries.

As for her own contributions, Emily says, "The big kids at Tanta's cry," in 7d, but then she contradicts this in 7f: "But the big kids don't cry." In addition, she attempts her own narrative, a conventional version of which might be "The infant seat was broken at Tanta's." But she is not yet able to sustain this theme in a conventional way, that is, to organize all the features of theme, style, and structure that a recognizable genre requires. This attempt is infiltrated by the father's stresses ("one") and tones ("*T-a-n*ta's") and is syntactically fragmented.

Even when Emily does not reproduce the same thematic content as her father (as in the "buy" and "cry" themes), she sometimes reenvoices his prosodic style with other content. The theme, style, and structure components of genre are separable in this sense. Each component is produced in the father's dialogues in a certain "shape"—a certain semantic, prosodic, and discourse shape. These are the inputs to Emily's hearing. Her monologues are characterizable as mixtures of repeated features of her parents' genres. She re-creates these according to her capability of the moment. And of course, she permutes the order of genre features in less conventional ways than her parents do.

More important, in order to understand the reenvoicement of the features of genre in monologue, we must see how the processes in monologue are analogous to the processes in dialogue. For example, Emily's Childworld monologue re-creates processes that are analogues of the processes in the Childworld dialogue: the successive rephrasings of the "buy" and "cry" themes, the successive listings of names, the same cadence and rhythm and distributions of emphatic stress and dramatic melodies. Even the mix of question, answer, and statement processes of dialogue is partially reproduced and permuted in monologue. So it is not the case that Emily merely imitates part of what her father said, or that she creates something entirely different from what was said. Rather, her monologues conflate these two overall processes of imitation and creation. She blends her own "voice" with that of her father.

Reen*voice*ment involves combinations of what Bakhtin called the "voices of authority" and "one's own internally persuasive voice." In this case we have the "official" conventional versions in the father's voices (his BT cajoling, his AT explanatory argument, and so on) and Emily's own efforts (her fairly clear contributions to the dialogue, and her underdeveloped genres in the monologue). In the dialogue she asks, "Who cries?"; she categorizes herself as "I big kids," extends her father's argument in "babies cry at Tanta's," adds "Linda" to the list of names, and so on. Her monologic efforts not only are longer and more complex but also mix pieces of her own dialogic contributions with those of her father; for example, segment 4 mixes her introduction of "Tanta" with her "broken seat" theme *and* her father's dramatic prosodic style.

Emily's own contributions to her monologue, apart from closely analogous reenvoicements of her father's features, are best described not as mistakes but as efforts to learn how to weave the features of genre together. For example, she generalizes the list of names to "*any*body," combining her own content ("any") with the father's stress style (*any*). Recall also that Emily asks the questions during the dialogue. So, considering the genre hypothesis proposed here, even a line like her "Do big kids like Emmy and Carl and Linda don't cry" is not a grammatical error. Rather, it is a blend of her voice (the questioning voice) and her father's stating-and-listing voice (*"Big* kids, like Donny and Leslie and *Carl* and Emily and Neil, they don't cry").

This analysis of the reenvoicement of the features of the genres in the Childworld dialogue in Emily's monologue of the same night reveals Emily's speech ability at that point in her development. What develops is not only the components of grammar (phonology, syntax, and semantics) but also the processes of genre (of thematic construction, of stylistic rendering, of discursive processes). If we look for fixed products, such as repeated sentences, or exact prosodic rhythms or imitated story lines, we will be misled. Features of genre are more fluid than the more stable features of grammar. One can produce a perfectly grammatical sentence (as occasionally happens in Emily's monologues of the first three months), but a perfect genre performance is a misnomer. Rather, speech is performed only as approximations of "ideal" genre formats.

Analysis of Earlier Monologues

The first monologue in the transcripts I analyzed was as follows:

Seven and eight-nine-ten . . . (little bit) seven *and* eight (?) ring around the rosey pocketful of posey . . . ashes ashes we all fall *down* [Emily banging crib] boom . . . boom pocka . . . and posey . . . ring around the ro-ey rosey pocketful of rosey . . . ashes ashes . . . all . . . fall . . . *d-o-w-n* ring around-a- . . . pocketful of rose . . . ashes-all-fall-down p- . . . f- . . . oh pocka . . . pocketful of po-ey . . . ashes as- (?) all fall down boom boom boom. (22 months, 16 days)

This monologue has several features that are essential for understanding Emily's monologues in general. It is entirely sung. It seems as if a melodic rhythm is established and then words are "backfilled" into it, as it were. In this monologue there is also an action corresponding to the words ("all fall *down*" followed by the banging of the crib), then an echo of that action ("boom boom"). This suggests that there is some amalgamation of word-action-echo in Emily's system of mental representation at this time.

Also, the initial phrase of the song, the conventional one, had to be imitated. In this sense it must be an imitation of the "voice" of another. Yet the singing of the numbers may not be taken from another, and the words sung at the end of the monologue are almost certainly not imitated. Thus we have the first weave of voices in our data. Another musical feature is the variations on a theme here: the two "number" phrasings vary, as do the "all fall down" phrases. We also see abbreviations ("p- . . . f- . . .") and other rearrangements ("pocketful of rose") of elements. Further, a few days later Emily's mother sings the first line of "Ring around the Rosey" in the midst of their dialogue before sleep, thereby weaving the voice of that song into their conversation. The mother reports that she and Emily had sung this song before.

Example 3 in the appendix gives some of the dialogue of the next day. After the father and Emily negotiate the "blanket" condition, the father promises: "And when you wake up we're gonna go to Carl's, but you have to go to sleep now." This is produced in a very high-pitched, rapid, singsong intonation. Emily's monologue that night following the dialogue suggests that at least part of Emily's monologue here is an attempt to reenvoice the father's promissory sequence. And further, other sequences are being worked out at the same time. That is, in addition to the core clauses of the promissory genre (Emmy wake, Daddy and Emmy go to Carl's, Emmy sleep now), there seem to be elements like "Emmy go/come in Daddy's car"; "Carl come then go"; "Carl sleeping"; "the baby coming"; "Emmy coming after my nap." Table 1 presents an abstract schema for comparing their talk.

In table 1 the clauses of the father's promissory sequence are numbered consecutively; we might abbreviate these as the "Emmy," the "go," and the "sleep" clauses. Emily uses these in her monologue as three frames in the narrative sequence. Her first two clauses use a reference to herself ("my") and the "go" from the second narrative frame; the third to fifth clauses reflect the "go" frame also, but she substitutes "come" for "go"; and the sixth and seventh clauses reflect the "sleep" and "now" of the third frame. Then her monologue roughly recycles the theme again. It seems she is struggling toward some formulation of a sequence that would be an analogue to her father's theme, but here she does not approximate it closely.

The theme produced by the father is in a promissory genre. But in the monologue Emily is trying instead to work out the theme of who is going (coming) where, and who is sleeping. Operations to note in the monologue are the following: She produces semantically opposed verbs in the same predicate slot ("go come") and then alternates them. She seems to paraphrase the father's "when you wake up" with "after my nap," adding the formulaic expression "not right now." She has "Carl

Table 1 Schema for comparing Emily's talk with that of her father.

Father's dialogue	Abstract schema	Emily's monologue	
1. and when you wake up	when Emmy (verb)	when my go come	1–2
		my go in Daddy's (?) car	2
2. we're gonna go to Carl's	X go/come Y	when Carl come	2
		then go to (?)	2
		go [Peabody]	2
3. but you have to go to sleep *now*	X sleep	Carl sleeping	3
		not right now	1–3
	X come	the baby coming	2
	Y	Carl coming m' house	2
	Z	Emmy coming	2
		after my nap	1
		not right now	1–3
		the baby coming *now*	2–3

come" instead of her father's "we're gonna go to Carl's." She says "Carl sleeping" instead of her sleeping, and "Emmy coming" instead of Carl. Then she lists names of who is "coming" (the baby, Carl, Emmy). Instead of the father's "sleep *now*," she produces "not right now" and "the baby coming *now*." In sum, in her monologue Emily doubles the verb slot, substitutes one object phrase for another, reverses directionality ("Carl come"), lists several names before her verb slot of "coming," interjects a formula ("not right now"), and introduces the theme of her brother's birth ("the baby coming now"). What is more, she ends with the same word and with the same emphatic stress on it as her father does in his version. These latter borrowings from her father, and the different analogues of the father's model in dialogue, reveal how this early monologue of Emily's reenvoices only small parts of the preceding dialogue.

In addition to more singing and people coming and going, waking and sleeping, the monologues, at 22½ months, show Emily both calling out to her parents and working out various statements to herself. At the end of that week, for example, a monologue begins with "I blew my nose [crying] I blew my nosey . . . Daddy clean my nosey. Clean my nosey! I need clean my nosey." So here she calls out to her father again, and she also refers back to their nose-wiping routines. Although this routine is not mentioned in our data, we can safely suppose that Emily is here again reenvoicing a family ritual.

By the end of the next week there are several new developments. She fantasizes that someone other than her parents will get her ("Dindo come and get Emmy"), thereby beginning to mix the imaginary ("Dindo") with her actual wishes (for her parents to get her). She recounts family scenes that may not have been discussed with parents; for example, referring to her mother's morning showers, she says, "So Momma all clean." She works toward formulating for herself descriptions and statements about other family rules: "I didn't drink my . . . this little bitty juice . . . I need drink my little bitty more juice . . . I need my juice." She begins to state her wishes clearly in her monologues: "I don't want to go nap!" And she relates these to "argumentlike" structures, as in "I don't need go nap today."

At almost 23 months, we hear her working out her next day's agendas: "Pretty soon Emmy get up and go Mormor's . . . Tanta's . . . house or Mormor's Tanta . . . maybe afternoon when my wake up." Compare this with the preceding dialogue: The father says, "You've got to be rested for tomorrow cause it's a Tanta day tomorrow"; Emily replies, "A Mormor day"; and the father concludes, "Maybe you'll see Mormor later but mostly a Tanta day tomorrow." It is this kind of collaboration with her father about the next day's events that becomes transformed into the apparently confused material of Emily's monologues ("Mormor/Tanta," and so on).

In the next night's monologue we see a shift back to more emphasis on melody (as a prosodic style) than on narrative continuity. Emily produces clear beats in melodic lines—for example, "kiss . . . kiss . . . kiss . . . mmm . . . mmm . . . mmm." She spells out the letters of words in song: "B-i-n-g-o." But in the same monologue she fails to sustain semantically coherent narrative lines. It is as if the melody (prosodic style) is worked out here partly independent of the narrative content (theme).

The next night's dialogue, at 23 months, 9 days, shows how Emily modulates her linguistic forms in line with her father's input. A dialogic exchange goes as follows:

E: I don't want boat
F: You don't want a what?
E: Boat
F: You don't want a boat.

The father provides the conventional form of the noun phrase with the "a" determiner, which Emily adapts in her monologue of that night. And she elaborates: "When my woke up, then Daddy come my went . . . out and took the boat out and took Emmy out in . . . Emmy the boat." In this monologue we also see the reenvoicement of conversational exchange structures: after she mentions "alligator," she says, "No-o-o . . . no . . . no . . . no . . . n- . . . n," which is the frequent response of the parents in the dialogues. Moreover, we see further signs of the opposition of Emily's voice to the parent's voice blended in rapid monologic succession. She says, "Now sleeping time. Now *not* sleeping time," as if to disagree with her parent the way she does in the dialogues.

The closest Emily comes to sustaining more than three semantically coherent clauses in the same narrative theme during this part of the analysis occurs a few days before the Childworld episode, when she says, "Now Emmy fix the bed. Tuck it down. And tuck it down. Tuck it down. Now over here." This reflects how she reenvoices talk rituals in monologue. The last phrase must be a part of how her mother or father talks while making a bed. Her monologues to this point, though they pervasively reenvoice bits of the parents' speech in all the ways described above, are still fragmented as recognizable genre performances.

Later Developments in Emily's Monologues

In the opening lines of the monologue after the Childworld episode, Emily finally succeeds in sustaining a coherent narrative for a familiar theme: "Oh Carl sleep in bed and Carl's daddy took the blanket back . . . and Carl didn't like that . . . Carl liked his blanket (a whole bunch) in the bed." There had been talk that night of blankets, as usual, but not of Carl's blanket or Carl's daddy or what Carl liked. Rather, Emily spoke of her own blankets, daddy, and likes. So at this point she can systematically substitute multiple items from dialogue in her monologues. The mother reports that they had talked about a "special blanket" that Carl had but Emily did not. Also in this monologue she first distinguishes several of her own blanket designs (another standard dialogic routine): "This is kinda blanket . . . Emmy blanket . . . her bear blanket and star blanket . . . mother goose goose blanket and some *n-e-w* blanket Daddy Mommy put the bl—." This list having been performed, however, she cannot yet add on coherent related clauses.

But at 24½ months related narrative themes begin to become woven together. For example, "Later when I wake up we put my jamas in the laundry and down in the basement they get *washed* . . . These okay but they're dirty . . . It's okay but they're dirty . . . and down in the laundry my (?) . . . After I take these jamas off I wear my red pajamas to *bed so* Mamma can wash these jamas." This narrative combines, first of all, a description of the clothes-washing scene with some dialogue typical of that family scene ("These okay but they're dirty"). Second, it makes a transition from the washing scene itself to a pajama-changing scene, while still preserving narrative continuity about washing.

Two weeks later, at 25 months, Emily struggles in a monologue to internalize some of her father's evaluations: "Cough really makes my better here . . . on my tomach. My back is *this* and my tomach is *this* . . . Oh good tomach ache oh . . . This is . . . good really good side my because it's really good . . . for Emmy . . . for Emmy *likes* this side." This monologue would be incomprehensible had we not had the father's talk in the dialogue: "It's better for your cough on the other side . . . That side is not good for your cough because what happens is that the stuff in your nose drips down into your throat and makes you cough and if you are on your *stomach* it's better." Not only does Emily work out the contrast between stomach and back and evaluate which side is better, but she also internalizes the father's preference by claiming to herself which side she "likes" better.

Two months after the Childworld transition, at 25 months, 18 days, we hear Emily weaving several voices in a dramatic reading. She had taken a book called *Dandelion the Lion* to bed with her, and it happened to be raining outside at the time. She begins: "I am Dande- (?) and it's raining outside and you better come outside with me. I am Dandelion. I want to come with you . . . 'Why don't you take out (?) because it's not raining' . . . 'I'll keep Dandelion. Mother' . . . 'Mother you *cannot* keep it' (?) . . . 'Now Mother' . . . Dandelion, I am coming to your party. I came already. It was good." So Emily merges lines from the book, facts from the context (rain), and dialogue she addresses to both her mother and Dandelion. Moreover, her voice tones shift to impersonate other characters in the book, and some utterances narrate other facts about the story in a more neutral voice.

These sophisticated developments far surpass Emily's efforts of her twenty-third month. At that point she could only minimally reenvoice a few features of genre components at a time. At the Childworld episode she reached a maximum of reproducing the complex sets of features she had heard in the preceding dialogue. After that she had apparently internalized enough of the abstract format of some genres to reenvoice them while using her own content or style or structure. By her twenty-sixth month her monologues weave together many voices, and Emily begins to coordinate more than one genre at a time.

Some Implications of Genre Theory

The theory of the speech genres of everyday life I propose here is meant to help us discover the "deep functions" of language. It provides some reliable tools for examining the functional organization of talk beyond the level of single utterances. It is a rich theory of discourse, capable of describing any exchanges in conversation as well as the narrative lines of monologue to oneself (perhaps even those chains of mental events we call verbal thinking, insofar as such data are available). In this sense the genre theory of language functioning fulfills Foucault's definition of discourse: "The concrete link between representation and reflection . . . the path by which representation communicates with reflection."[15] This is a theoretically useful way to understand Emily's monologues in particular: she is using discourse genres to work through what she can already represent on the one hand and her reflections on those representations on the other.

I propose the notion of speech genre as the largest manageable unit of linguistic functioning. It is Wittgenstein's "language game" writ large. The features of genre performance will be partly determined by the particulars of the social scene and the scenario in which it occurs. Each performance is actualized with a different set of features. This accords with Wittgenstein's point that the applications of word uses to new situations will continually vary. And it meets Bakhtin's sense of the "live utterance" as ever renewing itself. Genre describes the experience of speaking, not knowledge of language.

Apparently, the formatting of speech genres emerged in this child's mind in at least partial separation from grammatical development. We saw how Emily's monologues developed more sophisticated genre formats across time. Yet even in her later monologues there is a good deal of syntactic fragmentation, semantic anomaly, and phonological inconsistency. Also, one can imagine a child acquiring the structural properties of a grammar on the basis of limited speech input. However, learning something as subtle and variable as a genre seems to require much more "practice," that is, the ongoing experience of being in dialogue with others and of reprocessing the voices of dialogue in one's own monologic versions. Genre performance is less fixed, less stable, and less computational than grammar. It seems that the learning of genre requires more repetitions and routine productions, indeed even ritualizations, of varieties of talk in context than does grammatical learning.

Given the emphasis on the social determination of genre learning, if this theory has merit, we will have to reconsider one of the basic premises of linguistics. We all readily believe that "children acquire language" in some sense. We are less ready to believe that "language acquires children." Yet the genre conceptualization of what language is requires some such principle: that the agency that enables a child to speak ever more appropriately must extend beyond the child's cognitive capacity; genre meanings and functions are first co-constructed with more fully socialized agents of language (parents). The voices of others in close coproduction and coarticulation are involved not only in the child's social talk but in her thinking itself.

Linguistics needs at least a more deeply interactionist view of language development. Obviously, interaction must occur between the patterns of speech the child hears and the ability to internalize knowledge and skill about these. But many of the nuances of genre performance emerge in the child's speech long before she can assimilate them to any knowledge structure: consider, for example, the many "frozen" voices of others appearing in Emily's early monologues, long before they are integrated into her own versions of talk. Utterance meanings and functions become most alive when they pass from passive hearing to active speaking. We need a theory of what happens *between* speakers and, especially, a theory of the interaction between how the child acquires language cognitively and how a society acquires the child functionally.

Appendix

Example 1. The "Childworld" Text Coded for the Elements of Genre

Dialogue	Style	Structure
E: I sleep in here [crying]		State
F: You know—		
You're gonna sleep right there! Yes you are.	BT	Agree
You know what we're gonna do		
[Emily crying] . . .		
~~Y...~~		~~Q...~~
We're gonna go . . . to Childworld . . . and we're		State
gonna buy some *dia*pers for *St*ephen, and		List
some *dia*pers for *Em*ily, and we're gonna buy		List
an *in*tercom system, so that we can hear	AT	Explain
Stephen in different parts of the *house* . . .		
I think you're gonna like it because we'll be		Evaluate
able to hear Stephen downstairs when Stephen's		Explain
upstairs . . . It's gonna be a neat gadget . . .	BT	
E: Say that 'gain.		Request
F: When we . . . we're goin' to Childworld and buy		State
*dia*pers for *St*ephen, and *dia*pers for Emily,		List
and what is called an *in*tercom system, that		
plug in . . . Stephen, into Stephen's room . . . and		Explain
then we go downstairs and we plug it in . . .		
and we get to hear Stephen . . . we'll see who		State
wakes up . . . we'll hear him cry . . . through the	AT	
intercom system . . . It's a neat gadget.		Evaluate
E: Say again.		Request
F: One more time . . . and then we go to bed.		Comply/Command
On *Saturday* . . . we're gonna go to Childworld	BT	State
and we're gonna buy *dia*pers for *Em*ily and		List
*dia*pers for Stephen and an *in*tercom system		
so we can hear Stephen in different parts of	AT	Explain
the house . . .		
Good night . . . Hon. I love you.	BT	Leavetake formula
E: I sleep in here.		State
F: Yeah . . . I love you Sweetie.		Leavetake
E: [crying] I want [crying]		
F: You want . . . you want that right like that?		Question
That's fine . . . Hon.		Evaluate
E: [crying]		
F: Okay, night-night.		Leavetake
E: [crying] I wanna sleep in there . . .		Request
F: Night-night . . . Sweetie . . . I'll see you in the morning.		Leavetake
E: I wanna sleep in there [crying].		Request
F: Now, remember, y-, remember, Emily what we	AT	Command

Dialogue	Style	Structure
said about . . . member what we said about big kids?	BT	Question
Big kids don't cry, do they?	AT	Tag question
E: I big kids, the b-l-a-nket.		Request
F: What do you want Daddy to do with the blanket?		Question
E: [crying]		
F: You know *Carl* doesn't cry . . . Hon	BT	State
E: [crying] (?) Alligator		
F: N-o-o-o. There's no alligators. You know . . .		Disagree
would you like to have the blanket on *top* of you?		Question
Would that be fun? Let me show you . . .		Request
I can take this pretty blanket and put it on *top* of you.		State
E: [crying]		
F: Now remember, Em. Know when I say	AT	Command
[whisper] *Carl* doesn't cry, and *Carolyn*, and *Neil*	BT	List
doesn't cry.		
E: Neil		Repeat
F: Neil doesn't. You know who cries when they go to bed?	Contrast	
Stephen cries, cause Stephen's a little baby.	AT	Explain
But *big* kids like you and Neil	BT	Contrast
and Carolyn and *Carl*, they don't cry.		List
They just go to sleep.		Explain
E: The big . . . what do- . . . *what* do *one do?*		Question
F: Carol . . . Carol who's still a little bit of a baby . . .		Answer
she's kind of a still a baby, and Stephen,		State
they cry . . . and Angela cries sometimes . . . and Lilly,		
they cry.		List
But *big* kids, like Donny and Leslie		Contrast
and *Carl* and Emily and Neil, they don't cry		List
cause they're big kids . . .		Explain
Mommy and Daddy don't cry and Mormor doesn't cry		List
. . . Tanta doesn't cry . . .		
You could talk to yourself a little bit before	AT	
you go to sleep if you want.		Suggestion
E: Th- th- th- th- *babies* cry at Tanta's when baby		State
F: *Yeah,* but *big* kids *don't.*		Agree/Contrast
E: Eh- th- th- *one* at . . . house. Eh . . . who cries?		Question
F: The babies cry, huh, but not the big kids.		Answer/Contrast
E: Um . . . who cries . . . at . . . who cries?		Question
F: Lilly . . . and Angela . . . and Stephen	BT	Answer/List
E: And Linda		List
F: No . . . Linda's a big kid . . . Carol, the little girl	AT	Disagree
who was here tonight . . . *she* cries sometimes		Explain
E: Oh . . . baby!		Exclaim
F: Yeah . . . Okay, Sweetie . . .	BT	Agree
Well I'll see you in the morning. [Emily crying]		Leavetake
F: Now remember . . . no crying . . . remember?	AT	Command
E: I sleep in . . . up this!		?

Dialogue	Style	Structure
F: Yes . . . Okay, I love you. I'll . . . [Emily crying]	BT	Agree/Leavetake
F: Now remember what I said about crying, Hon!	AT	Command
E: Tell me what . . . buy at Childworld!		Request
F: We're goin a Childworld on . . . S-a-turday	BT	Comply
So you have a good sleep Hon . . . I love you.		Leavetake

Example 2. Emily's Monologue after the Childworld Dialogue

1a. I can't sleep with the *bl-a-n*kets [crying] . . .
  b. I member the (?)   [crying] I went to sleep

2a. e- *D-a-d*dy said buy *dia*pers for *St*ephen and Emmy
  b. and buy *sok*ething for 'tephen . . .
  c. plug in . . . and say ahhh . . . and put . . . the . . . in . . .
  d. on *Sa*turday go Childworld . . . buy *dia*pers for Emmy and *dia*pers for the
    baby
  e. and then buy (chocalik) for the . . . and . . .
  f. see . . . for . . . that baby plug in and
  g. get diapers for *any*body . . .
  h. and buy more (?) that day . . . at Childworld . . .
  i. and buy (croutes) . . .

3a. and my *blan*ket . . .
  b. Childworld cause . . .

4a. that *one* is broken at *T-a-nt*a's . . .
  b. the one (is) broken . . . the one that broken . . . here
  c. the . . . infant seat . . . bed (actually) and (?) . . .
  d. Oh, they . . . at *Tant*a's . . .

5a. do . . . big . . . big kids like Emmy and Carl and Linda don't cry.
  b. *They* big kids. *They* sleep like big . . . kids
  c. the baby cry at Tanta's.

6a. And the (next over) the next people that came. Then . . .

7a. babies can cry but—big kids like Emmy don't cry . . .
  b. they go sleep but the *bab*ies cry . . . (?)
  c. everbod- the big kids like Emmy don't cry.
  d. The big kids at Tanta's cry
  e. and (say d-a-h)
  f. but the big kids don't cry.

Example 3. Excerpts from the Father-Emily Dialogue of 22 months, 17 days, and from Emily's Monologues of 22 months, 17 days, and 22 months, 18 days.

FATHER–EMILY DIALOGUE

F: I'll put a blanket . . . you lie down. Daddy'll put a blanket on you.
E: [muttering under her breath]
F: [higher-pitched, "optimistic" tone] And when you wake up we're gonna go
    to Carl's, but you have to go to sleep now. You're *such a* good girl, Pookey.

E: I sleeping on my *bunny.*
F: That's okay.
E: [Tearfully, emphatically] I don't *want* sleep on my . . .
F: [Quickly] Oh, I know you don't want to sleep on your bunny. No! Okay.
E: The bad *bunny!*
F: Okay. Have a good . . . Hon. I love you.
E: The bad—[Father exits, closing door]

MONOLOGUE OF 22 MONTHS, 17 DAYS

Maybe when my go come, maybe my go in Daddy's (blue) big car maybe maybe when Carl come again go to back home go Peabody Carl sleeping. Not right now. The baby coming and Carl coming m' house . . . *a-n-d* Emmy (???) coming after my nap. Not right now cause the baby coming *now* . . .

EXCERPT FROM MONOLOGUE OF 22 MONTHS, 18 DAYS

Because then Emmy go to sleep Emmy have go to sleep. When Emmy wakes up, Carl come after my nap then Carl come over my house. When Daddy wake up sleep when Emmy wake up Emmy has—then alligator come get me.

Logosphere and Semiosphere: Bakhtin, Russian Organicism, and the Semiotics of Culture

Amy Mandelker

Bring this vision actually before your sight, so that there shall be in your mind the gleaming representation of a sphere, a picture holding all the things of the universe.
—Plotinus, *Enneads* 5.8

In memoriam Jerry Leo

Semiotics and the Big Bang:
Revising the History of Origins

The evolution in Moscow-Tartu school semiotic theory during the 1980s might be compared with the shift from Newtonian to relativistic physics. The recent paradigm shift from a theory based on Saussurean linguistics to a biological, organismic approach influenced by Vernadsky and Bakhtin resembles the type of cultural explosions and "big bangs" that Iurii Lotman describes in his latest work, *Culture and Explosion* (1992). Western critical theory has comfortably assimilated semiotic theory in its earlier structuralist mode, yet this appropriation has often distorted the basic premises of Slavic theory, resulting in elisions, misreadings, or impoverished interpretations. The current vogue for the work of Mikhail Bakhtin has in its turn obscured recent trends in semiotics, in particular the concepts of the "semiosphere" and "cultural explosion." Bakhtin's own influence, together with that of the geologist Vladimir Vernadsky, has been one of the main stimuli behind the paradigm shift in contemporary semiotics.

In a series of largely untranslated articles from the 1980s, Iurii Lotman, the leading figure of the Moscow-Tartu school of semiotics, carves out a new direction for semiotic inquiry in proposing the model of the "semiosphere," a metaphor based on principles of cell biology, organic chemistry, and brain science. In the work of Lotman and his colleagues, the sphere is also a dialogic model, by analogy to the asymmetrical function and interplay of the two hemispheres of the human brain. Terminologically and conceptually, Lotman's semiosphere derives from Bakhtin's logosphere, itself adapted from a source that also inspired Lotman directly: Vernadsky's notion of the biosphere. Bakhtin's logosphere is a response to problems in discourse theory that supplies an ecological and organismic approach to the concept of embodiment and speech. The organicist strategy, picked up by Lotman, is compelling because it revivifies some moribund issues in epistemology. As a result, the recent work of Moscow-Tartu semioticians, especially Lotman's "On the Semiosphere" and *Culture and Explosion*, has moved far beyond classic structuralism.[1] Current semiotic theory explodes the bipolar grid of significance erected to fit a Saussurean model and adopts a less mathematical-linguistic, more biologically based method of modeling, experimentation, and inquiry.[2] Saussurean linguistics no longer serves as the privileged "primary modeling system"; instead, current semiotics pursues a nonlogocentric model.

This recent development in semiotics in fact chronologically parallels the Western phase of deconstructive post-structuralism. If the earlier period of Soviet semiotic research retains its accepted designation as "structuralist semiotics," it becomes tempting to term the latest semiotic theory a "post-structuralist semiotics."

Russian "post-structuralism," however, is discontinuous from Western post-structuralism. So-called Slavic structuralism (Prague school structuralism) is more accurately a "post-Formalist" movement, and Russian Formalism is arguably already structuralist in its intent, especially in the culminating publications of the Russian Formalists Jakobson and Tynianov[3]. By contrast, Western structuralism (especially French structuralism, as represented by such figures as Roland Barthes and others of the Tel Quel school) more closely resembles early Russian Formalism. Indeed, French structuralism in the practice of its adherents Girard or Guiraud is often more formalist than the Formalists themselves, in its reliance on the types of Proppian maneuvers that can reduce texts to a series of functions and strategies. This type of mathematical textual analysis in a contextual vacuum provided an impetus for a recontextualization of discourse analysis among the opening moves of what has come to be known as post-structuralism. But the term *post-structuralism* does a disservice to Slavic structuralism, which was way ahead of its European homonym.

Although Western theory can claim its own pragmatic developments in semiotic theory before the French structuralist movement (for example, the work of the Anglo-American philosophers Charles Sanders Peirce and Charles Morris), it is of greater concern to recognize and recoup the large-scale movement in the Russian and Slavic tradition that has been obscured in the Western appropriation of Russian Formalism and Slavic structuralism. As Thomas G. Winner recently commented in his essay "Prague Structuralism and Semiotics,"

Francophilia inhabits the American academic establishment where concepts and fashions originating in the Parisian intellectual ambiance . . . [acquire] a cultist "mainstream" character which may attain a superficial dogmatism. . . .

A Saussurean structuralism has been followed by a reinterpretation of Russian Formalism leading to so-called post-structuralism dubbed deconstruction in the eighties. The story leaves out more of the broad structuralist-semiotic program than it includes . . . [in particular] Prague Structural Semiotics of the thirties."[4]

In fact, the standard nonspecialist work on Russian Formalism and the structuralist movement excises Prague structuralism altogether: "[Structuralism's] rise . . . may be conveniently dated from the publication of Lévi-Strauss' *Tristes tropiques* in 1955, and . . . may be said to have reached a zenith of sorts (following such important sign-posts as the foundation of *Tel Quel* in 1960 and the publication of Lévi-Strauss' *La Pensée sauvage* in 1962) with the twin appearance, during the 1966–67 season, of Lacan's already legendary *Ecrits* and of Derrida's three major texts." Jameson also "deliberately exclude[s] . . . any treatment of . . . Soviet Structuralism" (semiotics?), thus closing off his account of Slavic structuralism with the demise of Russian Formalism.[5]

In fact, the Russian Formalists, in their last publications by Jakobson and Tynianov (1929), were already debating and probing the issues that became critical not only to structuralists but also to Western post-structuralist debates more than half a century later. Therefore, if we are going to fall in with the contemporary critical practice of "post"-al designations, Slavic structuralism would have to be considered equivalent to Western post-structuralism, since Slavic structuralism from its inception rejected isolationist heuristic methodologies, that is, critical focus on the structures of a text to the exclusion of all "extraliterary" factors. *Mutatis mutandis*, Western post-structuralism could be considered a persistent or an unreconstructed structuralism, since such theorists as De Man and Derrida continue to operate within an essentially Saussurean conception of language, viewing signification as arbitrary, at least to the extent that Derridean deconstruction posits ruptures, gaps, or aporias in language as inescapable problems in communication.[6] A post-structuralist semiotics in the Russian context, which posits spherical enclosures and generative explosions that blast away the logocentrism of post-structuralist thought, would thus have to be registered as post-post-structuralist in Western terms.[7]

From Prison-House to Ecosystem: Russian Dialogics

Creating a post-post-structuralist camp is useful, as it offers an acceptable categorization for such sui generis figures as Bakhtin, whose impact on Western criticism arguably occurs at a post-post-structuralist moment in the history of the theory of discourse. It is the Bakhtin of the Rabelais book who has most captivated Western readers—the Bakhtin whose celebration of the subversive and the carnivalesque casts him as an apostle of "antinomian freedom," championing absolute metaphysical openness. This aspect of Bakhtin's work should not be taken out of the context in which it was written—Stalinist Russia—a backdrop that renders more urgent Bakhtin's resistance to systematization but that simultaneously makes the characterization of Bakhtin as a revolutionary problematic. Bakhtin seems to belong to the political "other" of both Western and Soviet society: what is conservative by Western standards becomes a more profound kind of radicalism by contemporary Soviet standards and vice versa. The current engagement with Bakhtin has caused his earlier and later work in epistemology to be overlooked. Yet it is precisely in this area that Bakhtin's influence on Soviet and post-Soviet semiotics has been most profound.

The emphasis of recent semiotic theory on dialogue is clearly Bakhtinian, if not post-Bakhtinian.[8] Yet Bakhtin's own response to developments in structuralist theory was primarily negative: "My attitude towards structuralism: I am against enclosure in a text."[9] In his notes written in the 1970s, Bakhtin criticized semiotic theory for its reliance on a concept of textual context as a grammar in codified form, since "a code is a deliberately established, killed context," while, in distinction, Bakhtin's own theory continually emphasizes the living speech act. Critiquing the Saussurean notion of *langue* versus *parole* and the concepts of grammatical competence and "deep structure" we have come to associate with Chomsky, Bakhtin attacks the "deep structuralism" in semiotics: "Semiotics deals primarily with the transmission of ready-made communication using a ready-made code. But in live speech, strictly speaking, communication is first created in the process of transmission, and there is, in essence, no code. The problem of changing the code in inner speech."[10]

In other words, Bakhtin rejects a view projecting an artificial code (*langue*) onto individual speech acts (*parole*) and focuses on the internal mechanism of language as a living speech act, that is, on mental representation or "inner speech."[11] The concept of inner speech proves to be a critical notion for separating Slavic and Western linguistics and social theory. In the accepted view based on Piaget's child psychology, the individual possesses what Piaget terms an "autistic" form of presocial, preverbal signifying mentation that is subsequently lost, deformed, or co-opted when it is made to conform to general, arbitrary, linguistic practice during language acquisition and socialization. Piaget's account of the loss of "autism" parallels the loss of preverbal communion with the mother in Freudian and Lacanian psychoanalytic theory, generating the nostalgia and desire that Lacan and Derrida, among others, have seen residing in the conventional relationship between signifier and signified. Language, in this Western view, becomes the site of anxiety, nostalgia, and eternal failure.

In the alternative Russian view represented by the psychologist Lev Vygotsky, V. N. Voloshinov, and Bakhtin, the individual is social from the moment consciousness occurs: "The conscious psyche is a socioideological fact."[12] There is no question of arbitration or separation or loss: I and the other are an I-other in an embodied discourse of inner speech.

Lotman increases the complexity of these earlier theories of inner speech by replacing the generalized notion of interiorized thought (the region of anxiety for logophobes) with a specific, scientific model of intracerebral communication between the two hemispheres of the brain. He characterizes this type of inner speech as a "dialogue" consisting of an alternating current of receptivity and transmission, or noise and silence. Lotman acknowledges his debt to Bakhtin's suggestive notion of the logosphere, that "dialogic sphere where the word exists."[13] Bakhtin's logosphere encompasses the regions where a speech acts "unrepeatable" and, therefore, uncodifiable moments occur: "Through the utterance, language joins the historical unrepeatability and unfinalized totality of the logosphere." The space around the utterance is, first and most simply, silence: "Silence—intelligible sound (a word)—and the pause constitute a special logosphere, a unified and continuous structure, an open (unfinalized) totality."[14] While the bare elements of the utterance may be examined and codified by linguistics or semiotics, Bakhtin argues that the living space of the logosphere, a living space with a plenitude of unfinalizable meanings, requires its own science: "The utterance (speech product) as a whole enters into an entirely new sphere of speech communication (as a unit of this new sphere), which does not admit of description or definition in the terms and methods of linguistics or—more broadly—semiotics. This sphere is governed by a special law, and its study requires a special methodology and, it should be said outright, a special science."[15] The importance of the logosphere in this thinking motivates Katerina Clark and Michael Holquist's observation that for Bakhtin "language is not a prison house; it is an eco-system."[16] This characterization tacitly acknowledges Bakhtin's reliance on the ecological biosphere theory of the Russian geochemist, earth scientist, and philosopher of science Vladimir Vernadsky (1863–1945).[17]

The Ecology of Meaning: Vernadsky, the Biosphere, and Dialogic Semiotics

Vernadsky was the first to hypothesize that, in addition to an atmosphere, the earth has a "biosphere": a conceptual "membrane" over the planet surface comprising all living matter and functioning as a unified totality.[18] The metaphor of the biosphere may become clearer if compared with the cellular slime mold (*Dictyostelium discoideum*), whose units—individual organisms—bond chemically to form a supraorganism that can function physically and cognitively in a manner impossible for each individual organism to achieve. The biosphere may be understood analogously as a kind of superior intelligence of the planet. The notion of the biosphere thus requires conceptualizing the multiformity of all planetary life as integrated into a singular organismic mechanism dedicated to the functioning of the earth and to perpetuating its photosynthetic incorporation of solar rays into the order and structure of life. Vernadsky's ecological theory situates humanity's role in the biosphere by positing the presence of conscious thought on the planet as a new geologic force; that is, he defines the emergence of human consciousness as simply another stage in the development and refinement of the biosphere and its processes.[19] Vernadsky terms this stage of the manifestation of human consciousness on earth the "noösphere" (from the Greek *noös*, "mind").[20] This concept, which Teilhard de Chardin and Richard Dana referred to as the "cephalization" of nature, or the initiation of the "psychozoic era," was considered by Chardin to incorporate the culmination of cosmic consciousness, permitting nature to contemplate and cognize itself: in this view, humanity as a macrocosm is the universe's cognitive organ.

Bakhtin engages this particular application of Vernadsky's view of planetary evolution when he writes:

When consciousness appeared in the world (in existence) . . . the world changed radically. A stone is still stony and the sun still sunny, but the event of existence as a whole (unfinalized) becomes completely different because a new and major character in this event appears for the first time on the scene of earthly existence—the witness and the judge. . . .

. . . This cannot be understood as existence (nature) beginning to be conscious of itself in humanity, beginning to reflect itself. . . . No, something absolutely new has appeared, a *supra-existence* has emerged.[21]

Bakhtin resists the teleological, Hegelian overtones of Chardin's model of humanity's historical phase in the development of the *Weltgeist* and remains loyal to Vernadsky's biological model for the production of life and energy.

This model is based on the principle of specularity, or mirroring, on the interplay in nature of symmetrical and asymmetrical structures, and the reproduction of life through the union of enantiomorphic (mirror-image) pairs. Vernadsky derived his theory of the symmetrical-asymmetrical paired structure of life-forms from the work of Louis Pasteur and Pierre Curie, who studied the asymmetrical disposition of the crystals of biomolecules and investigated piezoelectricity, a form of electric polarity in crystals. Vernadsky observed asymmetrical pairing to be the essential (or universal) pattern in the replicative function of life-forms. He suggests that the same pattern underlies both molecular asymmetry and the sexual dimorphism of complex organisms that reproduce by sexual intercourse. The life force becomes universalized in the principle of functional asymmetry—from cytoarchitectonics at the biomolecular level to cerebral lateralization at the cognitive level, to sexual dimorphism at the reproductive level.

Attributing a biological, or living, energy to events in consciousness, Bakhtin similarly argues that developments in self-awareness, the production of thought—like the production of beings—can only take place via contact with an other. Comparing the emergence of conscious thought in the individual mind to the birth of the noösphere on the planet, Bakhtin observes:

> Something absolutely new appears here: the supraperson, the *supra-I*, that is, the witness and the judge *of the whole* human being, of the whole *I*, and consequently, someone who is no longer the person, no longer the *I*, but the *other*. [N.B.: That is, the development of individual consciousness allows the self to know the self, as if it had the status of an observing other, A.M.] The reflection of the self in the empirical other through whom one must pass in order to reach *I-for-myself* (can this *I-for-myself* be solitary?). The absolute freedom of this *I*. But this freedom cannot change existence, so to speak, materially . . . —it can change only the *sense* of existence.[22]

Bakhtin's conclusion here implicitly interrogates Vernadsky's theory: How do shifts in consciousness (the plane of the noösphere) affect material reality (the plane of the biosphere)? Bakhtin rejects Vernadsky's view of an active noösphere cultivating the biosphere and instead adopts an almost Husserlian subjectivity where the inner dialogic relationship between existence and consciousness functions only to alter perception.

The Semiosphere: Breaking with Semiotic Totalitarianism

Lotman explores the dialogic relations between existence and consciousness by narrowing the focus of his work to the biochemical processes of the mind—that is, to the communication between the functionally asymmetrical hemispheres of the brain. The dialogic relations Lotman describes at the intracranial level he then interprets as microcosmic models for larger events in life and in the universe of meaning. In this passage he traces his commitment to resolving these questions: "The biologist V. I. Vernadsky [found] it more productive to study the interrelationship of structures that are binary, asymmetrical, and at the same time, unitary. This is the approach we [in current semiotic theory] will be adopting."[23]

Lotman builds on the biosphere and logosphere theories by developing his own bioecological, neuroculturological theory of the semiosphere in articles from the 1980s entitled "Asymmetry and Dialogue," "Culture and the Organism," "The Text, the Brain, Culture, and Artificial Intelligence," and "On the Semiosphere."[24] He investigates the issues attendant on the functional assymmetry of the human brain in a series of technical neuropsychological and neurolinguistic experiments.

Together with his collaborator, the neurolinguist Nikolai Nikolaenko, Lotman explores the types of functions allocated to each hemisphere and, more important, the mode of dialogic exchange—the transmission of information—between the two hemispheres.

This work expands on psycholinguistic models that posit two modes of cognition. In his study of aphasic patients, Roman Jakobson observes that the two prominent forms of aphasia (Wernicke's and Broca's) are the result of deficits either in the process of verbal selection (the axis of similarity) or combination (the axis of contiguity) and argues that the literary tropes of metaphor and metonymy could be allocated to each axis respectively. It has been claimed that these two modes of consciousness represent the division of labor between the two hemispheres of the brain: the left hemisphere forms sequential differentiations (linguistic function is known to be situated primarily in the left hemisphere), while the right hemisphere performs holistic, synthesizing functions (facial recognition, musical phrase analysis, and so on).[25] The performance of each hemisphere is impaired or impoverished, however, if the neurochemical circuits between the two hemispheres are severed. The hemispheres seem to require each other in order to interpret the input they synthesize.[26]

Lotman emphasizes the communication patterns between the two hemispheres, which he characterizes as the essential interplay between somatic experience (the right hemisphere) and the cognitive aspect of recollective and retroactive understanding through languages (the left). Bakhtin's statement that we have not experienced an event until we re-present it to ourselves in words (through inner speech) is thus reiterated in Lotman's model of brain function where the left brain cognizes and interprets the impulses received by the right. Information is thus exchanged in the brain between an asymmetrical pair that is functionally united into an autonomous, teleologically harmonized sphere.

Lotman promotes this model into a universal principle for all dialogic semiosis on the micro-, macro-, and metalevels. In culture, for example, it is the left hemispheric function that "civilizes," since it is liberated from inarticulate experience to generate a "free play" of signs within the codes of cultural conventions. Curiously, this interpretation reverses the more popular perception of the right hemisphere as the source of creativity. However, in Lotman's view, the right hemisphere is nonfecund and inarticulate, merely absorbing sensory perceptions that are cognized and re-created when the information is transferred to the left hemisphere. Only the left hemisphere, therefore, is capable of the free play of signs liberated from the senses. Since the right hemisphere requires the left in order to comprehend extrasemiotic reality, dialogue between the two hemispheres becomes a necessity. The image of the sphere, a space uniting the asymmetrical pair, becomes imbued with the mission of facilitating communication and of developing consciousness. Lotman terms this model the semiosphere, "that space outside of which semiosis cannot exist."[27] A semiosphere enters into dialogic relations with other semiospheres, as well as nurturing dialogic relations within itself in the interactions between its interior elements and their correlative functions.

Lotman makes the asymmetrical dialogue of the cerebral hemispheres emblematic of cultural trends and transitions, asserting a principle of polarization in cultural evolution and explosions. In "Reconsidering the Mysterious 'Golden Mean'" Lotman and the neurologist Nikolai Nikolaenko suggest that the history of art and architecture may be described according to trends that popularize the style formation preferred by each of the brain's two hemispheres.[28] This thesis is based on clinical studies demonstrating that the way a subject conceives of space when drawing or viewing art becomes polarized after one of the subject's hemispheres is impaired or excluded through pathology or experimentation. Left hemispheric dominance causes vertical drawings with elongated, ectomorphic figures, while right hemispheric dominance stimulates the production of horizontal drawings with rounded, mesomorphic figures. Lotman and Nikolaenko propose that the "golden mean," the desirable ratio of spatial asymmetry described by the Greeks, results from dialogue between the two hemispheres and represents the tension of that interplay in the visual field. Lotman and Nikolaenko offer periods and trends in the history of art when one tendency may be said to predominate. For example, the Gothic period would reflect left hemispheric preferences for elongated, vertically elevated forms, and the Baroque period, right hemispheric predilections for the ornate, rotund, and earth-directed.

The spatialized and biologized concept of the semiosphere enhances the earlier Moscow-Tartu school model of inner and outer cultural perspectives.[29] First, the spherical model presumably escapes the gridlock of the traditional, bipolar structuralist schema. Since the circle cannot be squared, we may assume there are elements within the ovoid spaces of a sphere that cannot be predicted by the graphics of intercorrelated functions and binary oppositions erected by traditional structuralist analyses. Further, the use of a spherical model permits mapping the concepts of center and periphery, in addition to organizing cultural dynamics hierarchically. The sphere also invites the borrowing of some suggestive topics from biophysics and cell biology: enclosure and disclosure, resistance or responsiveness to penetration, and the assimilation of intruding and extruding elements.

The progression in modern Russian theory from the biosphere to the logosphere and then to the semiosphere constitutes a new organicism that restructures Russian structuralism in a way paralleling post-structuralist reconsiderations of Formalism, structuralism, and semiotics. In the Western philosophical tradition, the metaphors and paradigms of organicist philosophy frequently become associated with gender, as Donna Haraway demonstrates.[30] Whether this feature opens up or closes down the production of meaning or applies to Russian theory at all, remains at issue.

Circling the Problematics of Organicism

Organicism, the philosophical strategy of attributing organic status to inorganic objects, is predicated on a vision of a polyphonic and harmonized totality of life that is isomorphic at its every level—from the microorganism to the human brain and its manifest behaviors and beyond to the macrocosm of the universe.[31] Most important, the organicist approach rejects as reductionist the traditional biochemical method of analysis, emphasizing instead the organic interconnections of a system or organism that produce a whole greater and more meaningful than the sum of its parts: "Now the essential feature of an organic unity is that the parts manifest the whole—that, since the whole as a unity is what it is, the parts must be what they are. This, as we have seen, is really the case with all wholes, and therefore all wholes are really organic unities."[32]

The organicist metaphor is both liberating and confining. In addition to the driving rhythm of an apparently unalterable orbit through the historical development of the universe, the model of the sphere organicizes as it organizes; it operates both positively as a figure of autonomous enclosure in the geologic theories of cyclical oscillation and dynamic equilibrium of the homeostatic steady state system. It also functions discriminatively as a figure of definition—distinguishing between the external and the internal, demarcating what is alien and what is native to the enclosure. In its culturological function it becomes a mechanism for delimitation or, alternatively, translation.

From the metaperspective, the sphere reads as the circle of necromancy that establishes the need for communication between the inside and the outside and thus privileges the necromancer. The necromancer must own a special language and ritual in order to bridge the uncrossable line, representing human intellectual control over or manipulation of the vegetative body that is an enclosure (the noösphere's cultivation of the biosphere). The organic nature of the sphere, the figure of enclosure, like that of the female body, suggests the mysteries of the creation of life and of meaning that the necromancer must penetrate and acquire.

Such figuration of the acquisition and cultivation of meaning through the union of opposites can be traced back to mythological, early Christian, and gnostic conceptions of sexual intercourse and marriage as the fundamental sign of a creative God in Nature and hence as the emblem of the divine creation of life and meaning. Tracing the metaphor of the union of opposites in the Western tradition from Plato through alchemy, Evelyn Fox Keller finds that a critical reevaluation during the Industrial Revolution resulted in the degradation of what she considers the "feminine" component.[33] Attendant upon the separation of gender roles in the marketplace, the feminine poles of the philosophical categories of mind/body, science/nature, reason/emotion, public/private, official/domestic, were simultaneously degraded and pedestalized. The division of the natural world into the simply beautiful (conceived in feminine terms) and the sublime (valorized as masculine) was the keystone of Romantic aesthetics, and Kant's elaboration of these categories made them the basis of most subsequent aesthetic philosophy. Furthermore, the view that the Life principle is refracted into different particulates whose conjunction generates new life is obviously basic to many philosophical traditions and to natural science.

The feminist critique of scientific thought has indicted the tendency for epistemological speculation to erect binary oppositions that acquire gendered qualities.[34] As Keller has commented à propos of post-Baconian scientific thought, "Gender ideology [was] a crucial mediator [at] the birth of modern science." Thus there was a significant "role played by metaphors of gender in the formation of the particular set of values, aims, and goals in the scientific enterprise."[35] A feminist critique of Lotman's recent work would note that he discusses the means by which meaning is generated and transmitted in biological terms. For example, in describing the interactions of semiospheres, Lotman contrasts the stasis of a barren, isolate semiosphere with the productivity of a semiosphere in dialogue: intercourse is required in order to create something new and meaningful.

The sphere, the cell membrane, the boundaries of cultures, the limits of language, require dialogue with what is beyond and dialogue between the elements that are within. Does Lotman's vision and extension of Bakhtinian dialogue run the risk of reinstantiating certain stereotypes developed in Western theory within Russian semiotics? An earlier feminist critique was leveled against narratology and against Lotman's narratology in particular. For example, Teresa de Lauretis asserts that Lotman ascribes the active plot functions to masculine heroes and restricts passive plot functions to the heroines.[36] Lotman also relies on a spherical, or cyclical, model to account for the universals of narrative structures. Inscribing a formation similar to Joseph Campbell's "monomyth," Lotman suggests that plot events are constituted of transgressive passages across boundaries, interpreted by de Lauretis as active, penetrating movements performed by male heroes.[37] As Rachel Brownstein has observed, the heroines of narrative, by contrast, remain static; they are territory to conquer or obtain.

The acquisition of gender by metaphor seems unavoidable in the spatialization of meaning that creates embodiment for discourse. For example, when Derrida spatializes meaning and attempts to square the circle of traditional aesthetics by emphasizing the square frame of the picture in his *Truth in Painting*, he exploits the sexy connotations of his imagery: "I write right on the *passe-partout* well known to picture framers. . . . right on this . . . virgin surface . . . open in its 'middle'. . . . [the work of art] thus slides into the *passe-partout*."[38] Having aroused our interest, Derrida leaves us unsatisfied by his failure to consider the way in which sexual stereotypes have enfolded conceptualizations to provide ready-made spaces for the implantation of meaning.

The use of gendered metaphor in literary criticism and philosophy often becomes automatic in the attempt to spatialize meaning or describe an embodied discourse. The persistence of these metaphors throughout the debate in epistemology over the separation between body and thought or between experience and cognition suggests a mental habit of labeling cognitive styles "masculine" or "feminine." Thus brain scientists readily sexualized the two cerebral hemispheres in ways that have since proved to be unscientific.

By exploiting Bakhtin's dialogic model, Lotman succeeds in expanding the reproductive analogy beyond its somatic parameters. Lotman's model of dialogue itself might still be seen as problematic, because, although dialogue unites the two hemispheres of the brain in a larger totality, their union is based on the need for *silence*: "Under normal conditions of the simultaneous functioning of both hemispheres of the brain, we see the well-known inter-inhibitory activity of each hemisphere, as it were, the exclusion of one hemisphere and the stimulation of the other's activity. . . . It must take turns by means of pauses during which it suppresses its activity and directs its attention to the reception of the partner's activity."[39] The passing of electrical impulses between the neural circuits of the brain's two hemispheres and, by extension, the semiotic transmissions between individuals and cultures acquire a hegemonic and potentially violent character, necessitating interruption, suppression, submission, and silence. Lotman's sphere of silence embraces, encloses, and embodies the utterance, just as the biosphere, figured as the earth goddess Gaia, embraces all life and lies passively open to men's husbandry (the action of the noösphere).[40]

But perhaps silence need not be the result of oppression. Bakhtin considers the "I-for-myself" to be without words until its thought is structured responsively by the "I-for-others."[41] In Bakhtin's version, silence is gestational, free, and productive, while the verbalization of experience is secondary and enculturated. To the extent that he differs from Bakhtin, Lotman exalts the creative free play of verbal signification that occurs, in his model, only when semiosis is liberated from experience.[42]

Lotman's most recent work on cultural models, *Culture and Explosion*, somewhat attenuates the model of somatic passivity overinscribed by semiotic creativity. In his latest monograph Lotman sketches a cataclysmic model for cultural change that seems partly motivated by recent events in the former Soviet Union, as well as a sign of drift from Vernadsky's soft-Hegelian position of evolution and change, both geologic and socioideological. In his latest theory, which he only began to articulate, Lotman continues to assert a reproductive model for the production of meaning. He affirms the unification of opposites in a "singular, simultaneous working mechanism," but he stresses the dynamics of an internally heterogeneous semiosphere, a cacophonous plurality of semiologically ordered elements unified through interrelations "so complex as to facilitate the possibility of a breach [*proryva*] in the determined space. This function is fulfilled in the moment of explosion [*vzryv*] which constitutes a window in the semiotic layer."[43] Although the interior of the semiosphere is now increasingly active so as to invite its own puncture or rupture, the explosion is no implosion; the aperture still requires penetration, dialogue is still essential. We can anticipate and extend Lotman's thinking to accommodate a more Bakhtinian model that appreciates the role of each partner in the dialogue.

Rounding Off: Conclusions

Lotman's model of the semiosphere, in its adaptation of organicist strategies, risks perpetuating the use of gendered metaphors in the philosophy of science and epistemology that constrain the feminine to passivity while valorizing the masculine action and word. However, the dialogism of his model attenuates this reinscription of masculinist paradigms. Bakhtin's own dialogics are apparently neuter, although critics are divided over whether his logosphere gives adequate space to the issue of gender difference.[44] While Bakhtin never assayed a model of intracerebral dialogue, his musings in epistemology on the body-mind problem (in the early essay "Toward a Philosophy of the Act") propose a polyphony or heterophony of embodied voices rather than a voice raised over silence.[45] Lotman's semiosphere model requires the transfer of an event from one hemisphere or semiosphere to another, a procedure that dilutes the salience of what Bakhtin termed "eventness" and that privileges the actions of the semiotizing hemisphere and, by extension, the realm of systematization and theorism.[46]

By contrast, for Bakhtin, existence cannot occur within a theoretical vacuum: "It is impossible for any practical orientation of my life to occur in the theoretical world; it is impossible to live there." This would be an aesthetic form of existence in which "not I but my pseudo-self [*dvoinik-samosvanets*] is found."[47] Existence and experience for Bakhtin occur only in carnate action—uniting the somatic ontological moment with the cognitive apprehension of it. Bakhtin's philosophy of the act juxtaposes the semiotic realm with the existential realm but locates life and self in the latter, death and pseudo-consciousness—false transcendence—in the former. For Bakhtin the word is spoken by an embodied voice; any other word is "a word removed from dialogue . . . spreading everywhere, limiting, directing and retarding both thought and live experience of life."[48]

For both Bakhtin and Lotman, Vernadsky's concepts of biosphere and no-ösphere offered seductive organic metaphors for figuring the embodiment of discourse. In opposition to the structuralist tradition, where *parole* is ancillary to *langue*, the Russian organicism outlined here privileges an embodied and living discourse, which the system of meaning would fix and pin to the page. In his critique of structuralism, Jameson dismisses the philosophical premises of organicism: "The relationship of part to whole reflects an older logical model, which is no longer useful in the solving of the new kinds of problems posed by the peculiar nature of language."[49] In the deconstructionist view, *"parole* is irrelevant." Recording the Slavic tradition of organicist thought in the history of structuralism—pre-, post-, and prop(p)er—suggests a different shape for outlining the problems of discourse and the production of meaning. The reordering of event, meaning, and discourse in a bioecological model liberates the production of meaning from the prison-house of theory. Within the ecosystem of organic substance and living speech, the dialogue of difference continues.

Notes

Introduction

1. A. K. Shevchenko, *Kul'tura. Istoriia. Lichnost'. Vvedenie v filosofiiu postupka* (Kiev: Naukova dumka, 1991), 3. In this book Shevchenko places Bakhtin among other European thinkers, from Aristotle and Augustine to Heidegger and Berdyaev, who have produced typologies of responsible action in the world. His four major divisions are I. "Virtuous Man," II. "Juridical Man," III. "Metaphysical Man," and IV. "The Meaning of History and the Problem of the Utopian in Culture."

2. Stephen Toulmin, "The Marginal Relevance of Theory to the Humanities," *Common Knowledge* 2, no. 1 (Spring 1993):75–84, esp. 77.

3. M. M. Bakhtin, "Toward a Methodology for the Human Sciences" (1974), in *Speech Genres and Other Late Essays*, trans. Vern W. McGee, ed. Caryl Emerson and Michael Holquist (Austin: University of Texas Press, 1986), 159–72.

4. The expression is W. Wolfgang Holdheim's; see his "Idola Fori Academici," *Stanford Literature Review* 4 (1987):7–21, esp. 11.

5. Gary Saul Morson, *Narrative and Freedom: The Shadows of Time* (New Haven, Conn.: Yale University Press, 1994).

6. For the most lucid exposition to date on this matter of objective-subjective values in Russian neoidealism common to many of the *Landmarks* authors, see Philip J. Swoboda, "The Philosophical Thought of S. L. Frank, 1902–1915: A Study of the Metaphysical Impulse in Early Twentieth-Century Russia," Ph.D. diss., Columbia University, 1992, esp. chap. 3, pp. 218–92.

7. Aleksandr Shchelkin, "Russkaia ideia: Iskusheniie dukhovnost'iu," *Nevskoe vremia*, 30 Dec. 1992, p. 3. He continues, overgeneralizing but with some grounds: "To Russian political maximalism [these authors] counterposed, as a way out, not a gradual, normal, constitutional, rule-of-law state, but something altogether different. . . . Personal freedom and creativity would be achieved by the heroic deed of humility and service."

8. M. M. Bakhtin, *Toward a Philosophy of the Act*, trans. Vadim Liapunov, ed. Michael Holquist and Vadim Liapunov (Austin: University of Texas Press, 1993), 54.

9. Consider *Toward a Philosophy of the Act*: "I can perform a political act or a religious ritual in the capacity of a representative . . . but . . . [o]ne has to develop humility to the point of participating in person and being answerable in person" (52).

10. For more on Bakhtin's "novel imperialism" of the 1930s and 1940s and a general hypothesis about the shape of Bakhtin's career, see Gary Saul Morson and Caryl Emerson, *Mikhail Bakhtin: Creation of a Prosaics* (Stanford, Calif.: Stanford University Press, 1990), chap. 2, esp. pp. 89–95.

11. In 1974, as part of a memoir series on early Soviet cultural life, the Mayakovsky scholar Viktor Duvakin recorded on tape sixteen hours of reminiscences from the aged Bakhtin, largely on the war years and the 1920s. Duvakin asked his interviewee whether he was "more a philosopher than a philologist." Bakhtin replied: "More a philosopher. And thus have I remained to the present day. I'm a philosopher. A thinker." Bakhtin noted that in those years philosophy itself was an uncertain field, it did not "give one a profession," and one "had to be a specialist," so he chose to be trained as a classicist. "Razgovory s Bakhtinym," preface by S. G. Bocharov, in *Chelovek*, no. 4 (1993):137–53, esp. 152.

12. *Arethusa* 26, no. 2 (Spring 1993). Guest co-editors were Paul Allen Miller and Charles Platter.

13. T. G. Mal'chukova, "Nasledie M. M. Bakhtina i izuchenie antichnoi literatury" (The Legacy of M. M. Bakhtin and the Study of Ancient Literature), in *M. M. Bakhtin: Problemy nauchnogo naslediia* (Saransk: Mordovskii universitet, 1992), 52–68, esp. 64–65.

14. Mikhail Bakhtin, *Problems of Dostoevsky's Poetics* (1963), ed. and trans. Caryl Emerson (Minneapolis: University of Minnesota Press, 1984), 182.

15. For an efficient statement of Nussbaum's position, see Martha C. Nussbaum, "Perceptive Equilibrium: Literary Theory and Ethical Theory," in *Love's Knowledge: Essays on Philosophy and Literature* (New York: Oxford University Press, 1990), 168–94.

16. Nussbaum, "'Finely Aware and Richly Responsible': Literature and the Moral Imagination," in *Love's Knowledge* 148.

17. See S. S. Khoruzhii, "Kak sdelan 'Uliss': Priemy poetiki Dzh. Dzhoisa" (How *Ulysses* Is Made: Devices in the Poetics of James Joyce), in *Dialog. Karnaval. Khronotop* 1, no. 2 (1993): 52–66, esp. 56.

18. M. M. Bakhtin, "Iz chernovykh tetradei" (From Working Rough-Draft Notebooks) [1940s–1960s]), ed. Vadim Kozhinov, in *Literaturnaia ucheba*, knigi 5 and 6 (Sept., Oct., Nov., Dec. 1992):153–66. Cited material appears on p. 155 and p. 154 respectively.

19. From a discussion with Bakhtin on 21 November 1974, recorded by Sergei Bocharov. See S. G. Bocharov, "Ob odnom razgovore i vokrug nego" (About and Around a Certain Conversation), *Novoe literaturnoe obozrenie*, no. 2 (1993):70–89, esp. 70–71. The essay has appeared in English as "Conversations with Bakhtin," trans. Vadim Liapunov, *PMLA* 109, no. 5 (Oct. 1994):1011–24.

20. The best, most compressed discussion of Bakhtin and (anti)-modernism is by Clare Cavanagh, in one page-long footnote in her essay "Pseudo-Revolution

in Poetic Language: Julia Kristeva and the Russian Avant-garde," *Slavic Review* 52, no. 2 (Summer 1993):283–97, esp. 290. In three important ways, Cavanagh notes, do modernist appropriators of Bakhtin (Kristeva being the case in point) get him wrong. First, "Bakhtin's favored canon of truly 'dialogic' writing ends with the demise of the nineteenth century," where modernists place their revolutionary "scriptural break"; second, Bakhtin shows little sustained interest in avant-garde writing, considering "the best and highest form of aesthetic language" to be "simply everyday speech, in all its many variants"; and lastly, contra the Formalists and Futurists, Bakhtin insisted—wrongheadedly or no—that *poetic* language narrowly construed was monologic, dogmatic, authoritarian in a conservative sense, not, as those modernists claimed, subversive or disruptive of an undesirable status quo.

21. Mikhail K. Ryklin, "Bodies of Terror: Theses toward a Logic of Violence," trans. Molly W. Wesling and Donald Wesling, in *New Literary History* 24, no. 1 (Winter 1993):51–74. The essay first appeared in the premiere issue of the *Bakhtinskii sbornik* (Moscow, 1990).

22. K. G. Isupov, "Bakhtinskii krizis gumanizma (materialy k probleme)" (Bakhtin's Crisis of Humanism [Material on the Problem]), *Bakhtinskii sbornik II: Bakhtin mezhdu Rossiei i zapadom* (1991):127–55.

23. A. F. Losev, *Estetika Vozrozhdeniia* (The Aesthetics of the Renaissance) (Moscow: Mysl', 1978), 586–93 (entry on Rabelais). Cited material occurs on pp. 588, 589, 591. The polemic over the Abbey of Thélème (whether it deserves utopian or ironic treatment) has been seen properly as a central focus for understanding Bakhtinian carnival. See, for example, V. S. Vakhrushev, "'Bitva' vokrug Telema (F. Rable, M. Bakhtin, A. Losev i drugie)," in *Dialog. Karnaval. Khronotop* 2, no. 7 (1994):23–32.

24. Elsewhere Isupov expands on this idea, which is of central importance to the Russian recuperation of Bakhtin. "The legacy of our own Russian thinkers shows with exceptional clarity the historical stages of both extremes of humanism: egoistic self-affirmation (classical humanism) and collectivistic madness (proletarian humanism)." See his essay "Istoricheskie uroki gumanizma" (The Historical Lessons of Humanism), in *Dialogi o gumanizme: Mezhvuzovskii sbornik nauchnykh trudov*, ed. K. G. Isupov (St. Petersburg: Obrazovanie, 1992), 44–53, esp. 44.

25. Readings of the Fall are common in Russian religious thought, and as an interesting contrast to Isupov's humanist interpretation one might consider Lev Shestov's reading of Genesis in his *Athens and Jerusalem*. How odd, Shestov remarks, that we always assume that the Serpent (the Spirit of Lies) is telling the truth in the Garden! And in any event, why should knowledge equal godhood? Might not godliness reside in some utterly other value? Shestov suggests that this other value is freedom—not freedom in the choice between good and evil but freedom in one's power, through faith, to prevent evil's entry into the world. According to Shestov, when all freedoms were reduced to the cognitive, that is, when humanity agreed

to measure itself and its freedom by knowledge rather than by faith, then God was exiled from the Garden and its crestfallen residents, Eve and Adam, stayed where they were—and were lost.

26. "Postmodernizm i kul'tura (materialy 'kruglogo stola')," *Voprosy filosofii*, no. 3 (1993):3–16. The four participants are well-known Russian academic philosophers: O. B. Vainshtain, V. I. Novikov, V. A. Podoroga, and L. V. Karasev. Summarized or cited material occurs on pp. 3, 4, 8, 10, 15.

27. Bakhtin, "From Notes Made in 1970–71," in *Speech Genres*, 143–44.

28. Bakhtin, "The Problem of the Text in Linguistics, Philology, and the Human Sciences: An Experiment in Philosophical Analysis" (1959–61), in *Speech Genres* 126. See also the section "The Superaddressee" in Morson and Emerson, *Mikhail Bakhtin: Creation of a Prosaics* 135–36.

29. Bakhtin, "Toward a Methodology for the Human Sciences," in *Speech Genres* 167, 169.

30. For a very suggestive account of the "search for essences" that gripped European thought from 1880 to 1920 and that formed a background for Bakhtin's early development, see Steven Cassedy, *Flight from Eden: The Origins of Modern Literary Criticism and Theory* (Berkeley: University of California Press, 1990), esp. chap. 7, "Numbers, Systems, Functions—and Essences" (135–47).

31. For more on Bakhtin's resistance to "presentism" (Morson's term), see Gary Saul Morson, "Bakhtin and the Present Moment," *American Scholar* (Spring 1991):201–22.

32. See Bakhtin, "The Problem of Speech Genres" (1952–53), in *Speech Genres* 78–81, esp. 80.

33. M. G. Yaroshevskii, "Perezhivanie i drama razvitiia lichnosti (Poslednee slovo L. S. Vygotskogo)," *Voprosy filosofii*, no. 3 (1993):82–91. Yaroshevsky is a well-known Russian historian of psychology and a biographer and translator of Vygotsky.

34. Yaroshevsky provides more detail on this art-psychology connection in his excellent, and excellently translated, biography *Lev Vygotsky* (Moscow: Progress Publishers, 1989). See esp. the chapters "Art: A Social Technique for the Emotions" and "Psychology in Terms of Drama."

35. In the study of child psychology that Vygotsky was working on at the time of his death, metaphors from the dramatic (and/or tragic) stage figure prominently. Noting that psychologists had found it easier to systematize stable or durable developmental periods, he turns his attention to the "crisis," epogee, and "turning point" (perelom) as standard components in the plot of an emerging self (cf. the chapter headings "The Crisis of the First Year of Life," "The Crisis at Three Years," "The Crisis at Seven Years"), and also to "experience" understood as successful performance under high expectation or pressure. For Vygotsky, a "crisis of personality" for the child was not a negative event—although it can

be accompanied by "obstinancy, stubbornness, negativism, capriciousness and selfish willfulness"—but rather a highly creative one requiring different types of reinforcement and analysis. See "Voprosy detskoi (vozrastnoi) psikhologii," in L. S. Vygotskii, *Sobranie sochinenii v 6-i tomakh*, t. 4, *Detskaia psikhologiia* (Moscow: Pedagogika, 1984), 244–415, esp. 251.

This final work, never prepared for publication by Vygotsky himself, would be of special interest to John Dore and other "linguists of the crib narrative."

36. See G. P. Aksenov, "O nauchnom odinochestve Vernadskogo" (On Vernadsky's Scholarly Loneliness), *Voprosy filosofii*, no. 6 (1993):74–87, esp. 75; in the same issue see also M. B. Turovskii and S. V. Turovskaia, "Kontseptsiia V. I. Vernadskogo i perspektivy evoliutsionnoi teorii" (Vernadsky's Concept and the Future of Evolutionary Theory), 88–104. Interest in Vernadsky's eccentric (although highly successful) career and utopian theorizing about the cosmos remains high in Russia today, especially in connection with environmental preservation and evolutionary theory. Nor is this cosmism perceived to be in conflict with humanist goals; for as Aksenov puts the proper link between *"Kosmos* and *Lichnost,"* "Cosmos" and "Personality": "Each person is obliged to become aware solely of his own unique and unrepeatable means for connecting with the Whole, a means that corresponds to his own stores of knowledge and his own character" (77). For a provocative forum, in English, that links Bakhtin, Vernadsky, and contemporary Russian thinking about culture and science, see the special issue of *Configurations* 1, no. 3 (Fall 1993), on "Communities of Science and Culture in Russian Science Studies," esp. Daniel Alexandrov and Anton Struchkov, "Bakhtin's Legacy and the History of Science and Culture: An Interview with Anatoli Akhutin and Vladimir Bibler," 335–86; and Vadim M. Borisov, Felix F. Perchenok, and Arsenii B. Roginsky, "Community as the Source of Vernadsky's Concept of Noösphere," 415–38.

37. L. M. Batkin, "Dva sposoba izuchat' istoriiu kul'tury," *Voprosy filosofii*, no. 12 (1986):104–15, esp. 111. Bakhtin provided an excellent and balanced review of Bakhtin's monograph on Rabelais on its appearance in the Soviet Union (1965): L. M. Batkin, "Smekh Parurga i filosofiia kul'tury," *Voprosy filosofii*, no. 12 (1967):114–23.

Prosaic Bakhtin

1. Gary Saul Morson and Caryl Emerson, eds., *Rethinking Bakhtin: Extensions and Challenges* (Evanston, Ill.: Northwestern University Press, 1989); and Morson and Emerson, *Mikhail Bakhtin: Creation of a Prosaics* (Stanford, Calif.: Stanford University Press, 1990).

2. Mikhail Bakhtin, "Response to a Question from the *Novy Mir* Editorial Staff," in *Speech Genres and Other Late Essays*, trans. Vern W. McGee, ed. Caryl Emerson and Michael Holquist (Austin: University of Texas Press, 1986), 2.

3. Bakhtin, "From Notes Made in 1970–71," in *Speech Genres* 147.

4. Citations from *Landmarks* are to the recent English translation, published as *Signposts: A Collection of Articles on the Russian Intelligentsia*, ed. and trans. Marshall S. Shatz and Judith E. Zimmerman (Irvine, Calif.: Schlacks, 1986); reprinted as *Vekhi/Landmarks: A Collection of Articles about the Russian Intelligentsia* (Armonk, N.Y.: M. E. Sharpe, 1994). References, provided in the text, identify the contributor and the page. For the Russian edition, I have used the 1967 Posev reprint of *Vekhi: Sbornik" statei o russkoi intelligentsii* (Moscow, 1909). The collection was first published in the Soviet Union by Novosti in 1990.

5. Christopher Read, *Religion, Revolution, and the Russian Intelligentsia, 1900–1912: The "Vekhi" Debate and Its Intellectual Background* (London: Macmillan, 1979), 7.

6. On Struve in this period, see Richard Pipes, *Struve: Liberal on the Right, 1905–1944* (Cambridge: Harvard University Press, 1980).

7. As cited in Leonard Schapiro's superb study, "The *Vekhi* Group and the Mystique of Revolution," in *Russian Studies*, ed. Ellen Dahrendorf (New York: Viking, 1987), 71.

8. "'Landmarks' Printed for the First Time in Soviet Russia," *Moscow News*, no. 31 (1990): 2. This article, which prods the reader by mentioning the book's "ridiculously low price of 60 kopeks," describes the collection in a way that makes its current relevance unmistakable. The contributors "believed that class struggle and social revolution were catastrophic and ruinous for society. According to them, atheist materialism, political radicalism and violence . . . and utter disdain of individual interests were characteristic features of democratic and socialist ideology which brought Russian society into deadlock. To oppose such ideology, the seven thinkers put forward their own positive programme which envisaged, in particular, that the democratic intelligentsia should take up responsibility for what was happening."

9. Joseph Conrad, *Under Western Eyes* (New York: Doubleday, 1963), lxi. The novel was originally published in 1911, two years after *Landmarks*; the "Author's Note" I have cited is dated 1920. The successor to *Landmarks*, a collection entitled *Out of the Depths*, was published in 1918 and, like Conrad's note, reflected on the revolution's confirmation of the warning in the earlier book. There is thus an interesting parallel to be drawn between the Conrad novel and author's note on the one hand and *Landmarks* and *Out of the Depths* on the other.

10. Jeffrey Brooks, "*Vekhi* and the *Vekhi* Dispute," *Survey* 19, no. 1 (Winter 1973): 21.

11. This is presumably part of Nabokov's point in the chapter about Chernyshevsky in *The Gift*.

12. The comparison to a religious order is developed in the opening chapter of Nicolas Zernov, *The Russian Religious Renaissance of the Twentieth Century* (London: Darton, 1963).

13. For a study of Chernyshevsky's key contribution to the intelligentsia's mythology and ways of living, see Irina Paperno, *Chernyshevsky and the Age of Realism: A Study in the Semiotics of Behavior* (Stanford, Calif.: Stanford University Press, 1988).

14. Tolstoy in fact criticized the *Landmarks* contributors for not distinguishing themselves *enough* from the intelligentsia. He made fun of their own intellectual language, inaccessible to simple peasants. He objected to their moderate reformism on the grounds that politics are totally irrelevant. At times Tolstoy's article reads as if Chekhov had written it to parody Tolstoyanism. It was evidently a great disappointment to Gershenzon in particular. Characteristically, Tolstoy did not publish it but let its contents be known in detail in a published interview with him. The article itself can be found in volume 38 of the 90-volume edition of his complete works, pp. 285–90. See also Nikolai P. Poltoratzky, "Lev Tolstoy and *Vekhi,*" *Slavonic and East European Review* 43, no. 2 (June 1964): 332–52.

15. Leo Tolstoy, *Resurrection*, trans. Mrs. Louise Maude (New York: Dodd, 1899), 210.

16. Citations of Chekhov's letters, given in the text, are to the following sources: Ernest J. Simmons, *Chekhov: A Biography* (Boston: Little, Brown, 1962), abbreviated as S; and A. P. Chudakov, *Chekhov's Poetics*, trans. Edwina Jannie Cruise and Donald Dragt (Ann Arbor, Mich.: Ardis, 1983), abbreviated as Chudakov. Citations of *The Duel* are from Chekhov, *Ward Six and Other Stories*, trans. Ann Dunnigan (New York: Signet, 1965).

17. Leo Tolstoy, *Anna Karenina*, the Garnett translation edited by Leonard J. Kent and Nina Berberova (New York: Random, 1965), 350. Further references, given in the text, are to *AK*.

18. Caryl Emerson first called my attention to the importance of considering the relation of Bakhtin to *Landmarks*. See her recent article, "Russian Orthodoxy and the Early Bakhtin," *Religion and Literature* 22, nos. 2–3 (Summer-Autumn 1990): 109–31. I have also profited from conversations with Alexandar Mihailovic and from his paper at the 1990 MLA conference, "Mikhail Bakhtin at the Borders of Theological Criticism in 'Art and Answerability,'" which focuses on connections between Bakhtin and *Landmarks*. Mihailovic points to the importance of the parallels in terminology used by both, particularly their emphasis on *lichnost'* (the individual, the personality, which was "out of place in a traditionally Soviet Marxian context"). I differ from Mihailovic in a number of places where it seems to me he softens the harshness of the attack by *Landmarks* on the radical intelligentsia, and I cannot accept his observation that "Marxist schemata are deeply imbedded in 'Art and Answerability.'" In general, I do not think it wise to make thinkers acceptable by presenting them as more politically radical than they are.

Mihailovic is probably right that in some broad sense Bakhtin's early work belongs to the Russian religious renaissance, in the sense that this diverse movement allowed for discussion of concepts traditionally neglected or excluded, such as the individual personality and "a kind of existentialist meta-criticism." The religious aspect of *Landmarks* is highly attenuated and has little in common with the other wing of the Russian religious renaissance, which tended toward extremist and apocalyptic formulations of a distinctly unprosaic sort. Read observes that "these religious thinkers cannot be classified together as a school even in the loosest possible sense of the term" (*Religion, Revolution* 13), and he divides them into two groups, one that tended toward a moderate philosophical liberalism and the other that tended toward mystical anarchism of various degrees and sorts. Struve cannot be reasonably classed with Rozanov. In *Landmarks*, religion is invoked principally to affirm the infinite rather than the utilitarian value of the individual, to advocate personal self-improvement, to oppose the reduction of ethics to politics, and, interestingly enough, to recommend Western forms of Christianity that encouraged daily work and the accumulation of material wealth for a society.

Randall Poole is also exploring the relation of *Landmarks* to Bakhtin.

19. But in the United States, where it is now fashionable for similar reasons to speak of "literary production" rather than individual creation, the polemical edge of Bakhtin's original title might be restored.

20. Ivan Turgenev, *Fathers and Sons*, the Garnett translation revised by Ralph Matlaw (New York: Norton, 1966), 104.

21. One instance in which Bakhtin uses this image is cited later in the present essay. The other occurs in the "Concluding Remarks" of Bakhtin's chronotope essay.

22. Bakhtin, "The Problem of the Text," in *Speech Genres* 120.

23. Ibid.

24. Osip M. Brik, "T. n. 'Formal'nyi metod," *LEF* 1 (1923): 213.

25. Anatoly Lunacharsky, "O 'mnogogolosnosti' Dostoevskogo" (originally published in *Novy mir*, no. 10 [1929]), as cited in Mikhail Bakhtin, *Problems of Dostoevsky's Poetics*, ed. and trans. Caryl Emerson (Minneapolis: University of Minnesota Press, 1984), 35. Further references to this book, given in the text, are to *PDP*.

26. Bakhtin, "Toward a Methodology of the Human Sciences," in *Speech Genres* 162.

27. *Chekhov: The Major Plays*, trans. Ann Dunnigan (New York: New American Library, 1964), 191.

28. M. M. Bakhtin, "K filosofii postupka," in the 1984–85 issue of *Filosofiia i sotsiologiia nauki i tekhniki*, a yearbook (*ezhegodnik*) for the Soviet Academy of Sciences (Moscow: Nauka, 1986), 102. Further references, given in the text, are to KFP.

29. Bakhtin's approach might usefully be compared with the tradition of casuistry as sketched, defended, and revived in Albert R. Jonsen and Stephen Toulmin, *The Abuse of Casuistry: A History of Moral Reasoning* (Berkeley: University of California Press, 1988).

30. The term *politicism* is my own, not Bakhtin's.

31. In spite of the hostility to *Landmarks*, a debate did ensue along liberals and socialists about the morality of surrendering responsibility to a party or dogma and about the assumption that the ends justify all means. The Bolsheviks maintained the old dogma and regarded the very asking of such questions as a betrayal of intelligentsial traditions. But by the time the Bolsheviks seized power, Lenin and Gorky were on the defensive in making these arguments. In these observations, I paraphrase Aileen Kelly's fascinating article, "Self-Censorship and the Russian Intelligentsia, 1905–1914," *Slavic Review* 46, no. 2 (Summer 1987): 193–213.

32. Bulgakov 27. The translators here correct a misprint in the original, which reads "historical" when "hysterical" is evidently meant. But upon reflection, the resulting pun is not bad.

33. Bakhtin, "Toward a Reworking of the Dostoevsky Book," as translated in the second appendix in *PDP* 297.

34. I of course allude to Karl Kraus's famous dictum that psychoanalysis is the disease it purports to cure. The same might be said of Marxism (in this case, the name of the disease is social injustice).

35. Fyodor Dostoevsky, *The Brothers Karamazov*, trans. Constance Garnett (New York: Random, 1950), 281.

36. Alexander Herzen, *"From the Other Shore" and "The Russian People and Socialism,"* trans. Moura Budberg and Richard Wollheim (Oxford: Oxford University Press, 1979), 36–37.

37. See Emerson's gloss on this passage and its relation to earlier Russian thought on love in "Russian Orthodoxy and the Early Bakhtin" 118.

38. Mikhail Bakhtin, "Forms of Time and of the Chronotope in the Novel: Notes toward a Historical Poetics," in *The Dialogic Imagination: Four Essays by M. M. Bakhtin*, trans. Caryl Emerson and Michael Holquist (Austin: University of Texas Press, 1981), 148. Further references, given in the text, are to FTC.

39. Could that be the deeper meaning of the long sleep that in utopian fiction transports the hero to the Promised Time, the Time That Matters?

40. Bakhtin, "The *Bildungsroman* and Its Significance in the History of Realism (Toward a Historical Typology of the Novel)," in *Speech Genres* 26.

41. Bakhtin, "Response to a Question," in *Speech Genres* 5.

42. The phrase "intentional potential" occurs in Bakhtin, "Discourse in the Novel," in *Dialogic Imagination* 421. For more information on this complex of ideas, see Morson and Emerson, *Mikhail Bakhtin: Creation of a Prosaics* 284–90 ("Meanings and Potentials") and 361–65 ("Canonization and Reaccentuation").

43. Bakhtin, "Response to a Question," in *Speech Genres* 5.

44. I pursue the aspects of this essay that deal with the philosophy of time, in Bakhtin and more generally, in *Narrative and Freedom: The Shadows of Time* (New Haven, Conn.: Yale University Press, 1994).

Inventing the Novel

This essay was originally written for a joint session of the International Conference on the Ancient Novel and the Dartmouth School for Criticism and Theory (July 1989).

1. M. M. Bakhtin, *The Dialogic Imagination*, ed. Michael Holquist, trans. Caryl Emerson and Michael Holquist (Austin: University of Texas Press, 1981); further citations to this book appear in the text. The essays were first published in Russian in Moscow in 1975.

2. P. N. Medvedev/M. M. Bakhtin, *The Formal Method in Literary Scholarship: A Critical Introduction to Sociological Poetics*, trans. A. J. Wehrle (Cambridge: Harvard University Press, 1985); V. N. Voloshinov, *Marxism and the Philosophy of Language*, trans. Ladislav Matejka and I. R. Titunik (Cambridge: Harvard University Press, 1986).

3. Tzvetan Todorov, *Mikhail Bakhtin: The Dialogical Principle*, trans. W. Godzich (Minneapolis: University of Minnesota Press, 1984), 90.

4. As characterized by Alastair Fowler in *Kinds of Literature: An Introduction to the Theory of Genres and Modes* (Cambridge: Harvard University Press, 1982), 235.

5. Georg Lukács, *The Theory of the Novel: A Historico-Philosophical Essay on the Forms of Great Epic Literature*, trans. Anna Bostock (Cambridge: M.I.T. Press, 1987), 56.

6. See B. P. Reardon, *The Form of Greek Romance* (Princeton, N.J.: Princeton University Press, 1991).

7. M. M. Bakhtin, *Speech Genres and Other Late Essays*, trans. Vern W. McGee, ed. Caryl Emerson and Michael Holquist (Austin: University of Texas Press, 1986), 65.

8. Cf. Stephen Jay Gould, "The Episodic Nature of Evolutionary Change," in *The Panda's Thumb: More Reflections in Natural History* (New York: Norton, 1982), 179–85.

9. Walter L. Reed, *An Exemplary History of the Novel: The Quixotic versus the Picaresque* (Chicago: University of Chicago Press, 1981), 4.

10. Pace Michael McKeon, who in *The Origins of the English Novel, 1600–1740* (Baltimore: Johns Hopkins University Press, 1987) misreads Bakhtin as a mere inversion of Northrop Frye's "archetypalism" and can therefore relegate ancient fiction to one of two precursor revolutions "whose innovations are suggestively analogous" to those leading to the English (or modern) novel (23). McKeon does not examine any particular work of ancient fiction or question the relation between Greek and Roman traditions.

Response and Call

1. See Gary Saul Morson's characterization of the "Bakhtin Industry" in *Slavic and East European Journal* 30 (Spring 1986):81–90, and, especially, Caryl Emerson's

judicious account of problems with Bakhtin's poetics, in *Slavic and East European Journal* 32 (Winter 1988):503–25.

2. It is generally accepted that Mikhail Bakhtin was the Socratic inspirer, the *eminence grise* behind, if not the chief author of, three extremely sophisticated quasi-Marxist refutations of Formalism, Freudianism, and Saussurean linguistics that were officially published between 1927 and 1929 under the names of P. N. Medvedev and V. N. Voloshinov. The correct ascription of actual authorship is a highly debatable matter. The discussion of the disputed texts in Katerina Clark and Michael Holquist's biography, *Mikhail Bakhtin* (Cambridge: Harvard University Press, 1984), has led to turbulent polemics against their alleged "Bakhtinolatry." See, for instance, I. R. Titunik, "The Bakhtin Problem," *Slavic and East European Journal* 30 (Spring 1986):91–95, and Nina Perlina, *Funny Things Are Happening on the Way to the Bakhtin Forum*, Kennan Institute Occasional Papers, no. 231 (Washington, D.C., 1989). Recently, Morson and Emerson have resolved their doubts and declared for a dialogic colloquium among the three authors; see their introduction to *Rethinking Bakhtin: Extensions and Challenges*, ed. Gary Saul Morson and Caryl Emerson (Evanston, Ill.: Northwestern University Press, 1989).

3. To be specific, Bakhtin's oddly single-minded notion of the "carnivalization" of Rabelais's total discourse in *Gargantua and Pantagruel* has been taken to task in Richard M. Berrong's *Rabelais and Bakhtin* (Lincoln: University of Nebraska Press, 1986). Earlier, Dominick La Capra, in *Rethinking Intellectual History* (Ithaca, N.Y.: Cornell University Press, 1983), had summarized the substantive reservations of historians regarding the supposedly therapeutic "gay relativism" inscribed, for Bakhtin, in every social carnival. Many Western Slavists have remained unconvinced that Dostoevsky could be said to have composed a truly "polyphonic," decentered narrative; see, for instance, Réné Wellek, "Bakhtin's View of Dostoevsky: 'Polyphony' and 'Carnivalesque,'" in *Russian Formalism: A Retrospective Glance*, ed. Robert Louis Jackson and Stephen Rudy (New Haven, Conn.: Yale University Center for International and Area Studies Publications, 1985). Finally, Emerson, in the article cited in note 1, admirably acknowledges the litany of objections to date, including Bakhtin's sentimentalizing of "folk laughter" and his privileging of "novelistic" form and crude schematization of "monologic" expression in the lyric.

4. The term for linguistic structuralism's confinement of meaning to relational pairs is taken from Richard Terdiman's interesting critique in *Discourse/Counter-Discourse* (Ithaca, N.Y.: Cornell University Press, 1985).

5. There is an excellent discussion of Bakhtin's closeness to, and distance from, the Derridean correction of structuralist linguistics in Michael Holquist's essay, "The Surd Heard: Bakhtin and Derrida," in *Literature and History: Theoretical Problems and Russian Case Studies*, ed. Gary Saul Morson (Stanford, Calif.: Stanford University Press, 1986), 137–56. Morson's own commentary (192–201) sharpens the distinction by emphasizing Bakhtin's focus on the interpretive moment as a

cultural process that always strives to reconstruct situationally given codes and thereby to reduce the inherent uncertainty of utterances.

6. M. M. Bakhtin, *Speech Genres and Other Late Essays*, trans. Vern W. McGee, ed. Caryl Emerson and Michael Holquist (Austin: University of Texas Press, 1986), 5.

7. V. N. Voloshinov, *Marxism and the Philosophy of Language* (New York: Seminar Press, 1973), 94.

8. M. M. Bakhtin, *The Dialogic Imagination*, ed. Michael Holquist, trans. Caryl Emerson and Michael Holquist (Austin: University of Texas Press, 1981), 354–55. Further citations from this volume will be noted in the text.

9. Perhaps the fullest account of the important generational shift between an "integrationist" and an exclusivist understanding of what constitutes "African American expressive culture" appears in chapter 2 of Houston A. Baker Jr.'s *Blues, Ideology, and Afro-American Literature* (Chicago: University of Chicago Press, 1984), 64–112 (hereinafter cited in the text). The crucial turn toward a vernacular and ear-attuned perception of African American texts and their complex signifying was heralded in Stephen Henderson's influential book *Understanding the New Black Poetry* (New York: Morrow, 1973).

10. Henry Louis Gates Jr., "Criticism in the Jungle," in *Black Literature and Literary Theory*, ed. Henry Louis Gates Jr. (New York: Methuen, 1984), 6.

11. Exactly contemporary with the work of Gates and Baker, Michael G. Cooke, in *African American Literature in the Twentieth Century* (New Haven, Conn.: Yale University Press, 1984), was also locating a culturally specific expressivity in two forms constitutive of an African American "critique oblique." The blues and oral signifyin' "by their obliquity . . . enabled the culture to exist without demanding, indeed without provoking recognition" (21–22).

12. Henry Louis Gates Jr., *Figures in Black: Words, Signs, and the "Racial" Self* (New York: Oxford University Press, 1987), 240.

13. Mikhail Bakhtin, *Problems of Dostoevsky's Poetics*, ed. and trans. Caryl Emerson (Minneapolis: University of Minnesota Press, 1984), 196.

14. Houston A. Baker Jr., *Modernism and the Harlem Renaissance* (Chicago: University of Chicago Press, 1987), 84.

15. Henry Louis Gates Jr., *The Signifying Monkey: A Theory of African American Literary Criticism* (New York: Oxford University Press, 1988), 1. Further citations from this influential volume will be noted in the text.

16. A similar recent attempt to enlist Bakhtin's dialogics in a campaign to promote a Black American exceptionalism may be located in Michael Awkward's *Inspiriting Influences: Tradition, Revision, and Afro-American Women's Novels* (New York: Columbia University Press, 1989). Awkward argues for the existence of "non-expropriating refigurations of precursorial texts" as a distinct tradition among African American female writers, invoking Bakhtin's discussion of "the necessity

of discursive appropriation" but also claiming a cultural and gendered privilege of "noncompetitive revision" within the African American community of women writers.

17. Zora Neale Hurston, *Their Eyes Were Watching God* (Urbana: University of Illinois Press, 1978), 16, 285.

18. Barbara Johnson, "Metaphor, Metonymy and Voice in *Their Eyes Were Watching God*," in Gates, *Black Literature* 205–19.

19. I have in mind, specifically, the sensitive, nuanced literary transcription of the bicultural divide between peasant performances and aristocratic auditions in the Russian tradition of "rural sketches" since Turgenev's *Sportsman's Sketches* of 1852. There is, by the way, a remarkable parallel between Ralph Ellison's often-cited definition of the origin of the blues—"an impulse to keep the painful details and episodes of a brutal experience alive in one's aching consciousness, to finger its jagged grain, and to transcend it . . . by squeezing from it a near-tragic, near-comic lyricism"—and Turgenev's depiction of the auditory impact of Yasha's soaring folk song technique in his famous tale "The Singers." Ellison's quote is from his 1945 essay, "Richard Wright's Blues," as reprinted in *Shadow and Act* (New York: Random, 1964), 78.

20. An intelligent cautionary word about the institutional and "dialogic" pressures driving critics of a marginalized literature toward reductionism has been voiced by Wahneema Lubiano: "The single greatest difficulty facing Afro-American scholars is the need to figure out, in the space of an article or a book, how to convey the full complexity of periods or genres or intertextual relationships. . . . The summarizing that is so much a part of the work of an Afro-Americanist is information organization that concretizes the amorphous at the cost of simplifying. Furthermore, because we are speaking of and to a discourse that is racialized and marginalized, the summaries construct essentialist categories. The abuse of the 'Afro-American tradition' is continual and assured"; Lubiano, "Constructing and Reconstructing Afro-American Texts: The Critic as Ambassador and Referee," *American Literary History* 1 (1989):432–47. See also Mae G. Henderson's response to Baker's theorizing about the poetics of African American women's writing, a "dialogical engagement" that resists the "totalizing character of much theory and criticism," in *Afro-American Literary Study in the 1990's*, ed. Houston A. Baker Jr. and Patricia Redmond (Chicago: University of Chicago Press, 1989), 155–63.

21. Hazel V. Carby, *Reconstructing Womanhood: The Emergence of the Afro-American Woman Novelist* (New York: Oxford University Press, 1987), 17.

22. Bakhtin, *Problems* 196, 203.

23. Toni Morrison, "Unspeakable Things Unspoken: The Afro-American Presence in American Literature," *Michigan Quarterly* 28 (Winter 1989): 8–9.

24. M. M. Bakhtin, *Estetika slovesnogo tvorchestva*, ed. S. G. Bocharov (Moscow: Iskusstvo, 1979), 269.

25. The central article of faith about the culturally constructed "Russianness of Russian literature" was voiced by modern Russia's first literary critic, Vissarion Belinsky. In Morson's paraphrase, "Belinsky defined the Russian literary tradition as an antitradition. He described its major works as self-conscious challenges to the basic presuppositions of Western thought and to the inscription of those presuppositions in literary genres. To know a work as Russian . . . is to recognize the European conventions they invert, parody, or ostentatiously defy" (*Literature and History* 24).

26. Ralph Waldo Emerson, "Experience," in *Essays: Second Series* (Boston: Houghton Mifflin, 1903), 75. As early as 1844 Emerson anticipates that the full enunciation of human particularity entails the deconstruction of generic discourse and the inevitable onset of an age of linguistic suspicion.

Moral Perception and the Chronotope

I want to thank Maria DiBattista, Caryl Emerson, A. Walton Litz, and especially Gideon Rosen for their help.

1. M. M. Bakhtin, "Forms of Time and of the Chronotope in the Novel," in *The Dialogic Imagination*, ed. Michael Holquist, trans. Caryl Emerson and Michael Holquist (Austin: University of Texas Press, 1981), 248.

2. Ibid.

3. Henry James, *The Portrait of a Lady* (New York: Vintage, 1992); this edition follows the Houghton Mifflin edition (1881) and not Scribner's New York edition. James, *The Golden Bowl* (New York: Penguin, 1985); this edition follows the New York edition (Scribner's, 1909), vols. 23–24. Further citations of both works appear in the text.

4. The chief sources for this moral view are the prefaces to the earlier novels. The prefaces were written late, of course, but on my view they represent, in their moral outlook, a return to an early view that James had abandoned in *The Golden Bowl*. Nussbaum's essays on James are collected in Martha C. Nussbaum, *Love's Knowledge: Essays on Philosophy and Literature* (New York: Oxford University Press, 1990), hereinafter cited as *LK*.

5. The classic modern expression of this view is Iris Murdoch's *The Sovereignty of Good* (London: Ark, 1985). For the attribution to Aristotle, see John McDowell, "Virtue and Reason," *Monist* 62 (1979):331–50. The assimilation of moral judgment to vision depends crucially on the prior view that ordinary vision is not just a matter of passively taking in the scene before the eyes, but involves rather the active application of concepts in judgment.

6. Cf. Immanuel Kant, *Groundwork of the Metaphysic of Morals*, trans. H. J. Paton (New York: Harper Torchbooks, 1964), 69.

7. M. M. Bakhtin, *Toward a Philosophy of the Act*, trans. Vadim Liapunov, ed. Michael Holquist and Vadim Liapunov (Austin: University of Texas Press, 1993), 62.

8. Cf. Kant, *Groundwork* 56.

9. See John Cooper, *Reason and the Human Good in Aristotle's "Ethics"* (Cambridge: Harvard University Press, 1975).

10. Sallie Sears, *The Negative Imagination: Form and Perspective in the Novels of Henry James* (Ithaca, N.Y.: Cornell University Press, 1963), 200–201.

11. Henry James, *The Complete Notebooks of Henry James: The Authoritative and Definitive Edition*, ed. Leon Edel and Lyndall H. Powers (New York: Oxford University Press, 1987), 15. James's entry, dated 16 March 1879, reads: "The obvious criticism of course will be that it [*The Portrait of a Lady*] is not finished—that I have not seen the heroine to the end of her situation—that I have left her *en l'air.*—This is both true and false. The whole of anything is never told; you can only take what groups together. It is complete in itself—and the rest may be taken up or not, later."

12. Ruth Bernard Yeazell, *Language and Knowledge in the Late Novels of Henry James* (Chicago: University of Chicago Press, 1976).

13. Cf. "her birth as a woman," in *LK* 149.

Literature as Social Knowledge

1. James Clifford and George Marcus, eds., *Writing Culture: The Poetics and Politics of Ethnography* (Berkeley and Los Angeles: University of California Press, 1988).

2. Herbert Marcuse, *The Aesthetic Dimension* (Boston: Beacon Press, 1978).

3. M. M. Bakhtin, *Speech Genres and Other Late Essays*, trans. Vern W. McGee, ed. Caryl Emerson and Michael Holquist (Austin: University of Texas Press, 1986), 3–6. In the interview with the cultural journal *Novy Mir*, which appeared in November 1970, Bakhtin reveals clearly his argument that one may not consider the literary text apart from "the history of culture." He explicitly resumes his earlier critique of the Formalist tendency to abstract text from context.

4. George Bataille, *Inner Experience*, trans. Leslie Anne Boldt (Albany: State University of New York Press, 1988).

5. George Herbert Mead, *Mind, Self, and Society* (Chicago: University of Chicago Press, 1934).

6. "Insofar as stratification of the communal whole into social classes occurs, the complex undergoes fundamental changes; the motifs and narratives that correspond to those strata are subject to a reinterpretation. A gradual differentiation of ideological spheres sets in. Cultic activity separates itself from undifferentiated production; the sphere of consumption is made more distinct and to a significant extent compartmentalized. Members of the complex experience internal decline

and transformation. Such elements of the matrix as food, drink, the sexual act, death, abandon the matrix and enter *everyday life*, which is already in the process of being compartmentalized"; M. M. Bakhtin, *The Dialogic Imagination*, ed. Michael Holquist, trans. Caryl Emerson and Michael Holquist (Austin: University of Texas Press, 1981), 211. In this description, Bakhtin accounts for the appearance of everyday life through the critical idea of differentiation.

7. C. P. Snow, *The Two Cultures and the Scientific Revolution* (Cambridge: Cambridge University Press, 1959).

8. However, Bakhtin's referent is the "rich treasury of folk humor" in his study of Rabelais or, as in the studies of Dostoevsky's poetics, the multiplicity of voices or "consciousnesses" that do not reduce to a series of "types," as in Lukács's Weberian formulation.

9. V. N. Voloshinov, *Marxism and the Philosophy of Language* (New York: Academic Press, 1973).

10. Carlo Ginzburg, *The Cheese and the Worms: The Cosmos of a Sixteenth-Century Miller*, trans. by John Tedeschi and Anne Tedeschi (Baltimore: Johns Hopkins University Press, 1980), xvi.

11. Ibid., xvii.

12. Ibid.

13. Ibid.

14. M. M Bakhtin "The Problem of the Text in Linguistics, Philology and the Human Sciences" in *Speech Genres*, 103.

15. Ibid.

16. Bakhtin, *Dialogic Imagination*, 84.

17. Ibid., 206.

18. Georg Lukács, "Reification and the Consciousness of the Proletariat," in *History and Class Consciousness* (London: Merlin Press, 1971). Of course, Lukács would not agree with the judgment that popular culture is "displaced, but not destroyed" by the penetration of the commodity form to all corners of the social world, the division of labor and its consequent alienation-effects.

19. Bakhtin, *Dialogic Imagination*, 217.

20. Norbert Elias, *The Civilizing Process* (New York: Urizen Books, 1980).

21. Bakhtin, "Discourse in the Novel," in *Dialogic Imagination*, 103–4.

22. M. M. Kamshilov, *Evolution of the Biosphere*, trans. Minna Brodskaya (Moscow: MIR, 1978), 40–41.

23. Bakhtin, "The Bildungsroman" in *Speech Genres*, 37.

24. Bakhtin, "The Problem of Speech Genres," in *Speech Genres* 72–73.

25. The boom in Benjamin studies was initiated by Hannah Arendt, who in 1967 edited the first collection in English of a selection of Benjamin's essays: Walter Benjamin, *Illuminations*, ed. with an introduction by Hannah Arendt (New York: Schocken Books, 1967). But it was not until Fredric Jameson's discussion of

Benjamin in *Marxism and Form* (Princeton, N.J.: Princeton University Press, 1972), and articles in *New York Review of Books* and other periodicals in the 1970s that he was recognized by scholars and critics beyond the Germanists and Frankfurt school mavens.

26. Andrei Zhdanov, "The Richest in Ideas, the Most Advanced Literature," *Soviet Writers Congress, 1934*, by Maxim Gorky et al. (London: Lawrence and Wishart, 1977), 15–26.

27. These themes are repeated in the various works of Michael Holquist, Caryl Emerson, Gary Saul Morson, and Tzvetan Todorov. Todorov's pithy remarks on the subject of Bakhtin's relation to Marxism are extremely instructive in this regard. While, as he points out, Bakhtin never published a "single polemical text under his own name," there is, according to Todorov, little doubt that the Marxist works of members of the circle with which he was affiliated had his approbation and that their debates with various orthodoxies were conducted from inside Marxism. See Tzvetan Todorov, *Mikhail Bakhtin: The Dialogical Principle* (Minneapolis: University of Minnesota Press, 1984), 9–10.

28. Bakhtin, *Speech Genres*, 42.

29. Mikhail Bakhtin, *Problems of Dostoevsky's Poetics*, ed. and trans. Caryl Emerson (Minneapolis: University of Minnesota Press, 1984).

30. Ibid., 18.

31. Julia Kristeva, "Word, Dialogue and the Novel," in *Desire in Language* (New York: Columbia University Press, 1980). In this essay, Kristeva underlines dialogism as "transgression giving itself a law" (71).

32. Bakhtin, "Discourse in the Novel," in *The Dialogic Imagination* 366–67.

33. Ibid., 278.

34. This point is elaborated in Bakhtin, "The Problem of Speech Genres," in *Speech Genres* 60–102.

The Postmodern Crisis

1. Walter Benjamin, *The Origin of German Tragic Drama* (London: NLB, 1977), 177–78.

2. Linda Hutcheon, *A Poetics of Postmodernism: History, Theory, Fiction* (New York: Routledge, 1988), 11.

3. See Linda Hutcheon, *A Theory of Parody: The Teachings of Twentieth-Century Art Forms* (New York: Methuen, 1985), for extensive discussion and bibliography.

4. Silvio Gaggi, *Modern/Postmodern: A Study in Twentieth-Century Arts and Ideas* (Philadelphia: University of Pennsylvania Press, 1989).

5. Jean-François Lyotard, *Le postmoderne expliqué aux enfants* (Paris: Galilée, 1988), 46.

6. Unlike the quotationalism of much postmodern architecture in which the "historical referent" is simply a marker of the postmodern—an architecture that quickly degenerates into kitsch—Johnson's elegant citations of the past, in the ATT building, for example, respect the cited past, the tradition, however artificial it may be. His citations are not self-referential. They do not proclaim membership in a school.

7. Fredric Jameson, foreword to *The Postmodern Condition: A Report on Knowledge*, by Jean-François Lyotard, trans. Geoff Bennington and Brian Massumi (Minneapolis: University of Minnesota Press, 1984), vii–xxi.

8. Fredric Jameson, "The Politics of Theory: Ideological Positions in the Postmodern Debate," in *The Ideologies of Theory: Essays, 1971–1986* (Minneapolis: University of Minnesota Press, 1988), 2:103–13.

9. Gianni Vatimo, *La fine della modernità: Nihilismo ed ermeneutica nella cultura post-moderna* (Rome: Garzanti, 1985).

10. Lyotard, *Postmodern Condition*. Since the publication of *The Postmodern Condition* in 1984, Lyotard has modified his position slightly, giving critical attention to his model of the narrative; see Lyotard, *Le postmoderne*.

11. Vincent Crapanzano, "On Dialogue," in *The Interpretation of Dialogue*, ed. Tullio Maranhao (Chicago: University of Chicago Press, 1990), 269–91; idem, "On Self-Characterization," in *Cultural Psychology: Essays on Comparative Human Development*, ed. J. W. Stigler, R. A. Shweder, and G. Herdt (Cambridge: Cambridge University Press, 1990), 401–23.

12. Paolo Portoghesi, *Postmodern: The Architecture of Postindustrial Society* (New York: Rizzoli, 1983); Hutcheon, *Poetics of Postmodernism*.

13. Mikhail Bakhtin, *Problems of Dostoevsky's Poetics*, trans. Caryl Emerson (Minneapolis: University of Minnesota Press, 1984).

14. Gary Saul Morson, "Parody, History, Metaparody," in *Rethinking Bakhtin: Extensions and Challenges*, ed. Gary Saul Morson and Caryl Emerson (Evanston, Ill.: Northwestern University Press, 1989), 63–86.

15. Bakhtin, *Problems* 189.

16. Hutcheon, *Theory of Parody* 11.

17. Morson, "Parody" 65.

18. Hutcheon, *Theory of Parody* 34.

19. Ibid., 32; for a more complete discussion, see Gerard Genette, *Palimpsestes: La littérature au second degré* (Paris, 1982). By calling attention to the two means of *para*, "against" and "beside," Hutcheon (*Theory of Parody* 35; *Poetics of Postmodernism* 57) underlines the fact that parody is "a personal act of supersession and an inscription of literary-historical continuity." Like Genette, she does not consider the importance of parody's domination of its target by both superseding it and affirming its position in tradition or context. In the nonliterary instances I am

discussing, this inscription of continuity is one of the devices for imposing a set of conventions on the exchange.

20. Morson, "Parody" 67.

21. Similar strains and similar responses, including the retrogressive, can be seen in family and personal histories where, for whatever reasons, their assumption is questioned and their incorporation of multiple positions revealed. (Deconstructionist and certain psychoanalytic readings of life historical texts reveal their multivoicedness, their several narrative positions, which are ideologically encompassed by the governing personal pronoun—the I.)

22. Hans-Georg Gadamer, *Truth and Method* (New York: Crossroad, 1982), 16.

23. Dennis Tedlock, *The Spoken Word and the Work of Interpretation* (Philadelphia: University of Pennsylvania Press, 1983).

24. Hugo von Hofmannsthal, "Ad me ipsum," in *Aufzeichnungen* (Frankfurt: Fischer, 1973), 211–44. For discussion of the allomatic, see also D. H. Miles, *Hofmannsthal's Novel: Andreas* (Princeton, N.J.: Princeton University Press, 1972), and Benjamin Bennett, *Hugo von Hofmannsthal: The Theaters of Consciousness* (Cambridge: Cambridge University Press, 1988).

25. Lyotard, *Le postmoderne* 115.

26. E.g., Robert A. Rosenstone, *Mirror in the Shrine: American Encounters with Meiji Japan* (Cambridge: Harvard University Press, 1988).

27. Benjamin, *Origin of German Tragic Drama* 178.

The Emergence of Language from Dialogue

1. M. M. Bakhtin, *The Dialogic Imagination*, ed. Michael Holquist, trans. Caryl Emerson and Michael Holquist (Austin: University of Texas Press, 1981); idem, *Problems of Dostoevsky's Poetics*, trans. Caryl Emerson (Minneapolis: University of Minnesota Press, 1984); idem, *Speech Genres and Other Late Essays*, trans. Vern W. McGee, ed. Caryl Emerson and Michael Holquist (Austin: University of Texas Press, 1986).

2. B. F. Skinner, in *Verbal Behavior* (New York: Appleton-Century-Crofts, 1957), argued that language developed in the child through imitation, reinforcement, and other stimulus-response techniques. Noam Chomsky, in *Aspects of the Theory of Syntax* (Cambridge: M.I.T. Press, 1965), severely critiqued this explanation and argued for a genetic ability to create novel sentences. Reenvoicement is intermediate between these two extremes, allowing for both individual and social contributions to the development of language.

3. Bakhtin, *Speech Genres.*

4. Gregory Bateson, *Steps to an Ecology of Mind* (New York: Ballantine, 1972), 319. Further citations of this work appear in the text.

5. Lev Vygotsky, *Mind in Society: The Development of Higher Psychological Processes*, ed. and trans. Michael Cole, Vera John-Steiner, Sylvia Scribner, and Elaine Souberman (Cambridge: Harvard University Press, 1978), 56. Further citations of this work appear in the text.

6. Lev Vygotsky, *The Collected Works of Lev Vygotsky*, vol. 1, *Problems of General Psychology*, ed. Robert Rieber and Aaron Carton, trans. Norris Minick (New York: Plenum, 1987), 259.

7. John Dore, "Feeling, Form and Intention in the Baby's Transition to Language," in *The Transition from Prelinguistic to Linguistic Communication*, ed. Roberta Golinkoff (Hillsdale, N.J.: Erlbaum, 1983); idem, "Holophrases Revisited: Their 'Logical' Development from Dialogue," in *Children's Single-Word Speech*, ed. Martin Barrett (Chichester: Wiley, 1985).

8. Lev Vygotsky, *Thought and Language*, trans. Gertrude Kaufmann (Cambridge: M.I.T. Press, 1962).

9. J. Searle, *Speech Acts* (Cambridge: Cambridge University Press, 1969).

10. Dell Hymes, "Ways of Speaking," in *Explorations in the Ethnography of Speaking*, ed. Robert Bauman and Joel Scherzer (London: Cambridge University Press, 1974).

11. Erving Goffman, *Frame Analysis* (New York: Harper and Row, 1974).

12. Bakhtin, *Speech Genres* 60.

13. L. Wittgenstein, *Philosophical Investigations* (New York: Macmillan, 1953).

14. H. Sacks, E. Schegloff, and G. Jefferson, "A Simplest Systematics for the Organization of Turn-Taking in Conversation," *Language* 50 (1974):696–735.

15. Michel Foucault, *The Order of Things* (New York: Random House, 1970), 83.

Logosphere and Semiosphere

I am indebted to a number of individuals who studied Lotman, Vernadsky, Bakhtin, and neurobiology with me and whose careful readings of this essay and suggestions for improvement I deeply appreciate: Carol Any, William Bleisch, Ellen Chances, Caryl Emerson, Richard Gustafson, Jerry Leo, Philip Lieberman, David Mandelkern, Alexandar Mihailović, Gary Saul Morson, Cathy Popkin, Stephanie Sandler, Domna Stanton, and Thomas G. Winner.

1. Iurii Lotman, "O semiosfere" (On the Semiosphere), *Trudy po znakovym sistemam* 17 (1984):30–45; idem, *Kul'tura i vzryv* (Culture and Explosion) (Moscow: Progress, 1992). A partial English translation of "On the Semiosphere" appears in Iurii Lotman, *The Universe of the Mind*, ed. and trans. Ann Shukman (Bloomington: Indiana University Press, 1991).

2. The writings of the Moscow-Tartu school of semiotics, formerly also known as the school of Soviet semiotics, appear primarily in its periodical, *Trudy po*

znakovym sistemam (Sign Systems). Most of the available English translations of works by Russian semioticians are drawn from writings published in the 1970s, which still retained a structuralist focus. The exception, Ann Shukman's excellent translation *The Universe of the Mind*, containing writings by Iurii Lotman, includes some more recent material, but the volume barely does justice to the innovative work Lotman accomplished in the 1980s before his death; see Lotman, *The Universe of the Mind*, ed. and trans. Ann Shukman (Bloomington: Indiana University Press, 1991). Critics have only begun to comment on Lotman's recent work and its indebtedness to Bakhtin and Vernadsky. See Allan Reid, "Who Is Lotman and Why Is Bakhtin Saying Those Nasty Things about Him?" *Bakhtin and Otherness: Discours social/Social Discourse* 1–2 (1990):325–38; Simonetta Salvestroni, "Bakhtin between the Russian Culture of the 1920s and New Contemporary Ideas," paper delivered at the Second International Bakhtin Congress; and Ann Shukman, "Semiotic Aspects of the Work of Jurij Michailović Lotman," in *The Semiotic Web, 1987*, ed. Thomas A. Sebeok and Jean Umiker-Sebeok, Approaches to Semiotics 81 (Berlin: Matonde Gruyter, 1987), 65–78.

Some pertinent articles have appeared since this work went to press, and thus they could not be considered in my discussion: see Daniel Alexandrov and Anton Struchkov, "Bakhtin's Legacy and the History of Science and Culture: An Interview with Anatoli Akhutin and Vladimir Bibler," *Configurations* 1, no. 3 (1993):335–86; and M. N. Sokolov, "Ikonosfery Bol'shogo Vremeni. K nelineinoi teorii kultury" (On the Iconospheres of Great Time: Toward a Nonlinear Theory of Culture), *Dialog Karnaval Khronotop* 4 (1994):19–33.

3. Roman Jakobson and Iurii Tynianov, "Problems in the Study of Literature and Language," in *Readings in Russian Poetics: Formalist and Structuralist Views*, ed. Ladislav Matejka and Krystyna Pomorska (Ann Arbor: Michigan Slavic Publications, 1978).

4. Thomas G. Winner, "Prague Structuralism and Semiotics: Neglect and Resulting Fallacies," paper delivered at the MLA annual meeting, December 1991.

5. Fredric Jameson, *The Prison-House of Language: A Critical Account of Structuralism and Russian Formalism* (Princeton, N.J.: Princeton University Press, 1972), ix, x.

6. That is, because the relationship between signifier and signified is considered totally arbitrary and conventional in Saussurean linguistics (the principle of *l'arbitraire du signe*), there is the inevitable sense of an unbridgeable gap between the concept of the thing represented and the manner of representing it.

7. This position is implied by Jurij Striedter in *Literary Structure, Evolution, and Value: Russian Formalism and Czech Structuralism Reconsidered* (Cambridge: Harvard University Press, 1989), and by Boris Gasparov in his introduction to *The Semiotics of Russian Cultural History: Essays by Iurii M. Lotman, Lidiia Ia. Ginsburg, and Boris A.*

Uspenskii, ed. Alexander D. Nakhimovsky and Alice Stone Nakhimovsky (Ithaca, N.Y.: Cornell University Press, 1985).

8. I must emphasize the distinction I am forming here between semiotic theory—that enterprise which explores the parameters of a theory of semiosis—as opposed to semiotic practice, or the analysis of texts to reveal their semiotic structures.

See V. V. Ivanov, "Značenie idej M. M. Baxtina o znake, vyskazyvanii i dialoge dlja sovremennoj semiotiki" (The Significance of Bakhtin's Ideas on Sign, Utterance and Dialogue for Modern Semiotics), *Trudy po znakovym sistemam* 6 (1973):5–45.

9. M. M. Bakhtin, "Toward a Methodology for the Human Sciences," in *Speech Genres and Other Late Essays*, trans. Vern W. McGee, ed. Caryl Emerson and Michael Holquist (Austin: University of Texas Press, 1986), 169.

10. Bakhtin, "From Notes Made in 1970–71," in *Speech Genres* 147.

11. For an excellent analysis of the concept of inner speech and its treatment in Bakhtin and Vygotsky, see Caryl Emerson, "The Outer Word and Inner Speech: Bakhtin, Vygotsky, and the Internalization of Language," in *Bakhtin: Essays and Dialogues on His Work*, ed. Gary Saul Morson (Chicago: University of Chicago Press, 1981), 21–40.

12. V. N. Voloshinov, *Marxism and the Philosophy of Language*, trans. Ladislav Matejka and I. R. Titunik (Cambridge: Harvard University Press, 1986), 25.

13. Bakhtin, "From Notes Made in 1970–71," in *Speech Genres* 150.

14. Ibid., 134.

15. Ibid., 135.

16. Katerina Clark and Michael Holquist, *Mikhail Bakhtin* (Cambridge: Harvard University Press, 1984), 227.

17. Vernadsky, one of the major founders of the sciences of ecology and geochemistry (termed "biogeochemistry" by the Vernadsky school of earth science), gave his name to the Institute for Geochemistry and Analytic Chemistry in the former Soviet Academy of Science in Moscow. Because of his role in the history of Russia's ecology movement, he has become popular in recent years, even figuring in Gorbachev's speeches. Bailes compares this notice with the fashion for Bakhtin but does not explore the connections in the author's philosophies; see Kendall E. Bailes, *Science and Russian Culture in an Age of Revolution: V. I. Vernadsky and His Scientific School, 1863–1945* (Bloomington: Indiana University Press, 1990), x–xi.

18. Vernadsky acknowledges that the term originated with Jean-Baptiste Lamarck and Eduard Suess in his article "The Biosphere and the Noösphere," *American Scientist* 33 (1945):10n1. Vernadsky's primary influence was probably his university professor, V. V. Dokuchaev, a soil scientist, who promoted a vision of soil as a heterogeneous totality of interacting organic and inorganic matter. For a thorough intellectual biography of Vernadsky, see Bailes, *Science and Russian Culture*.

19. Humanity's actions create a new stage in the activity of the biosphere, termed the "psychozoic era" by the American essayist Richard H. Dana.

20. According to Vernadsky, the term was jointly invented by Bergsonian philosopher Le Roy and the geologist and philosopher Teilhard de Chardin.

21. Bakhtin, "From Notes Made in 1970–71," in *Speech Genres* 137.

22. Ibid.

23. Lotman, *Universe of the Mind* 3.

24. Iurii Lotman, "Asimmetriia i dialog," *Trudy po znakovym sistemam* 16 (1983): 15–30; idem, "Kul'tura i organizm," unpublished manuscript; idem, "Mozg—tekst—kul'tura—iskusstvennyi intellekt," *Semiotika i informatika* 17 (1981); idem, "O semiosfere." All translations provided here are my own. A slightly different version of "On the Semiosphere" appears in the translation by Ann Shukman in *The Universe of the Mind*.

25. An enormous literature exists on the functional asymmetry of the brain. The interested reader is referred to Norman Geschwind and N. A. Galaburda, eds., *Cerebral Lateralization: Biological Mechanisms, Associations, and Pathology* (Cambridge: M.I.T. Press, 1987), chap. 5, "Asymmetry of the Human Brain"; and Michael Gazanaga, *The Social Brain: Discovering the Networks of the Mind* (New York: Basic Books, 1985).

26. The interdependence of the two hemispheres of the brain was first documented in studies of epileptic patients who had received the therapeutic surgical severing of the corpus colosum and thus had no intracerebral communication between the two hemispheres. These patients were able to draw pictures of objects seen only by the right hemisphere that they were subsequently unable to name. These split-brain studies are summarized in Gazanaga, *Social Brain*, chap. 3, "Split-Brain Studies, the Early Years."

The theory of hemispheric specialization and its possible gender basis has become widely popularized. According to this theory, males utilize the right hemisphere more than females, making males more spatially oriented and females more verbal. The gender biases of these views have been critiqued most extensively by Anne Fausto-Sterling in her *Myths of Gender: Biological Theories about Women and Men* (New York: Basic Books, 1988).

27. Lotman, "O semiosfere" 9.

28. Iurii Lotman and Nikolai Nikolaenko, "Snova èto zagadochnoe 'zolotoe sechenie,'" *Dekorativnoe Iskusstvo* 9 (1983):31–34.

29. In the 1970s the leading semioticians of the Moscow-Tartu school proposed a model for the cultural organization of information that juxtaposed interior membership to external marginalization as the basic principle. This model again set up the usual system of binary oppositions of inner versus outer, order versus chaos, us versus them, same versus different, and so on. See Iurii Lotman, "Theses

on the Semiotic Study of Cultures," in *The Tell-Tale Sign: A Survey of Semiotics*, ed. Thomas A. Sebeok (Lisse: Peter de Ridder, 1978).

30. Donna Haraway, *Crystals, Fabrics, and Fields: Metaphors of Organicism in Twentieth-Century Developmental Biology* (New Haven, Conn.: Yale University Press, 1976).

31. I use the term *organicism* comprehensively to include a common theoretical orientation within philosophy, biology, and aesthetics. See discussions in M. H. Abrams, *The Mirror and the Lamp: Romantic Theory and the Critical Tradition* (London: Oxford University Press, 1953); G. N. G. Orsini, "The Organic Concept in Aesthetics," *Comparative Literature* 21 (1969):1–30; D. C. Phillips, "Organicism in the Late Nineteenth and Early Twentieth Centuries," *Journal of the History of Ideas* 31 (1970):413–32; and Victor Terras, *Belinskij and Russian Literary Criticism: The Heritage of Organic Aesthetics* (Madison: University of Wisconsin Press, 1974).

32. J. McTaggart, *The Nature of Existence*, vol. 1 (Cambridge: Cambridge University Press, 1921), 161.

33. Evelyn Fox Keller, *Reflections of Gender and Science* (New Haven, Conn.: Yale University Press, 1985).

34. For a discussion of these issues, see, among others, Susan Bordo, "The Cartesian Masculinization of Thought," *Signs* 11, no. 3 (1986):439–56; Sandra Harding and M. B. Hintikka, eds., *Discovering Reality: Feminist Perspectives on Epistemology, Metaphysics, Methodology, and the Philosophy of Science* (Dordrecht: Reidel, 1983); Lynn Hankinson-Nelson, *Who Knows? From Quine to a Feminist Empiricism* (Philadelphia: Temple University Press, 1990); Sandra Harding, *Whose Science? Whose Knowledge?* (Ithaca, N.Y.: Cornell University Press, 1991); Keller, *Reflections*; and Nancy Tuana, ed., *Feminism and Science* (Bloomington: Indiana University Press, 1989).

35. Keller, *Reflections* 43–44.

36. Teresa de Lauretis, *Alice Doesn't* (Bloomington: Indiana University Press, 1987), chap. 6.

37. See Iurii Lotman, "The Origin of Plot in the Light of Typology," *Poetics Today* 1 (1979):161–84; and Joseph Campbell, *The Hero with a Thousand Faces* (Princeton, N.J.: Princeton University Press, 1949).

38. Jacques Derrida, *The Truth in Painting* (Chicago: University of Chicago Press, 1987), 12.

39. Lotman, "O semiosfere" 9.

40. See J. E. Lovelock, *The Ages of Gaia: A Biography of Our Living Earth* (New York: Norton, 1988).

41. Bakhtin, "From Notes Made in 1970–71," in *Speech Genres* 138.

42. I am indebted to Caryl Emerson for making me aware of these distinctions.

43. Lotman, *Kul'tura i vzryv* 25, 42–43.

44. Although many feminist critics, notably Dale M. Bauer (*Feminist Dialogics: A Theory of Failed Community* [Albany: State University of New York Press, 1988])

and those anthologized in Dale M. Bauer and Susan Jaret McKinstry, eds., *Feminism, Bakhtin, and the Dialogic* (Albany: State University of New York Press, 1991), find that Bakhtin's theory accommodates their aims, Caryl Emerson observes that the issue of gender is strikingly absent from Bakhtin's work. See Emerson, "Bakhtin and Women: A Non-Topic with Immense Implications," in *Fruits of Her Plume: Essays on Contemporary Russian Women's Culture,* ed. Helena Goscilo (New York: M. E. Sharpe, 1993), 3–20. From my perspective, Bakhtin arguably succeeds in creating a nonhegemonic model of dialogue.

45. See M. M. Bakhtin, "K filosofii postupka," in *Filosofiia i sotsiologiia nauki i tekhniki* (Moscow: Nauka, 1986), 80–138. All translations from "K filosofii postupka" in this essay are my own.

46. The translation of the term *sobytiinost'* as "eventness" is suggested in Gary Saul Morson and Caryl Emerson, eds., *Rethinking Bakhtin: Extensions and Challenges* (Evanston, Ill.: Northwestern University Press, 1989).

47. Bakhtin, "K filosofii" 88, 115.

48. Bakhtin, "From Notes Made in 1970–71," in *Speech Genres* 133.

49. Jameson, *Prison-House of Language* 25.

Notes on Contributors

Stanley Aronowitz is Professor of Sociology and Director of the Center for Cultural Studies at the City University of New York Graduate Center. He is the author of eleven books, including works on literature and aesthetics such as *Dead Artists, Live Theories and Other Cultural Problems* and *The Politics of Identity*.

R. Bracht Branham is Associate Professor of Classics and Comparative Literature at Emory University. He is the author of *Untimely Eloquence: Lucian and the Comedy of Traditions*, winner of the Wilson Prize for 1989, and co-editor of *The Cynics: The Cynic Movement in Antiquity and its Legacy for Europe*. He is translator and editor of Petronius' *Satyrica*.

Vincent Crapanzano is Distinguished Professor of Comparative Literature and Anthrolopogy at the City University of New York Graduate Center. His works include *Hamadsha Tuhami*, *Waiting*, and *Hermes' Dilemma and Hamlet's Desire*.

John Dore is Professor of Linguistics, Psychology, and Literature at Baruch College and the Graduate Center of the City University of New York. He is also Director of the Breakwaters Institute. He has published over fifty articles, books, and chapters on human development.

Lisa Eckstrom is a doctoral candidate in the Department of Comparative Literature at Princeton University, specializing in English and French nineteenth-century literature. This is her first publication. Her doctoral dissertation is on the topic of brother and sister love in the nineteenth-century female bildungsroman.

Caryl Emerson is Professor of Slavic Languages and Literatures and Comparative Literature at Princeton University. She has translated, edited, and commented on Mikhail Bakhtin for twenty years. She has also published on nineteenth-century Russian prose, music, and culture.

Amy Mandelker is Associate Professor of Comparative Literature at the City University of New York Graduate Center. She is the author of *Framing "Anna Karenina": Tolstoy, the Woman Question, and the Victorian Novel*. A former editor of the *Tolstoy Studies Journal* she has published articles on nineteenth- and twentieth-century Russian and European literature and literary theory.

Gary Saul Morson is Frances Hooper Professor of the Arts and Humanities and Director of the Center for the Writing Arts at Northwestern University. His most recent book is *Narrative and Freedom: The Shadows of Time.*

Dale E. Peterson is Professor of English and Russian at Amherst College and associate editor of the *Massachusetts Review*. His current project is a comparative study of Russian and African-American cultural nationalism, with emphasis on the construction of ethnic soul.